*To all local government chief executives
past present and future*

'ALL ANIMALS ARE EQUAL
BUT SOME ANIMALS ARE MORE EQUAL THAN OTHERS'

- George Orwell, Animal Farm, Secker & Warburg 1945 (quoted from in the Audit Commission's *Management Paper No 2, More Equal than others: the Chief Executive in Local Government*, London 1989).

' Like a skillful mariner to prick the card and to advertise and instruct the master how and in what order he is to keep his course and make his way'

- description of role of the chief executive's predecessor, the clerk of the council, by John Hooker, sixteenth century chamberlain and antiquary for the City of Exeter (quoted by Wallace T MacCaffery in *Exeter 1540-1640*, Harvard University Press 1975).

'Largo al factotum della città, largo!'
(Make way for the person who controls all the city's affairs, make way!)

- *Il Barbiere di Siviglia*, Cesare Sterbini 1816

THE ROLE of CHIEF EXECUTIVE

in

BRITISH LOCAL GOVERNMENT

its origins and development, present reality and future

Alan Norton

sponsored by the Royal Institute of Public Administration

and the Society of Local Authority Chief Executives

INSTITUTE OF LOCAL GOVERNMENT STUDIES

THE UNIVERSITY OF BIRMINGHAM
1991

First published 1991

Published by the Institute of Local Government Studies, The University of Birmingham
Edgbaston, Birmingham B15 2TT

Printed in Great Britain by
George Over Ltd, Somers Road, Rugby CV22 7DH

British Library Cataloguing in Publication Data
Alan Norton, 1926-
The role of chief executive in British local government - its origins and background, present reality and future
(Public administration, management and politics)
1. United Kingdom. Local government. Management.
I. Norton, Alan *1926-*

ISBN 07044 0980 1

CONTENTS

TABLES AND DIAGRAMS

Foreword on behalf of the sponsors

In 1962, TE Headrick published "The Town Clerk in English Local Government" as an authoritative account of the development of the office of Town Clerk up to the early 1960s. There has been no similar study produced since that time and it was Roger Morris, Chief Executive of Northampton, who first suggested to SOLACE that a book should be produced which would give an account of how chief executives have taken over the role of town (and county) clerks and developed it, especially during the period immediately after local government reorganisation in 1974. SOLACE readily agreed to the proposal, not least because by 1990, with the retirement of many of those who were appointed as the first chief executives in 1974, much first-hand experience might be lost if it was not recorded and analysed. The Society therefore sought a partner in the proposed enterprise and were delighted that the Royal Institute of Public Administration, under its then Director-General, William Plowden, agreed on the importance of commissioning the work as a joint enterprise.

The selection of the Institute of Local Government Studies at Birmingham University was a natural choice to produce the work, because of its in-depth knowledge of local government and its close association with the training and development of chief executives and senior managers in local government. Alan Norton, who has been a member of the Institute for many years has been painstaking in assembling information from chief executives about the nature of their jobs in a wide range of local authorities. The result is a fascinating and lively account of the inside working of local government today and how chief executives have played a key role in guiding, leading and managing their local authorities to meet the needs of their communities against a background of changing economic and social circumstances, new legislation and financial constraints. Alan Norton's book is an important contribution towards a greater understanding of what is really involved in being a local authority chief executive and how that role has evolved since 1974.

JEFFREY GREENWELL
(President – Society of Local Authority Chief Executives)
October 1991

Foreword on behalf of the sponsors

[illegible]

[illegible]

[illegible]

PREFACE

The origins of this book lie in a suggestion by Roger Morris, Chief Executive and Town Clerk for Northampton, carried forward by Jeffrey Greenwell, Chief Executive for Nothamptonshire, then Honorary Secretary and now President of the Society of Local Authority Chief Executives (SOLACE) and William Plowden, then Director-General of the Royal Institute of Public Administration (RIPA). Through them the RIPA and SOLACE came to be its joint sponsors.

Ken Young, then Director of the Department of Local Government Studies at the Insititute of Local Government Studies (INLOGOV) of the School of Public Policy in the University of Birmingham, was asked if my Institute would identify a suitable author. I agreed to undertake the work, not least because it gave me a chance to compare local authority management on the threshold of the 1990s with what I found as a researcher for the Committee on the Management of Local Government and other research in the 1960s. It framed in time developments with which I had been concerned and others which I had followed for a quarter of a century with constant interest.

An advisory committee was set up by the sponsors chaired by David Falcon, the new Director-General of the RIPA. The other members were Michael Clarke, Director of the Local Government Training Board; chief executives Roger Morris representing SOLACE, Rodney Brooke the London boroughs, Peter Daniels Scotland and Scottish districts, Michael Rush Wales and the counties, Bill (F W) Saunders the shire districts and David Spiers the metropolitan districts, joined later by Roger Jeffries as a London borough member; John Barratt, former chief executive nominated as a consultant by MSL Group International Ltd); and members of INLOGOV John Stewart and Ken Young. The committee met three times and gave most valuable advice prior to writing up. Members also gave helpful comments on early and very imperfect drafts of the text. The responsibility for the present text, which differs substantially from what was originally suggested by Roger Morris, is of course entirely my own although influenced and improved in many ways through the comments of the members of the committee.

For the finance of the project I prepared a research proposal to the Economic and Social Research Council (ESRC) which combined my interests in the historical origins of the role with its current realities and prospects. The ESRC approved the award in 1988 for the twelve months of the calendar year 1989 (no. R000 231390). The end of award report was submitted to it by 31 March 1990. The analysis and writing of this book continued until spring 1991, making it possible to take account of developments in the first half of 1991.

The award covered principally part of my own salary and research expenses and part of that of my colleague, Dr Liz Mills, now at the University College of Cardiff, who worked with me on the questionnaire and undertook the processing and analysis of the results. We were joint authors of the first publication based on the research, "The Role of the British Local Authority Chief Executive: some New Evidence' in *Local Government Policy-Making 1990*. It also covered help from a number of colleagues on the INLOGOV staff. The support of the ESRC is most gratefully acknowledged on behalf of all concerned.

Preface

The project as it developed was intended to meet a combination of objectives: to analyse the concepts, definitions and functions of the local authority chief executives as they vary between authorities; how the roles compared with that of their predecessors the clerks; changes in the roles through history; the core characteristics of the job and factors which could explain their variation; its formal definition; chief executives' characteristics and backgrounds; innovative approaches to the role; the effects of future developments; and generally to help provide a basis of understanding of the role to assist local councils to assess their needs in making future appointments.

The field of research included all types of main local authority in the United Kingdom. Over half the local authority chief executives in Great Britain replied to a complex questionnaire which required some one hundred individual responses. An interview programme entailed 23 visits to authorities, 17 of them selected to represent different parts of Britain, types of authority, length of experience and professional backgrounds of chief executives. Leading politicians including leaders of opposition parties were interviewed as well as chief executives in thirteen of these cases. A further six chief executives were selected from suggestions by chief executives on the advisory committee as innovators in the role. The information on chief executives in Northern Ireland was supplied mainly through a leading member of the regional branch of SOLACE and supplemented from written sources.

The scope of the research and extent of the information collected made it difficult to keep the book to the planned length. The tables of information alone, given the range of variables available for the analysis, would need a substantial volume in themselves. I have therefore regretfully been highly selective in the tabular information included. A file of the tables is however available to researchers on application to me through INLOGOV as well as print-outs, a copy of the questionnaire and the data stored on disc. Despite this there was still a problem of length within determined limits, which has been partly overcome by a decision taken at a very late stage to publish the historical material separately in a work that had already been planned in consultation with the Society of Town Clerks Education and Research Trust.

I have sought to reconcile obligations to five main audiences in writing this book and accept the risk that this will not altogether satisfy any of them. One is chief executives themselves. The total time and effort they have contributed to it in the completion of the long and demanding questionnaire as well as interviews is mind-boggling. A major element in the text consists of quotations from their written and interview responses, aimed to give an understanding of the great variety of situations in which they work as well as their diversity of approach and what they have in common. I hope the text will give them ample opportunity to reflect on their own interpretations of the job, what they have learnt about it from experience and how their individual approaches compare with those of their colleagues.

The second audience is of others in local government, not least those who may in future be chief executives themselves. I hope the book will help deepen their general understanding of the conditions, challenges and potentialities of the job. It may also help elected members to think through their needs and relationships at this level. In particular it casts light on the key relationship between council leaders and their first-ranking officers.

The third audience is members of the public who wish to understand how local authorities work, how officers relate to politicians and the contribution that chief executives make to the outcome, as well as the human aspects of the role.

Fourth is the academic world including researchers, teachers and students who are pursuing understanding of how democratic institutions work. The work was deliberately not framed within a particular academic approach, whether of administrative, management, political or historical studies. This was clear in the proposal submitted to and approved by the ESRC. I hope that, although satisfying no one academic approach, it will provide a source for those concerned with concepts and practice related to their fields and a springboard for studies which takes up specific aspects of the problems raised.

Fifth are those central policy-makers whose contribution to public decisions will determine the abilities of local authorities in the future.

To cover the wealth of information collected in such a short compass has necessitated a pithy style, lacking the looseness which can facilitate easy reading. I can only ask readers to forgive the lack of elegance and bear with the density of the style for the sake of the substance.

Acknowledgments

I owe a deep debt of gratitude to those mentioned above who enabled the project to take place and to the members of the advisory committee who contributed their most valuable time to advising on raw and sometimes rather inchoate papers. I was very sorry not to find time to follow up many of their excellent suggestions but trust that this will be done by others. I am especially grateful to John Stewart for reading and commenting on twice as much draft as anyone else, but I must emphasise however that I have ploughed my furrow largely alone and,again, that the responsibility for all contained in the book is entirely my own.

The indispensable cast of the book are the 263 chief executives who battled through the questionnaire and gave frank and committed responses, and also those who told me that they tried hard to complete it and gave up: together with those who gave their time to demanding interviews (not all of whom had completed the questionnaires). Equally I am very obliged to the senior councillors who expressed themselves so well about the role.

I am most grateful to Dr Liz Mills for her collaboration on the questionnaire, its administration and its analysis and to the administrative and secretarial staff, especially Dot Woolley, Mary Furamera and Kathy Bonehill. And more than anybody to the tolerance and support of my wife Susanne and others in the family to whom the work has been an unseen and unacknowledged burden.

Note on methodology, the response to the questionnaire and meaning

The ground covered in the research was wide and complex. A fuller description of methods is available in the end of award report submitted to the ESRC in March 1990 (available through the British Library, ESRC reference number R-000-23-1390: The

Chief Executive in Local Government: Role, Status and Future Effectiveness). The analysis was carried out on the standard statistical package SPSSX on the University of Birmingham's IBM3090 mainframe computer. The scope for analysis of the data has by no means been exhausted.

Some further information on methods is given in the text. A note on the questionnaire seems desirable here however since its findings figure prominently in all parts of the book.

The 263 chief executives responding were amongst the 504 whose titles included the words "chief executive' or whose job descriptions were understood to imply similar responsibilities. During the period for the completion of the questionnaire (June-September 1989) an unusually large number of relevant posts were vacant or filled by newly appointed officers who felt they were too inexperienced to make a reply worthwhile or their work too urgent to justify the loss of time. Some have apologised to me for this. Taking vacancies and recent appointments into account it is extimated that the response covers over 55 per cent of chief executives of the potential field. It was in the 50 to 60 per cent range for all types of authority with the exception of metropolitan districts and counties (where it was higher at 64 and 73 per cent respectively) and Scottish regions where it was 34 per cent. It represented 57 per cent of English chief executives, 56 per cent of Welsh and 37 per cent of Scottish. We found that the strongest response was from those who had been in the role for two to six years (79 per cent), followed by those with six to eleven years (58 per cent), over fifteen years (46 per cent) and under two years (28 per cent) in the office - the last figure perhaps accounted for not least by the difficulties and uncertainties of the settling-in period. The bias is therefore towards those who had been in post long enough to give settled assessments of their experience. Comparing the response with figures available for all or nearly all authorities and chief executives on political control, occupational backgrounds, size of authorities and population density of areas, it emerged that with regard to these matters it was proportionately a remarkably good representation of the authorities and chief executives in 1989 as a whole.

One recent development has been the welcome arrival of a number of women in the role, and that in some of the most complex and demanding posts. In most cases where appropriate I have used "he and she' and "him or her', but have occasionally felt that to avoid clumsiness of expression I should revert to the traditional understanding that the word "he' covered both sexes. The word "chairman' however is used to include chairwomen since repeated use of "chairmen and chairwomen' in the same paragraph can seem very clumsy and I am not happy with the alternative usages of "chairs' and "chairpersons', both being somewhat dehumanising. After trying alternatives I decided to keep on the whole to traditional usage with the clear intention the word chairman is common to both sexes, neither sex being more, nor less, equal than the other.

INTRODUCTION

In historical terms the British office of local authority chief executive is a recent innovation that connotes headship of staff and general responsibility for the management of the affairs of a local council - especially in those matters that go beyond the duties of individual departments and concern the council as a whole. A primary duty relates to the use of personal knowledge, skill and acumen to advise the council's members on policy and other matters of importance to the authority.

The principal elements of a modern local authority are a competitive political system that is commonly fragmented between competing parties and an officer system fragmented between competing departments. Competition for influence and resources is inevitable in both systems and indeed a sign of good health. There are normally close bonds of interest between matching elements across the boundary between the two systems - in particular between councillors and officers with a joint interest in and responsibility for particular services - leading to natural alliances in pursuit of joint aims. It follows that there is an imperative need for a role concerned with the integration of sectoral aims and activities to secure the common good.

While leaders of councils are normally seen to have responsibility for securing unity of policy, they are often largely dependent on chief executives to secure a decision-making process in which the contributions of officers and members are reconciled. Chief executives commonly serve their councils in securing reconciliation of aims in legitimate decisions within a political administration where politicians often cannot secure this themselves. In fulfilling such tasks chief executives are carrying out a function critical to the working and outputs of local democracy.

The effectiveness of chief executives in these matters depends on innumerable human relationships in which they not only need to give guidance and exercise leadership but also to mediate wherever appropriate. The very nature of the job makes it impossible to place a limit on what chief executives may be called upon to do in the service of their authorities, other than that they may not occupy a party political role.

This book examines the situation, practice and conditions of those who were chief executives in 1989-90 and concludes by considering the future of their role. Recognising the great variety of conditions to which chief executives respond, it examines their work in relation to differing political and organisational environments and seeks to draw conclusions on how the general purpose of the executive function in a local authority might be better met by alternative arrangements.

The research was conceived as an exploratory inquiry concerned with both the substance of the job, its perceived purpose and the contingencies involved. It approaches these tasks primarily through the subjective experience of those who seek to carry it out. The main purpose was an understanding of the role's demands - certainly not to put forward simple classifications and nostrums. In the late twentieth century physical science has led us to appreciate that there is an unpredictability and chaos in nature, most of all perhaps in human affairs, against which those in authority may be cast in the heroic role of stemming disorder. The local government chief executive acts in one such role, albeit a much less visible one than many. He or she is at the centre of an unpredictable microcosmos, seeking to realise purpose in the midst of uncertainty. He or she is no "bureaucrat' in any sense I can recognise.

Introduction

The role, as it has developed over the last twenty years, has acquired breadth of purpose and attributes of headship and service to local democracy. Its breadth enables individuals to develop their contributions in different directions according to their understanding of what is possible in a unique situation and their vision of the benefits a local authority can bring to the community.

Part A takes up briefly the origins of the role and its evolution since 1973. As mentioned in the preface the historical background will be covered in a second book. Part B is a study of the nature and conditions of the role on the threshold of the 1990s. It deals with contemporary realities, where chief executives' responsibilities lie, how they are interpreted, how they define and evaluate their tasks, their backgrounds, what they see as most valuable to them in the job and other information relevant to understanding their contribution to modern local government in Great Britain and Northern Ireland. Part C looks to the role's future. It examines how other countries meet the need for an executive role and how far this might contribute to the design of a more effective executive institutions in Britain, followed by a broad redefinition of the essence of the job as understood in 1991.

PART A

THE DEVELOPMENT OF THE CONCEPT OF THE LOCAL AUTHORITY CHIEF EXECUTIVE CONCEPT

Chapter 1

THE ORIGINS OF THE ROLE

Throughout the centuries local authorities have felt the need for an employee responsible to them for the management of the council's affairs as a whole and often, as much if not more important, to advise them on how they might best respond to needs and demands in the community and the demands made upon them by the law and central government[1]. That need was for long met in principle by the clerk of the council, the senior of the council's employees. Up to the early 1970s the basic role of the council's senior employee had not changed in essence since the middle ages, but in a few years from the mid-1960s it was reconceived and redefined as that of chief executive.

In 1963 criticisms of local government structure and management in the 1960s led the four main local authority associations for England and Wales to ask the minister for housing and local government to appoint a departmental committee on the management of local government. Its terms of reference were 'to consider in the light of modern conditions how local government might best continue to attract and retain people (both elected representatives and principal officers) of the calibre necessary to ensure its maximum effectiveness'[2]. (Management of Local Government (Maud Report): vol 1, 1967). The Committee and its twin the Mallaby Committee (Committee on the Staffing of Local Government, (Mallaby Report), 1967) set up to examine staffing matters were both concerned among other things with the definition of the role of the head of the local authority's paid service, but only the Maud Committee took a radical approach to the question.

The Maud Committee's research, under Dr Hedley Marshall, painted a picture of management responsibilities diffused over a wide range of committees which even in a small rural district could number over twenty without effective means of overall control to achieve shared interests. Departments tended to be bonded with individual committees. Management decisions were being dealt with mainly on an ad hoc basis: the postbag could be more or less opened out on the committee or sub-committee table or, in some county and London boroughs, councillors deluged with nearly a thousand sides of foolscap a month.

Typically the clerk operated at a weak centre of operations: a departmental officer for legal, secretarial and allied matters, including 'running the committee machine' and receiving and replying to correspondence for the authority as a whole, fielding as well as he could such issues such as were not the prerogative of departmental colleagues. Heads of department tended to lead the reporting to 'their own' committees although the clerk's department might put the papers together. The clerk was expected to see that people were consulted on matters that could not be pigeonholed as departmental. Major developments in services normally came about due to new legislation, statutory instruments and departmental circulars. The concept of 'policy' seemed unfamiliar. One county clerk reported that policy was understood to mean the introduction of new proposals for administrative action.

There was no committee or other body responsible for considering the priorities of the council as a whole and acting in a corporate capacity. Typically the clerk was not expected to lead but to do no more than overcome the inefficiencies that resulted from the system. Party leaders and clerks who sought to develop policies which put the interests of their own authorities and their political mandates first were left with little scope for shifting expenditure between major services. Except where a strong personality dominated the administration, the centre generally exerted influence only at the margins. Leaders' jobs tended to be seen as mainly to ensure that their party groups made as good a case in council as possible.

In the 1960s a few authorities had attempted to overcome some of these problems by the appointment of a strong leading officer: for example a Principal City Officer with Town Clerk in Newcastle upon Tyne (Elliott, 1971), a Town Manager without a department in Basildon answering immediately to a central executive committee of chairmen (The Basildon Experiment, 1966) and a county chief executive in Cheshire who was determined to convert his department from one primarily associated with legal advice to one concerned with the management of the authority's resources (Lee et al, 1974). The Maud Committee was influenced by such cases and also very strongly by Dame Evelyn Sharp, the permanent secretary to the Ministry of Housing and Local Government, who put the case with characteristic force that every authority needed a manager. The Committee took up the analogy with business management but recognised important differences. It recommended (1) the institution of a management board by every authority and 'that the Clerk be recognised as head of the authority's paid service and have authority over the other principal officers so far as is necessary for the efficient management and execution of the authority's functions', (2) that he 'be responsible to the management board and through it to the council' and (3) that 'the principal officers be responsible to the council through the Clerk and their terms and conditions of service be such that the Clerk's position and their own position are made clear' (para 179, Committee on the Management of Local Government, 1967).

The first recommendation would have extended the clerk's authority over other chief officers to an indefinite extent. The second would have removed his direct responsibility to the council. The fact that the clerk would be central to and responsible for the presentations on which policy and executive decisions were made implied that council decision-making matters across all services would be at the core of the role.

The Committee also recommended that the clerk's duties should include ensuring the effectiveness and efficiency of the organisation and the co-ordination (and integration where necessary) of its activities, the servicing of the management board with staff work, implementation of its decisions and those of the council, effective control systems, team working by the principal officers, secretarial services and the setting up of 'an effective establishment organisation to ensure economy in the use of manpower' (para 180).

It referred to the local authority's need to 'study the present physical and social environment of the area it serves, and assess its future needs and developments', and in the light of such a general study 'to come to conclusions on what its objectives are to be and the means to attain them. The problems cannot be studied in isolation; the objectives have to be reconciled with one another... Action needs to be co-ordinated, performance watched and timing and costs reviewed , so that corrective action can be taken when necessary' (para 144). This was the essence of what later came to be called corporate management.

No local authority is known to have adopted the management board system advocated in the Maud Report. Ten or so London and county boroughs joined the words 'chief executive' or 'chief executive officer' to that of clerk, adding to those who had already done so in response to the Town and District Clerks Joint Negotiating Committee's recommendation in 1949 (Greenwood et al, 1969). But more significantly, a reform movement of a radical nature developed during the five years from the issue of the Maud Report which was of a much more radical nature than the changes in Newcastle upon Tyne and Cheshire. It reflected new concepts and pointed the way to a new future, including direct concern with rational processes for policy-making, implementation and review (Greenwood, Norton and Stewart, 1969). Grimsby, Bradford, Coventry and Gloucestershire were amongst a small number of authorities where clerks, supported by political leaders, developed approaches which led directly to the recommendations of the Bains Report in 1971 (Conference Papers on Management and Administration in the Local Government Service 1969-70, 1970).

A critical examination of the Maud recommendations was developed in courses and conferences at the Institute of Local Government Studies (INLOGOV) at the University of Birmingham. INLOGOV, supported by the local authority associations for England and Wales, had begun its training activities for senior officers in British local authorities in 1967. A conference was held there in 1968 at the initiative of the Society of Town Clerks at which John Stewart, the director of the new courses, presented an influential theme paper on the future of the role. The conference concluded that clerks and chief executive officers should in future take the lead in policy formulation and development of control systems, provide integrated staff work to service the policy-making committees of their authorities, co-ordinate implementation of policy and as far as possible ensure the use of common management services throughout the authority. They believed that to fulfil these responsibilities they needed to lead a management group of chief officers and that their reports to committee should normally embody group opinion. The chief executive officer needed 'the authority to intervene in order to secure the execution of agreed plans where there is an avoidable failing on the part of a head of department, although this should be a last resort' (ibid). The tasks embodied in the approach were remarkably close to those which nearly all chief executives classified as essential personal responsibilities of a chief executive in our questionnaire survey over twenty years later (see chapter 7).

Eighteen months later another conference at INLOGOV initiated by the societies of town, county and urban and rural district clerks jointly reached similar conclusions but with a stronger emphasis on 'a participative cooperative style of management, in contrast to a more authoritarian approach, as more appropriate within the context of English local government... Some form of chief officers' group or management team', they thought, 'would be useful in drawing together chief officers and securing their willing co-operation and active involvement in the management process'. Not all county clerks present accepted the need for a formal definition of their authority over their fellow chief officers (ibid).

To investigate the position in English and Welsh authorities as a whole in 1971 INLOGOV invited clerks of county, county borough and London borough councils to answer a questionnaire on their councils' organisation. Out of the 126 responses on this subject 27 reported that there was no officer recognised by the council as having responsibilities for the whole of its activities; 49 that there was an officer with formal authority by council resolution over other chief officers 'except where the professional discretion or judgment of the officers is concerned'; and 50 cases where such authority was assumed without a formal resolution to back it (Greenwood, Norton and Stewart, 1975). The basis for the general management role of chief executives had been laid both in theory and practice.

New Model for Management: The Bains and Paterson Reports

The impetus for management reform grew with the issue of the Redcliffe-Maud Report in 1969 and the Labour government's acceptance of its crucial recommendations in the white paper *Reform of Local Government in England* (cmnd 4276) early in 1970.

The 1970 General Election brought to power a new Conservative administration under Edward Heath, with Peter Walker as a reforming Secretary of State for the Environment. He prepared and issued within eight months a new White Paper, *Local Government in England,* which set out the intention to carry through a massive programme of local authority amalgamations in the interest of efficiency. All existing main local authorities except in Greater London were to be superseded by new and in nearly all cases larger ones. Similar reforms were announced for Wales. The opportunity was created for radical change in the internal structures and management of local government in so far as the new councils wished it. Joint steering committees were to be set up and 'shadow councils' elected in 1973.

The Department of the Environment agreed with the local authority associations to set up a working group consisting of five officer representatives of the five types of authority plus a private sector representative under the chairmanship of Malcolm Bains, clerk to the Kent County Council. The group quickly became known as the 'Bains Committee' (The New Local Authorities: Management and Structure, 1971). It was overseen by a steering committee of representatives of the associations and industry. Malcolm Bains and the Treasurer for Gloucestershire, John Miller (later that county's chief executive and an early member of the INLOGOV courses) came from two counties whose progressive approaches were described in the discussion papers presented at the 1970 conference of clerks at INLOGOV. Two other members were well known exponents of management reform: John Bolton, clerk to Barrow and Soar RDC and the exceptionally trenchant Gordon Moore, town clerk to the County Borough of Bradford (invited to join the group not least because of the Bradford management reorganisation). The report in fact was one prepared predominantly by clerks or chief executives-to-be, embodying their conceptions of the future nature of the role of the head officer of the local authority of the future. The personal continuities are evident in that members of the group visited the Institute of Local Government Studies and used the facilities of the Institute to hold a two-day seminar at which they heard the views of second and third tier officers.

The 'Bains recommendations' contrast with those in the Maud Report in putting the emphasis on close partnership between members and officers rather than on a clearer division of labour between them. ('"Them and us" attitudes should be rejected as fostering distrust and dissipating effectiveness'). Secondly Bains' model of a central policy and resources committee serviced by a management team under the leadership of a chief executive and programme-orientated committees in place of traditional service committees was more acceptable to members and to chief officers than the Maud model of an executive board with the committees reduced to an advisory role. Moreover there was not the seemingly bitter attack on professionalism that the Maud Report contained - for example the expression 'professionalism feeding on departmentalism', a phrase that could come as a shock to officers who saw professionalism as motivation for the highest standards of behaviour and performance.

Most important in this context is the following main principle:

> Each authority should appoint a Chief Executive who should be of outstanding managerial ability and personality. His role would be very different from that of the traditional Clerk. Free of all departmental responsibilities, he would lead a team of Chief Officers to secure overall co-ordination and control and, in many ways, would set the whole tone and tempo of his authority.

The recommendations provided that the chief executive should act as leader of the officers of the authority (not just of the team) and be 'principal adviser to the council on matters of general policy'. 'The post of Chief Executive should be open to officers of any or no profession. The qualities of the man himself are more important than his professional or academic background.'

What other chief officers were asked to accept was 'somebody who is not merely primus inter pares, but is definitively their superior'. 'His first task is to gain the respect and esteem of his colleagues, because his true powers will come more from his own qualities and character than from anything written into his, or the Chief Officers' terms of appointment. There is much to be said for allowing the man himself to develop his own interpretation of the job within a fairly broad framework.' (ibid, paras 5.11-12)

The report includes as an appendix a model 'Job specification of a Chief Executive' (diagram 1-1) which, as the following chapters show, was commonly adopted. This is one of the most obvious achievements of the Report, along with the rather less common acceptance of the concepts of a policy and resources committee, the principle of directorships of groups of services and a much reduced number of committees (although in general these are still seen as 'service committees' instead of 'programme committees' as the Bains Group recommended). The recommendations set the norms to which most chief executives still work.

Following Local Government (Scotland) Act in 1973, the Scottish Office's equivalent to the 1972 Act for England and Wales, reorganisation process in Scotland ran about

Diagram 1-1

Extract from *The New Local Authorities: management and structure*, 1971 (Bains Report)

Appendix J

Job specification of a Chief Executive

1 The Chief Executive is head of the Council's paid service and shall have authority over all other officers so far as this is necessary for the efficient management and execution of the Council's functions.

2 He is the leader of the officers' management team and through the Policy and Resources Committee, the Council's principal adviser on matters of general policy. As such it is his responsibility to secure co-ordination of advice on the forward planning of objectives and services and to lead the management team in securing a corporate approach to the affairs of the authority generally.

3 Through his leadership of the officers' management team he is responsible for the efficient and effective implementation of the Council's programmes and policies and for securing that the resources of the authority are most effectively deployed towards those ends.

4 Similarly he shall keep under review the organisation and administration of the authority and shall make recommendations to the Council through the Policy and Resources Committee if he considers that major changes are required in the interests of effective management.

5 As head of the paid service it is his responsibility to ensure that effective and equitable manpower policies are developed and implemented throughout all departments of the authority in the interests both of the authority and the staff.

6 He is responsible for the maintenance of good internal and external relations.

---

a year later than that south of the border. The Scottish equivalent to the Bains Committee, the 'Paterson Committee', also correctly an advisory group, consisted of five clerks and a depute clerk, two chief finance officers and a deputy chief finance officer, two secretaries and treasurers, three secretaries of local authority associations, and an under-secretary from the Scottish Development Department. It set up a small body of experts named the 'Central Advisory Unit' consisting of three local government officers seconded from their authorities and a member of the staff of PA Management Consultants Ltd. Several members of the Committee were already known as reformers, knowledgable about corporate planning techniques (Midwinter, 1980). Contact was maintained with the Bains Committee, visits were paid to Bradford and also to Teesside whose Treasurer, Jack Woodham, had submitted an influential paper to the Bains Committee relating to member and officer involvement at all stages of the management process (ibid, para. 314).

Similarly to Bains the Paterson Report diagnosed the deficiencies in local authority management as fragmentation or lack of a 'unified approach', flexibility and response to change. It advocated 'corporate management', a concept developed like the Bains 'corporate approach' in two complementary ways. It gave 'the ultimate objective' as 'a situation where the needs of a community are viewed comprehensively and the activities of the local community are planned, directed and controlled in a unified manner to satisfy those needs to the maximum extent consistent with available resources'. It then stated these in terms of a process based on the management cycle of organisational theory interpreted in a way deeply influenced by the concepts of Policy Programming Budgeting Systems including a review of needs, specification of objectives, alternative means, evaluation of alternatives, action programmes and review and analysis in the light of objectives. It advocated a 'gradualist approach' to 'the ultimate objective of corporate management' - 'the integration of all planning and budgeting into a unified system carried out on a cyclical basis in phase with annual estimates procedures'.

Most of its other main recommendations had a close affinity to those of Bains, notably the integration of management structure through a policy and resources committee and a management team. Its concept of a comprehensive policy plan however seemed to demand a much more highly developed central staff than the one or two assistants to the chief executive working with inter-departmental groups that Bains envisaged. The committee therefore recommended the establishment of 'executive offices' consisting of the chief executive and the directors of finance and administration, except in the larger regions and where a new department of policy planning was to be added. The three person executives were soon dubbed 'triumvirates' or 'troikas'. A policy planning unit would be set up in the executive office consisting of 'a nucleus of permanent specialists together with a complement of staff seconded from the service departments as required'.

The Committee recommended a job specification for chief executives identical with that in the Bains Report with one exception. The Bains provision that the chief executive was to have 'authority over all other officers so far as is necessary for the efficient management and execution of the council's functions' was qualified by the clauses:

> except where:
> - principal officers are exercising responsibilities imposed on them by statute
> - the professional discretion or judgement of the principal officer is involved.

No evidence is known to the author that the addition of this clause made any practical difference, and as shown below, some chief officers in England and Wales still possess job descriptions that protect their authority in matters of professional discretion.

The Origins of the Role

The Great Reorganisation

In the three years from the setting up of inter-authority joint committees, through the period of elected shadow councils and the transfer of services to the new authorities to the initial shakedown of service delivery, clerks and chief executives were intensely involved in the enormous task of maintaining service areas in old authorities while substituting new and often much larger ones within strained resources. While the new legislation left local authorities free, apart from a few details, to adopt whatever internal administrative structure and distribution of authority they wished and the fundamentals of a new approach to management were clear and sanctioned by the local authority associations, in practice it was extremely difficult if not impossible to launch changes of a radical nature that required fundamental changes in the behaviour of members and officers. The over-riding priority was that on 'the appointed day' service delivery should continue smoothly over the crucial overnight transfer of powers as 487 new councils took over from the 1,821 that went out of existence. (Long and Norton, 1972; Richards, 1975; Pearce, 1982)

On top of this were the unprecedented conditions with which local government had to cope from 1973 associated with the world oil crisis. Councils and their staffs found themselves in a changed world where they could no longer assume that resources would in future be anything like what would be needed to match predicted need.

The research evidence on the response of chief executives to the problems of the transition will be described in detail in another publication. Not surprisingly over half (58 per cent) of the main problems in this period recalled by the 35 chief executives who responded to our questionnaires and occupied the role during reorganisation arose in setting up the new authorities - and not least coping with an unprecedented turn-over of staff as far more officers than expected took the opportunity of generous retirement terms for all who went aged 50 and above, inter-personal problems and the learning needs of those who had to fill the many gaps left in the exodus (Long and Norton, 1972).

On the other hand all these respondents recalled the period as one of unprecedented personal opportunities. For example one district chief executive wrote that he was the first non-solicitor clerk and although there were eyebrows raised at his appointment by members and chief officers, 'At the age of 28/30 life was beautiful and I believed I could handle anything!'

Difficulties were seen as challenges and the challenges as opportunities: this is a repeated theme in the responses, some chief executives refusing to acknowledge that any difficulty was to them seen other than an opportunity or challenge. Chief executives wrote that 'reorganisation presented an opportunity 'to create a new authority' and 'a new organisation', 'an efficient authority'; and another that his main opportunity was 'being given a free hand (and political support) to reorganise the committee and management structure'. A number of responses referred to style of leadership: 'to provide understanding leadership', 'putting right the dictatorial style of predecessor', 'imprinting own values and management style on a new organisation', and 'dragging authority into the twentieth century'. A number of chief executives placed high value on specific socially motivated opportunities: generating employment and improving trading aspects, overcoming multiple deprivation and 'helping the town to grow and respond without altering its character' for example. Politics entered in only two instances and then negatively, for example in a rural county with politically orientated centre city representatives, the 'development of policies acceptable to the majority of members'. In general these responses gave an impression of young men responding to challenge in a way not at all typical of the stereotype of the clerk of the past.

The New Office and its Holders

The need for a chief executive to head the officer force was generally appreciated. The acceptance of the new title was no doubt accelerated by the fact that the new legislation removed references to the office of clerk from the statute book and did not replace it with any other designation: the end of a tradition of statutory status starting in the middle ages. By the end of 1974, 502 local authorities had appointed heads of service whose titles included the word chief executive (or in two cases manager). This included some London boroughs unaffected in most respects by the reorganisation. All the new county councils and Scottish councils of every type appointed chief executives. Since then the number of chief executives has fluctuated only very slightly, varying by less than two per cent. After dropping to 493 around 1983 it had risen to 504 by 1989. (Figures derived from Municipal Yearbooks for 1975, 1979, 1984 and 1988). There are very few cases where the title 'chief executive ' has been abolished or replaced.

Even in 1989, 53 of the 257 chief executives replying to the questionnaire had job descriptions identical with the Bains or Paterson model and 169 had descriptions that were substantially identical. Out of a sample taken soon after the reorganisation which included 66 counties, 30 metropolitan districts and 185 shire districts in England and Wales, two-thirds appointed chief executives without departmental responsibilities (Greenwood et al, 1975). By 1989 the proportion was higher: 70 per cent of 38 counties, 59 per cent of 22 metropolitan districts and 75 per cent of 169 shire districts. Where chief executives had departments in 1974 they in many cases included personnel and management technique specialists. In 23 cases they had research and intelligence units and in 21 corporate planning staff.

The opening of the post of first officer to all professions and beyond was a recommendation by the Bains and Paterson Committees which echoed and strengthened conclusions by a succession of bodies from the Royal Commission of the 1920s onwards. What was the effect? In the former English counties in 1973 only one clerk, by profession a planner and chartered surveyor, is known to have been without a legal qualification, and seven in the county boroughs (six accountants and one professional secretary). In the new authorities in 1974 the figures were five in the county councils (including the new metropolitan county councils) and four in the metropolitan districts. Of course no great change could be expected overnight if only because since the new authorities understandably appointed experienced clerks in whom they had trust.

A survey of the professional qualifications of the chief executives of 1974 based on details in the Municipal Yearbook supplemented in some cases from other sources provides data for 426 chief executives throughout Britain. Some of the 91 omitted may in fact have had professional qualifications since in some cases lawyers and administrators are known not to have given their qualifications for the Yearbook. Apart from a professional soldier there were 272 (68 per cent) qualified in law, 59 (15 per cent) qualified in accounting, 59 (15 per cent) professionally or academically qualified in administration or secretaryship, 10 (2.5 per cent) in engineering and/or planning, and one ex-education officer. The figures are weighted by the exceptionally large proportion of administrators or secretaries in the English and Welsh districts: 58 (21 per cent).

The occupational backgrounds of the holders of the post have since become steadily more diversified (see table 10-1). A survey of the position in 1989 based on details in the Municipal Yearbook supplemented from other sources shows 46.5 per cent of chief executive posts to have been held by lawyers (a drop of over 11 per cent since 1974)), 20 per cent by accountants (an increase of 5 per cent 9 per cent by secretaries and administrators (a drop of 6 per cent) and ten per cent by planners and engineers (an increase of 6.5 per cent). Of the very few that came from outside local government professions three were from the civil Service and, as in 1974, one had been a senior officer in the armed forces.

There were few chief executives in the new authorities who had not previously been clerks or deputy clerks carrying central responsibility for guiding their elected members and officers in the quite extraordinary task of setting up the new authorities. This involved, as it had done in setting up of the first county councils and district councils in 1888-89 and 1894-95, formulating proposals on new structures and procedures and the leading role in reconciling inherited obligations and creating a new body of policies for the future. In theory there was a clean site for the building of a 'New Jerusalem'. In practice it could be a bed of nettles due to the conflicting concepts and interests amongst the mix of local and political interests involved. The theory that organisation should fit purpose or process was of little relevance where there was scant agreement on aims and objectives.

The strength of the Bains arguments and presentation resulted in much greater integration of business in committees and under directors of services. In 1975, over two-thirds in the 89 per cent of the counties replying to the questionnaire had eight or fewer main committees as contrasted with an average of 17 in the old ones. Nearly two-thirds among the metropolitan district respondents (92 per cent of all) had ten or under in contrast to an average of fifteen in the county boroughs - not such a sharp difference considering that the new authorities had a smaller range of functions. And 64 per cent of county districts respondents had eight or fewer committees. A survey in 1977-78 showed little change (Greenwood *et al*, 1980). The number of departments in the larger types of authorities was substantially bigger than that of committees: 71 per cent of counties had eleven to fifteen and 62 per cent of metropolitan districts more than ten, more justifiable in the latter case because of the much wider spread of functions. In other districts it seems that there was little difference: 76 per cent had from six to ten committees.

More significant for the role of the chief executive were those organisational innovations which integrated responsibilities at the centre: above all policy and resources committees and management teams led by the chief executive. It was here that the 'corporate approach', the dominant concept in the Bains Report, had to be given effect.

The 'corporate approach' was given little definition in the Bains Report beyond 'ensuring that authorities' resources were most effectively employed' - a trite formula which overlooks the inevitability and the desirability in a democratic body of conflicts in views and values concerning what effectiveness implies. The approach was put forward as the desired alternative to the 'departmental approach', somewhat misleadingly since in some respects the integration and centralisation involved conflicted with the principle, also put forward, that 'All decisions should be taken at the lowest practical level'. Departments remained and have continued to remain the basis of local government structure, both with regard to implementation and to the officer contribution to policy-making within programme areas.

Another complicating factor about the meaning of the 'corporate approach' was its use to cover the promotion of inter-authority and inter-sectoral work on community problems: a central concern for a chief executive, especially since state responsibilities were increasingly being fragmented through national legislation amongst a complex of special service and functionally organised public bodies.

Paterson, focusing on the 'corporate management process' with an emphasis on programming implementation and review, presented an approach by experts which, even in 'gradualist steps', would be extremely difficult to establish in the immediate post-reorganisation situation except, as it recognised, in very large authorities. To be meaningful it required central machinery at both committee and officer level which could produce a high level of commitment in the top levels of the political and officer administrations.

The great majority of local authorities were ready for the institution of cross-service central policy committees. In England and Wales there were by 1975 combined policy and resources committees in 35 county councils, 19 metropolitan districts, four metropolitan counties and 161 out of the 198 county districts that responded to a survey (Greenwood et al, 1975). In Scotland the regions and 37 of 53 district councils had such committees. But in ten smaller authorities they were committees for the whole council (Midwinter, 1980).

A large majority of authorities adopted the idea of chief officer groups or management teams, although their reality and performance is known to have been extremely variable. In nearly three-quarters of the 101 authorities in England and Wales on which information is available the teams met weekly. In Scotland the executive office recommended by the Paterson Committee for large authorities was adopted by five regions and five districts, but only two regions introduced the recommended policy planning departments. Two others (Grampian and Tayside) placed the function with the chief executive. All except three Scottish authorities set up some kind of management team. (Midwinter, 1982).

To the extent that the teams worked effectively they confirmed the commitment of chief officers to the idea of shared, collective involvement and responsibility for the preparation and formulation of policy advice. They appear to have provided chief executives with a most effective means of providing corporate general advice.

Notes

1 I am tracing the history of the work of the modern local authority chief executive's forerunner - the town, county and district clerk - in another book, along with a detailed account of its development into that of chief executive. Here there is space only for a few highlights in the development of the chief executive concept in the few years before the reorganisation of the 1970s.

2 Not least by Dame Evelyn Sharp, permanent secretary for the Ministry of Housing and Local Government, previously secretary to the Hadow Committee of the 1930s - a

committee that had urged that clerks should be educated as administrators rather than in the law (Sharp 1960, 1962).

Chapter 2

PROVING THE ROLE

The New World of Local Government

The setting up of the new authorities coincided with the collapse of the assumption of constant growth. Population growth fell sharply, belying the predictions on which the sanguine predictions of the need for expansion which was a driving force behind the drive for housing provision in the 1960s. Of more obvious impact the oil crisis following the war over Suez quadrupled the price of oil and led to a world-wide recession which cut world trade by 14 per cent. An attempt at reflation got out of hand. Inflation peaked at 25 per cent. A new Labour government, desperate for options, accepted the International Monetary Fund conditions for heavy support to overcome the rapidly expanding deficit in international trade. By 1973/74 local authority expenditure had soared to three per cent above the level in 1970 and was required by the government to bear a large part of the subsequent cuts. By 1977/78 it had dropped by four per cent. Central grant income fell rapidly over these years from 53 per cent in 1974/75 to 41 per cent by 1983/84. (Local Government Trends, 1987, 1989)

Central government policy became more concerned with cutting expenditure than with expansion. Specific grants were cut and policies of expenditure constraint beaten out between central and local government as the government struggled to meet its international obligations. Local government's share of the GDP dropped from 15.9 per cent in 1974/75 to 12.8 per cent in 1978/79.

The mid-1970s were marked by the onset of rising unemployment. In a few years the emphasis had swung from providing for economic expansion to offsetting the effects of depression. The decade ended in 1978/79 with a sharp deterioration in labour relationships, known to history as 'the winter of discontent'.

In a climate of financial austerity the need for a rational approach to local authority management was higher than ever. While it could be argued that rational corporate planning systems were the ideal means to this end, in practice ideals were frustrated. Targets were short-term and cuts made wherever practicable and acceptable. The savings had to be undertaken immediately after the new authorities had been set up. Many of the amalgamating authorities had deliberately launched programmes of capital investment to pass on to their successors. These had to be cut or replaced. The need to check incremental growth across the services made the new role of the chief executive critical in an unexpected way. Members' and officers' expectations had to be abated and new priorities identified. Chief executives had to help political leaders to negotiate a passage through the economic straits.

The extent to which titular chief executives acted as 'real' chief executives varied greatly. Many ex-clerks, with or without the motivation to play the role sketched in the

Bains Report, found themselves without the means or the support to do so. Research at INLOGOV on the organisation of the new authorities found sharp differences. Of 261 who replied to an inquiry in 1975, 36 per cent retained a department. It seems likely from the evidence that this was not because of the complexity of the job but rather because of the nature of local politics, local views of the role of officers and perhaps the feeling of chief executives that they needed their secretarial or accountancy staffs to keep them informed of what was happening in the authority. (Greenwood et al, 1975)

Three types of role were distinguishable. One was the traditional concept of the clerk - primus inter pares, typically low-profile, not concerned with matters within departments and not attempting to impose on the professions any coherent corporate management strategy. A second was the coordinator concerned with establishing efficient management practices corporately throughout the authority, generally associated with the use of management teams for this purpose. A third, typical of metropolitan districts, emphasised policy making and direction in a close relationship with the political leadership. This was often associated with a strong belief in corporate planning.

The chief executive job appears to have been determined in practice not so much by the job description, which was often quickly forgotten, but by the situation the chief executive met, his or her concept of the role, its political acceptance and how it was expressed in practice.

A later analysis of the nature of the role more in terms of its aspects than of types of chief executive, was made by a research team at INLOGOV in the late 1970s. (Greenwood et al, 1980). One aspect was 'the managerial role'. The coining of the phrase 'local government management' in a sense closely analogous to management in industry and commerce was almost an invention of the 1960s. It by-passed the approach to public administration dominated by concepts from the civil service and helped to justify drawing on the extensive literature on organisation and planning in the private sector. The findings of the researchers enabled them to say that 'The notion of the chief executive as a general manager has been fairly widely accepted by local authorities and the incumbents of the new role'. They detailed the differing means by which chief executives were securing necessary day-to-day knowledge: in particular retaining the secretary's department; building an 'executive office' (as recommended in the Paterson Report), enabling close liaison and understanding to be maintained through contacts with the heads of administration and legal affairs and finance; building up a department with key central functions such as personnel and corporate planning; and inner cabinets, personal assistants and leadership of crucial interdepartmental working groups. It is significant that the chief executives of metropolitan districts, who were among those with the most difficult problems of communication and control, were the most likely to retain a department as 'eyes and ears' to retain awareness of what was going on politically and administratively.

The second was 'the political role', more generally part of the job now that the great majority of authorities had adopted party system government. A minority of chief executives had undertaken to attend and service party groups. These were their main opportunity to achieve understanding of issues amongst members from the chief executive's perspective and to influence party decisions directly in many cases. The fact that the council leaders' role had become established through most of the system led to the development of the leader and chief executive axis, a critical means for two-way influence on general policy between majority group and officers on policy matters.

The third role was in external relations, where the county-district relationship was prominent but often frustrating and weakly supported by the members.

Difficulties and Opportunities 1975-79

The 67 chief executives in post in this period who answered the survey questionnaire represented a fair balance between type, size and political complexion of authority. How did they recall their problems and opportunities at the time?

Twenty-three replies related directly to the effects of reorganisation, including 'inter-authority rivalry' in the new authority, 'pulling together against urban-rural conflict', and 'welding together' disparate authorities. One chief executive described 'three years of establishing basic records and developing staff from small authorities'; another 'the establishment of a county council from scratch'. One found that his authority only settled down after major structural and political changes' and another reflected unresolved problems arising from the 'recognition that reorganisation had not got it right'.

Resource problems are prominent. Nineteen Chief Executives refer to 'financial constraints', 'stringency', 'retrenchment in the face of inflation' and identical matters. One refers to a rise in rate in the £ of over 70 per cent. Chief executives found difficulties in persuading their authorities to 'shift away from the traditional (free spending) economic stance'. On the other hand 'stringent cutbacks' in one case were seen as the result of a change in political control. Concern is reported about the difficulty of maintaining sufficient staff to provide adequate services.

Twenty-six respondents rated difficulties arising from elected members' attitudes as a major difficulty. Many of these problems related to uncertainties of leadership and political control, especially in the case of six hung councils. Four refer to the advent of party politics: 'parties became essential ingredients of the local authority mechanism' and there was 'conversion to political group style' and the 'advent of political control in a forceful manner'. On the other hand there are complaints about 'a non-party organisation lacking leadership', 'narrow concepts of the member's role', 'parochial attitudes', 'short-sightedness and parsimony' and an authority 'with much more traditional methods than I thought wise... with some suspicion of modern management methods'.

Problems included 'developing a broader view', 'persuading members to think corporately', to 'give time to corporate planning'. Another major difficulty was introducing and making sense of the 'Bains Structure'. Four chief executives complained of failures to establish clear policies and lack of commitment to policies and schemes. Problems relating to efficiency included five relating to establishing new or better management structures and two to departmentalism.

The period started with many difficulties relating to staff, particularly those at senior level, eg 'a management team with initially no idea how to cope', ' a total lack of senior management training and coordination', 'deadwood amongst inherited staff' and 'bad chief officer appointments'.

Regarding central government matters there were more and more restrictions', 'relations were under increasing strain' and there was a lack of national recognition of the problems'.

There is mention of leadership problems beyond those already implied above, including 'giving the city a belief in itself', dealing with a 'bruised ex-county borough (now within a shire county) and agency arrangements'.

There chief executives referred to personal problems of adaptation, including adjusting to a new role and area and taking over after a 'strained period with a predecessor, carrying out a chief officer's job as well as that of Chief Executive' and 'a heavy workload created by the Council's ambitions'. In general the responses show stress arising directly from the circumstances of reorganisation, including internal stress due to the failure of members to make policy-making and organisational decisions and of members and officers to accept new ideas and to adapt to new realities.

Responses on the opportunities of the new situation reflect the ambitions of chief executives at this time and some achievements of which they are most proud. Ten refer to the creation of a new authority: bringing together 'an unholy alliance of vastly different ambitions', 'shaping it' and turning it into one that has 'higher standards of service' and is 'responsive and forward-looking'.

Six show appreciation of the opportunity to develop a close relationship with politicians, working with the leader or chairman as an ally and, in one case, 'developing a position of trust... with scope apparently unlimited'. Two rate the building of officer-member relationships as a major opportunity. Eight refer to the implementation of corporate approaches. The word 'corporate' is used in different senses, as in 'a more corporate role in the chief officers Board' (sic), the 'introduction of corporate systems and process' and 'corporate management'.

Twenty-two instance responses to government policies of expenditure restraint as a major 'challenge' to manage with fewer resources, including a county chief executive implementing 'a three year programme with little resort to redundancies'. Ten give organisational restructuring and management processes: for example a corporate plan, a three year forward planning process and simply 'more modern processes'.

These references are however balanced by the 19 chief executives who refer to improvement of services and the environment and meeting community needs and aspirations, including six who mention specific re-development projects and five progress in housing provision amongst other services. Six gave opportunities for economic development and regeneration.

The final group of opportunities is one that relates directly to leadership achievement: 'more for less' leadership, team-building, leadership as an opportunity in itself, restoring staff morale, 'motivating staff to meet the challenge', creating recognition of the 'worth of local government, services and staff' and the 'questioning of values and modes of working (with the support of members). Several relate specifically to the leadership of elected members: challenging their attitudes, 'moving the Council into consideration of major policy issues' and 'bringing members from pre-1974 attitudes to the realisation that reorganisation had taken place and that new structures/systems had to be worked with'.

A few instance more personal matters: one to 'career progress', one to 'retaining position as head of the paid services' and another, much more positively, 'enjoyment of the management role in a large authority'.

The response as a whole belies the depressing picture often drawn of local government in the late 1970s. The assumption of a strong leadership and guidance role was seen as a possibility if not essential. The severe cutbacks in finance by no means prevented major achievements in services and development. 'Changing organisational culture', a phrase that came into common use during the 1980s, was clearly seen as a purpose and an opportunity by some chief executives. The newness of the authorities, the new philosophy of management that had been widely propagated and the need to compensate for the loss of resources from central government helped. Above all perhaps did close relationships with political leaders when they could be achieved. The need to achieve more with fewer resources, if only for political purposes, could change the relationship if a chief executive could deliver success.

The Need for a Chief Executive Under Question: Local Doubts and Tergiversations

From the start of the new authorities many councillors voiced criticism of the new machinery of government adopted to fulfil the 'corporate approach'. Advocates of medium or long-term planning processes often found themselves struggling against events. Grant expectations had to be scaled down repeatedly and new factors such as the onset of local unemployment changed priorities in mid-stream. Even two or three year programmes began to seem unduly optimistic. The cost of corporate planning staffs and the salary of the chief executive himself came under fire as wasteful and extravagant. Some chief executives without departments seemed to confirm such criticisms by taking on departmental responsibilities again as heads of secretarial or financial services.

By 1977 five English districts had made their chief executives redundant and not appointed a successor, or at least not one without a department - mostly it seems for reasons of economy. They were Rother, Exeter, Hart, Hinkley and Bosworth and Birmingham (all Conservative) and North Devon ('Independent'). The move was in most cases justified as a money-saving measure in the face of calls to reduce expenditure and was related to accusations in the press that local authorities had unnecessary, extravagant and top-heavy administrations. Typically they claimed that the appointments had not produced the streamlining and efficiency which had been promised for the 'Bains' system. The chief executive of Beaconsfield District Council argued in the press that the authority could not afford his salary and that he should be made redundant to save £10.000 a year (Municipal Journal, 6 February, 1976). An additional factor was that many councillors believed that the job chief executives were claiming to do was appropriately that of elected members and that the executive role in this sense should be theirs (Lomer, 1977).

The title of chief executive survived in four of these cases, coupled with the departmental designations of secretary or treasurer. Hinckley and Bosworth used the designation of principal chief officer together with that of a director of services. In 1989 it was principal chief officer and director of administration and finance. Hart on the other hand now has a non-departmental chief executive.

Political problems of a new nature had become central to the chief executive's difficulties in many authorities. It was not just that in many areas a well-developed party system was a new phenomenon and that party policies had tended to become more explicit and aggressive. If the political leadership insisted on dominating management, as there was no question they had every right to do, then to be effective in this area the chief executive required close relationships with the political leaders and knowledge of what was happening in the authority as a whole when sensitive political issues were at stake.

The Birmingham case is an outstanding example of the perceived incompatibility of chief executive authority with that of committee chairmen. The authority contrasts sharply with the other cases mentioned above because of its unique size, its range of functions and its long tradition of strong political leadership. It has had a highly developed 'Westminster' system of politics since the early nineteenth century. In July 1976 a new Conservative administration resolved to end the system of corporate management adopted by its Labour predecessor four years before on the grounds that 'it had not been conducive to the best administration of the council's officers and should be replaced'. Subsequently the so-called 'Bains machinery' - the policy and resources committee with performance review and land committees and a management team - was abolished and the chief executive role defined chiefly as one of ensuring working relationships with private and public bodies of concern to the city. The chief reasons given were that corporate working had not proved of value in Birmingham and ignored the importance of chairman-officer relationships at service level. The Conservative leader wrote that 'The close working relationship between the chairman of a committee and his chief officer' was 'incompatible with the corporate concept' and 'represented a partnership of immense value from which policy was often initiated' (Bosworth, 1976; Haynes, 1980).

The chief executive, F J C (Jim) Amos, informed me that he found his formal power to direct chief officers 'strangely conflictual'. Some members of the policy committee asked him to enforce 'caucus decisions' against a chief officer's will. Chairmen felt they, not the chief executive, should be directing the chief officers. Committees reported only every six months and were often unresponsive to central policy. The basic concept of information sharing, which the chief executive had found worked successfully in Liverpool (promoted by McKinsey consultants) proved impossible in Birmingham. He lacked the help of assistant chief executives who could work closely with departmental staff and keep him well informed of service developments. Added to which was the reaction of a new Conservative administration against the structures adopted by the previous Labour administration with which he was closely associated.

In 1976 the city treasurer was appointed principal city officer (but without the special status held by Frank Harris in Newcastle upon Tyne). The office of chief executive was re-instituted in 1982 with the appointment of Tom Caulcott, a dynamic ex-civil servant who had also been Secretary of the Association of Municipal Authorities for several years. This was a period of fluctuating control between parties when strong officer leadership was undoubtedly of value in securing continuity of programmes.

Authorities that rejected the concept of a chief executive in 1973, as in the case of Derby City and Adur District, or continued to use the designation of town clerk, all subsequently changed their minds and adopted or returned to the chief executive title with the one exception of the London Borough of Barking and Dagenham. Derby decided to rely on a management team of chief officers chaired in rotation by senior chief officers: the secretary, the treasurer and the planning officer. After four years experience of this arrangement the council appointed its housing officer as chief executive. In 1977 Exeter adopted a similar arrangement which lasted for several years.

One incident that involved a change of mind but not a change in the designation of the post was the appointment and dismissal of a chief executive within several months. Somerset County Council appointed Maurice Gaffney as chief executive. His previous career had been predominantly in the private sector until 1970 and he had little previous experience of the nature of west country county government. Mr Gaffney had a strong private sector management style and took up his post determined to run the authority corporately and as a business. A ten page 'indictment' of his behaviour was read out at the council meeting in July 1974. The council leadership's case was not made public but was reported to include rudeness to senior councillors, lacking consideration in parking his car and failing to pay his club subscription. It was clear that a sharp clash of cultures was involved: the county council leadership was not prepared to accept Mr Gaffney's style. He had no trade union membership and no protection from dismissal since the government's power to intervene in a clerk's dismissal disappeared on April 1 1974. His successor was the county treasurer, John Whitaker (BComm, IPFA) who had been assistant treasurer before reorganisation. He served with distinction for the following sixteen years in close collaboration with politicians and officers, playing a vigorous leadership role in the authority. The case demonstrated how easy it could be to 'sack' a chief executive and that cultural compatibility was a primary requisite for the post. To my knowledge there has been no other comparable case in the succeeding years.

Despite individual outstanding performances by chief executives it is difficult to avoid the sense that in the period after reorganisation there remained much confusion about the role amongst members and officers. Most chief executives adapted to the local political environment and did what elected members expected of them. Financial stringencies increased the need for the role wherever the search for economies was tackled in a corporate way, with strong political support or not.

The 1980s: Response to Challenge

The practice of partnership between central and local government survived under strain until the last years of the 1970s despite heavy pressures on local expenditure, but after the advent of the first Thatcher administration there was a breakdown. During the 1980s local authorities' resources were in general increasingly constrained by centrally imposed measures, including a system of penalisation for exceeding 'grant-related expenditure assessments' worked out on central formulas the basis of which was subjected to constant criticism. Selective 'rate-capping' followed and, at the end of the decade, the community charge or 'poll tax' and the uniform business rate, a tax over which local government had no control either in collection or distribution. Local government was attacked by the centre as profligate and extravagant in words that echo those of ratepayers' parties in opposition. Among other politically divisive issues were provisions for municipal tenants to buy out or opt out from local government landlordship; for schools to opt for independence; and, imposed in stages, competitive tendering for the carrying out of local government services, the legal provisions for which had fundamental effects on attitudes and organisation within local authorities described in the following part of this book. But these measures hardly reduced local government's activities or expenditures, and its number of employees increased marginally after a small initial drop.

The figures show that the government had in practice little success in reducing the scale of the local government sector, but local authorities had a hard game to play in meeting growing social need and demand. Most of all perhaps were the difficulties in meeting housing need. This was an impossible task in much of Britain. The responsibility remained in theory although local authority housing stocks declined along with the means available to them to build, improve and adapt stock.

At the beginning of the decade it quickly became clear that unless local authorities were in sympathy with the aim of the prime minister to minimalise their activity they would have to adopt a combative stance. In the outcome the conditions imposed by the centre were a great stimulus to innovative thinking.

The challenge was perhaps greatest in metropolitan areas where the policies and political orientation of the Greater London Council and the metropolitan county councils were seen as one challenge to central power. The metropolitan county council chief executives had the task of building up large new, novel and complex organisations while filling some of the traditional roles of their shire county colleagues, including clerkships to the police authorities and to the lieutenancies. Four of the six new chief executives came from county boroughs, bringing with them an approach and style of management more typical of boroughs rather than of the shire counties.

Rodney Brooke, former chief executive of the West Yorkshire County Council, commented in a personal communication that they were 'conceived in an era of overspill and strategic planning for growth which disappeared by the time of their arrival'. In the few years between establishing the new county systems and the battle for their survival, they 'engineered some striking successes in innovative services crossing their district boundaries, such as the creation of integrated transport systems and country parks'. In some respects their very success in promoting new strategic and in some instances very popular policies may have sealed their doom. (Norton, 1989).

The government's stance, style and innovations increased the dependency of elected members on their staff. Chief executives had the central responsibility for piloting members through the complexities of the legislation and central advice which fell on them in unprecedented volume. They were also faced with the task of overcoming resistance to innovations and economies from within the paid service, and as far as possible responding to hostility by demonstrating new and beneficial opportunities they opened up to both councils and staff.

During the decade new concepts of senior officers' role and style were given wide currency. Concepts of local government's role vis-a-vis the citizen were often redefined in private sector terms, especially those of client and consumer. The competitive tendering legislation in particular led to a stress on competitiveness. One highly successful book of research-based precepts on management in the private sector, Peters and Waterman's *In Search of Excellence* (1982), was widely referred to by senior local government officers. The central theme of the book is that management should be about the pursuit of excellence and that 'the dominance and coherence of culture' was proved to be 'an essential quality of excellent companies' such as IBM, Tupperware, MacDonalds and Kodak. Moreover 'the stronger the culture and the more it was directed to the marketplace, the less need there was for policy manuals, organization charts or detailed procedures and rules'. Phrases were coined such as 'action orientation', 'do it, fix it, try it', 'adhocracy' (specific action on issues that can be critical but do not fit into the bureaucratic framework of organisation and procedures), 'closeness to the customer', 'quality obsession', 'Management By Wandering Around' (MBWA), a philosophy of 'respect the individual', 'make people winners', 'let them stand out', 'hands-on, value-driven', and 'simple form, loose staff'. The central means to success in adapting to a hostile environment was to change the culture of the organisation from an 'administrative' one into a 'managerial' one', not so much by reforming organisation and procedures as by changing the values of its members. Peters and Waterman drew on a book by a political scientist, James MacGregor Burns (1978), for a general description of a leader's needs. They cover 'transactional leadership' - the agenda of management systems, shifting formal priorities, listening, 'building a loyal team', 'speaking with encouragement and reinforcing words with believable action': it calls for 'transforming leadership'... 'that builds on man's need for meaning, leadership and organisational purpose'; but in cases of outstanding achievement 'transforming leadership' that transforms cultural assumptions.

Many senior officers in the 1980s saw much relevance in this messianic approach from the private sector, although often expressing reservations relating to European cultural, political and public service contexts (eg Paine, 1985). The approach almost entirely neglects the values of public service propagated in earlier decades and may seem to reflect consumerist, 'shop-keeper' concepts dependent upon rapid short-term responses: a minimalist view of government as against views such as that of the Bains Committee which urged local authorities to secure 'the overall economic, cultural and physical well-being of their communities'. One chief executive defined the main difficulty of the period in his questionnaire as 'taking the long-term view': it may be that the philosophy of relating rapidly to the market in the short term was not the most appropriate approach in a period of uncertainty and lack of clear direction. The new approach has certainly had a practical inspirational effect for many in a period that called for a recasting of ideas on relationships within the authority and with its public. In fact, as we shall see, the impact of the Peters and Waterman book was associated with a rethinking of the relationship to the members of the community which local government serves, and more generally has had a wide effect on concepts of the chief executive role, whether directly or through other writers who have been deeply influenced by it and in some cases re-interpreted its meaning in terms of community government.

Difficulties and Opportunities of Chief Executives 1980-88

The difficulties and opportunities of the 1980s reported by chief executives are not especially characteristic of any particular size or type of authority, or except in a few cases indicative of the political complexion of the party in control. About a quarter of the 389 difficulties given by the 208 chief executives who answered this question on the period 1980 to 1987 gave chief weight to the problems arising from the government's constraints on recurrent and capital expenditure, compared with only about six per cent for the period 1974-79. According to one respondent the 1980s were a period of 'constant shortage' of resources. A number referred to the conflicting expectations of members who expected the maintenance or expansion of services and at the same time significant economies. There was a 'confusion of low spending with efficiency'. Maintenance of normal services left no space for innovation. Attempts at forward planning were frustrated. There was an 'excess of legislative change', a great workload and problems of adaptation.

This is not to say that chief executives did not associate themselves with the drive for greater efficiency or in most cases appreciate the work of the Audit Commission in its efforts to eliminate wasteful practice. In describing their role a few chief executives use phrases popularised by the Commission in this period, notably 'achievement of value for money' and the 'three es', (efficiency, effectiveness and economy).

In general chief executives appeared from their responses to see government policies as hostile to local authorities, describing the central stance as 'anti-Local Government' and 'antagonistic'. Problems set by government action alienated councils, leaving the chief executive to take much of the strain involved in maintaining progress within the space allowed. A response from a Somerset district where the Conservative Party lost power early in the decade illustrates what appears to be a common view: 'Whilst the authority had a majority party in control (the) difficulty was that new central government policies began to bite. We were already a careful and prudent authority'. A response from a firmly Conservative rural authority in Buckinghamshire reports that 'too many Government restrictions (were) mainly imposed to restrict a minority of councils spending on matters outside normal local government responsibilities'. A view which seems typical of Welsh authorities was that 'The Government appears determined to remove from local authorities the powers and duties it formerly exercised'. References to low member morale are not unusual, and in two cases deteriorating officer-member relationships.

The shocks of the 1980s probably struck hardest on authorities which had changed least in the previous decade. There are references to the difficulties of 'overcoming pre-1974 attitudes' and 'old-fashioned attitudes and procedures': to convincing 'members of the importance of radical change in our structures/approaches to service delivery to meet the challenges ahead', 'to agree clear objectives and to take unpalatable decisions', and 'changing the culture of the authority from one that is 'reactive' to one that is 'proactive'. The word proactive was a popular neologism of the period which indicated the need to initiate change rather than merely to react to demands. This reflects the difficulty stated by a Devon district chief executive of 'persuading an independent authority to respond to the opportunities that existed'; and one in a Hampshire borough of 'convincing members of the importance of radical change in our structures'.

In some cases the stimulus for change has come from elected members rather than officers. New members brought a fresh radicalism to both Labour and Conservative groups. In a County Durham district a chief executive faced difficulties in 'giving new (inexperienced) and strong-willed members the support and scope to effect their changes whilst maintaining stability'. Successes of the Liberal-Social Democrat Alliance in the middle years of the decade brought questioning of established practice and a variety of new approaches.

This new mixture of political attitudes often existed in a situation where no one party held majority control. By 1985 96 authorities were 'hung, including many large ones. Fourteen chief executives identified a 'hung' or 'balanced' council as one of the main difficulties of the period. A 'hung situation' often called for a mediatory role to produce decisions. When staid traditions stood in the way a chief executive might be accepted by political leaders as an activist, working on the 'culture' of the authority to produce a willingness for radical change among members as well as officers.

Uncertainties arising from central government action, together with those deriving from the internal politics of local authorities, made new demands on the chief executive's role. Chief executives, as heads of the paid service and chief advisers to a local authority, were typically expected to solve problems which neither elected members nor other chief officers could resolve themselves. The role was defined and developed by exceptions - those matters which it was agreed should be acted on but which no-one else in the authority but the chief executive was in a position to settle. He or she would then move in to fill what would otherwise be a vacuum.

One chief executive defined his main difficulty in this period as 'breaking the traditional role of the chief executive - making it more flexible and overcoming old-fashioned attitudes and procedures'. Clearly the chief executive was to a large extent himself defining the area of action needed and acceptable to the political leadership. The cultivation of a shared understanding of the demands and implications of new legislation required a bold role in the education of members - not a new area of action for chief executives but one that had to expand to cover more complex and radical challenges than ever before. Part of the problem was convincing members that the world had changed - 'making them realise that we shall never be the same'.

In stating the difficulties they faced some chief executives were also reporting their agenda for change - for example 'drawing together and developing a corporate organisation'. They might see, to select from similar responses, 'organisational inertia', 'lack of a modern style' and the 'need for major restructuring'. A chief executive of one of the largest of counties stated that there was 'a need to reorganise and restructure and reorientate a business with a £850 million turnover and about 50 thousand employees in no time at all'.

'Catalyst' was another word which entered into common use among leading chief executives in this period, indicating either a change in the 'organisational culture' of a local authority or promoting radical change in attitudes and practice. In defining the opportunities of the period chief executives used such phrases as 'to change the organisational ethos' and 'to achieve an enterprising culture for the organisation that was responsive to change'.

One area in which radical action was seen as essential by many was the mode and effectiveness of service delivery. Here competitive tendering was a demanding challenge to traditional attitudes and assumptions. It required organisational re-alignment of the organisation into client and contracting services, the former setting standards and the latter competing against outside bodies for survival. The curtain was still rising on this act of the drama in 1987. Only a few references were made here to 'preparation for competition' and the 'early stages of contractualisation'.

Competitive tendering was seen by some as a kind of Trojan horse, legitimising their quest for radical organisational change and bringing them the opportunity to develop a competitiveness conducive to efficiency and excellence of services: in the words of one district chief executive, to 'introduce a commercial approach'. Structural change, in dividing parts of the authority into clients and contractors, could make of the chief executive 'more of a referee between competing units', giving him a significant and new role. Fifteen respondents reported that they saw organisational restructuring as a major opportunity. For example one stated that he enjoyed the opportunity of 'restructuring the whole organisation to meet the perception of future needs'.

A larger proportion of chief executives cited the field of policy and decision-making as one of major opportunity: 43 per cent as opposed to 30 per cent for 1974-79. There are two strong emphases: policy formation and the promotion of economic development. The opportunities are described as the ability to 'demonstrate ability in guiding and advising the Council - to influence members' thinking' and to introduce new concepts. Sometimes they arise from the absence of political initiatives or political control within a council, particularly in the case of replies from some rural districts. A long-serving chief executive in a county wrote that a change in political control in 1985 made it possible for him 'to persuade all parties of the need to plan the service and introduce new systems'. From a large metropolitan district with firmly entrenched majority party control a newly appointed chief executive wrote that with a new leadership the opportunity arose 'for radical review and development of policy with considerable officer involvement'. In some cases the contribution to policy-making appears to have been particularly strong, as in a county where the opportunity was seen 'to introduce policies based on rational arguments rather than on political dogma'. Another chief executive claimed 'success in shifting the balance of expenditure to develop high priority services'. Another persuaded his authority to accept a 'commitment to growth'.

Several reported their success in persuading their councils or their majority groups to define their objectives. 'Setting the aims and objectives of the Council' was linked with the 'need for corporate management'. The 'corporate approach', is little mentioned but often implicit. One explicit reference came from a county chief executive who had welcomed the chance 'to begin to change the culture towards something which was more business-like, more product conscious, more client/consumer orientated, more corporately orientated', although he expected that 'it would be a long haul'.

Thirty-five per cent of the responses concerned with policy are related to economic development. Most of these show appreciation of opportunities for chief executives to implement their own ideas and aspirations concerning economic development or regeneration. They come chiefly from industrial areas with unemployment problems, but there are some from Conservative controlled districts in the south-east. In authorities which operated largely by consensual agreement some chief executives appeared to be able to spearhead economic development and regeneration initiatives with the support of their councils.

More than a fifth of the chief executives rated amongst their major opportunities the improvement of services or the planning and development of the environment. In some cases new chief executives found the scope to raise standards and make more general provision despite the tightness of the revenue situation: this was particularly so of authorities which benefited from housing sales and could rely on self-financing provision, particularly for leisure services.

The management team concept appears to have become firmly rooted in this period. It was the accepted answer to the need to create and to be part of a corporate approach. For a chief executive entering an authority without little previous knowledge of its human problems and resources it provided an immediate means to establish credibility, given a receptive political environment.

One chief executive appointed to an authority to fulfil recommendations of a report that emphasised the need for 'top direction' after it had lacked a team for nine years described his position as the occupation of an 'ivory tower post', implying a situation from which it was acutely difficult to relate to and influence the organisation as a whole. The problem was not so much need for 'top direction' as for team formation and leadership. But some teams presented serious problems, as in the case of a 'dispirited and fractious team' in the context of 'a non-corporate organisation'. Difficulties here as in other matters become a challenge and therefore an opportunity: 'the welding together of the chief officers group to introduce tighter approaches to corporate management and creating 'explicit priorities for the management team'. This may be part of establishing a new style of leadership to overcome established attitudes and to fight against 'a continuing apathy to strong leadership' or an organisation that 'totally lacks senior management training and co-ordination'. The central problem may become 'square pegs in round holes', 'getting good people and keeping them'.

The chief executive himself, if he cannot or will not adapt, can be a round peg in a square hole. One chief executive described his problem as 'getting to grips with the new age in an authority that had gone through three executives in ten years'.

It seems from the replies in general that the understanding of the role matured in the 1980s into one of comprehensive responsibility that generally permitted a high degree of initiative and/or exercise of authority. The chief executive often achieved a position where he could be described as the architect and developer of the general organisation and practical policies of an authority. There is little sign that his leadership role was generally questioned. Members' dependence on the chief executive's ability to explain and guide them in a period of unparalleled changes in the framework of legal control had established the role as a key one - not only on the evidence of the perceptions of chief executives themselves but also on that of statements of political leaders in 1989.

Reactions to the 'New Politics': Widdicombe and 'Propriety'

Political antagonisms became much sharper in the 1980s. This rose partly from the Thatcher ideology and its effects at national level and partly from the emergence of radical Labour politicians who not only attacked Thatcherism but who promoted practical policies which challenged its whole philosophy. For example they looked for means of attacking the power of private capital and redressing the disadvantages of the poor, women, ethnic and homosexual minorities by positive discrimination in their favour. The most conspicuous case was that of the Greater London Council, a problem that the government solved by abolishing it against the wishes of the majority of Londoners. As head servants of their councils chief executives could find themselves in a dilemma when expected by the controlling majority to promote policies within the staff and through the authority's means of communication to the public that were fiercely attacked by minority groups, putting in question the principle that the chief executive was the servant of the *whole* council. For example a Scottish district chief executive described one of his main difficulties in this period as 'fulfilling the "campaigning role" members saw for the chief executive on such matters as women's issues, contract compliance and peace related activities'. There was also a large grey area of 'creative accounting' and the use of loans where left-wing authorities would press the use of all feasible means to maintain expenditure against central government's attempts to constrain it. In a few cases senior officers also held elected office in other local authorities and were active in local politics. Liverpool City Council was a notorious case.

Except in some London boroughs and a few metropolitan districts the great majority of chief executives did not give problems of propriety in the behaviour of councillors as a major problem in the 1980s. In 1985 however the government, reacting to the concern of some of its members and their constituents over such cases, set up a small five person Committee of Inquiry under the chairmanship of David Widdicombe QC to look into 'the practices and procedures governing the conduct of local authority business', the 'rights and responsibilities of elected members', the 'need to clarify the limits and conditions governing discretionary expenditure by local authorities' and 'to make any necessary recommendations for strengthening the democratic process'. Democratic accountability, propriety and relationships of officers with members and groups were amongst matters they were asked to give particular regard to. They were not asked to look in particular at the role of the chief executive or at that of council leaders. The fact that the special position of the heads of the paid service or of the heads of the political administration were not focal points of the research commissioned by the Committee is perhaps due to this fact. Nevertheless the role of the chief executive became a chief focus of the inquiry and the subject of a series of their recommendations.

The Committee recommended that authorities 'should be statutorily required to appoint a chief executive, who should be head of the authority's paid staff with overall managerial responsibility for the discharge of functions by officers; that statutory functions relating to the propriety of council business 'should be vested in the chief executive including powers which were specifically defined, and should 'provide advice at the request of any councillor as to the legality of any proposed action or inaction by the council'. They also recommended that he or she should be statutorily responsible for ensuring the application of a provision that council committees should reflect as far as practicable the composition of the council as a whole and for 'the appointment, discipline and dismissal of staff below the rank of principal officer, except where they are appointed to serve the political groups or their leaders', and for initiating action for the discipline and dismissal of staff at principal officer level or above.

These recommendations went strikingly against the evidence submitted by The Society of Local Authority Chief Executives (SOLACE). It was acknowledged that there were difficulties in 'serving the whole of the Council whilst accepting that priority in terms of time must be given to the majority group'. A minority of chief executives believed that there was a case for moving 'more explicitly towards the Westminster model', and some that some senior officers at least should be appointed for the period of one administration only. But the majority felt that both the responsibility to all councillors and an acceptance of a special responsibility to the majority group must be reconciled.

The Association of Chief Executives of London Boroughs made a submission of its own that was appended to the main SOLACE evidence, confirming the special character of London's local politics. The London chief executives remarked on the emergence of full-time chairmen of committees who wished to be involved in 'areas of management previously regarded as the concern of officers'. They mentioned that the majority group election manifesto was used as the policy framework in some cases; that this had undoubtedly enabled members to exercise greater control of the policy process than in some other authorities; and that research had 'tended to suggest a greater reluctance to face' choices on submitting advice that 'will not be popular to one Group or other on the Council'. But they felt that 'developments in assertive politics' could not be reversed even if it was felt necessary to do so, and that it was indeed the right of democratically elected members to make policy, challenge professional advice and decide the level to which their involvement was necessary to ensure that the implementation of their policies should be protected rather than undermined. They felt that it would be inappropriate in this country to clarify formally the respective roles and rights of members, although an explicit statement might be required on this subject from every authority.

Against such evidence the recommendations of the Widdicombe Committee relating to chief executives came as a surprise and created wide debate within the membership of SOLACE. The original formal response to the Committee's recommendations in December 1986 was to reverse the view implied in the evidence by accepting that there should be a statutory requirement for local authorities to appoint a chief executive as head of paid staff with overall managerial responsibility for the discharge of functions by officers, but rejected the recommendations relating to propriety of business and the composition of committees as matters on which the chief executive should arbitrate.

The outcome, in the Local Government and Housing Act 1989, was to require authorities to designate a senior officer as head of paid service with the duty of carrying out certain duties specified in the Act. Local authorities retained the discretion to appoint or not to appoint a chief executive. All but a very small number were generally expected to do so and to include the duties of statutory head of paid service among his or her responsibilities, although it would in theory be possible to appoint a chief executive free of these duties if they could be borne by another member of staff. The new legal requirements included reporting to the authority on 'the manner in which the discharge of their different functions is co-ordinated', 'the number and grades of staff required for the discharge of their functions', 'the organisation of the authorities' staff' and the appointment and proper management of the authority's staff', and also sending such a report to each member of the council. The council was obliged to consider it within three months.

As may be seen from the job's history and the details of its functions given in the following part of this book, the provisions touch only slightly if at all on areas that most chief executives consider essential to their role. The provisions differed little from what had been normal practice in many and probably the great majority of local authorities. They obviously fall short of the 'overall managerial responsibility for the discharge of functions by officers' which the Widdicombe Committee recommended.

The Committee's recommendation that statutory functions relating to the propriety of council business should be vested in the chief executive was met by the requirement that councils should designate a 'monitoring officer' who would be empowered to suspend action on 'any proposal, decision or omission by the authority or one of its committees, sub-committees or joint committees' on which the council is represented which he or she considers might contravene the law or the council's statutory code of practice, subject to issuing a report on the matter to the members within 21 days. An authority could designate its chief executive or another officer as monitoring officer. Under the new legislation the monitoring officer was also given the duty of issuing a report to council members on acts of maladministration and injustice reported by the local government ombudsman. He has also, by implication, the responsibility to report on any contravention of provisions for proportionate representation of party groups on committees required under the Act. The Monitoring Officer has been dubbed the 'whistle-blower' for the authority. Views on the implications of these provisions for the role of chief executive on these matters are given below.

On the Threshold of the 1990S: The Pace Hotter Than Ever

In the last two years of the decade the external pressures on local authorities accelerated. Local government's response was a rapid adaptation to the pressures in which the chief executive contribution appears to have become more prominent than ever before. Of the 222 chief executives who replied to our question on the main difficulties of this period the great majority gave answers which referred directly or by clear implication to the effects and pace of new legislation. Forty-four cited the new legislation and its pace as a main difficulty. Sixty-two referred specifically to compulsory competitive tendering, which had been enforced more generally by the Local Government Act 1988 and backed by wide discretionary powers conferred on the secretaries of state. Twenty-five gave housing legislation, 17 the community charge (although not due for collection until about nine months after the submission date for the questionnaire), and 17 new financial controls (mostly those over capital expenditure). Some of the responses describe the reactions of elected members, for example 'the depression and demise of local government', 'frustration' and 'sense of instability'. Many chief executives faced the problem of persuading the members to face up to the need for decision on these matters. They described difficulties of 'making the members realise that change is inevitable' and that 'local government is under threat'. Those serving 'hung' councils and those without a strong party group system faced difficulties in winning the members' support for action: for example 'convincing a hung council to first face reality and adopt an aggressive self-help policy', and in a Scottish regional authority not organised politically where 'it was extremely difficult to carry out policy formulation in a meaningful way'. Others faced 'more overt political divergences', 'polarised political attitudes', 'a disintegrating political situation' and 'rapidly changing political stress within and between parties'.

In many cases responses reflect chief executives' conviction that it was necessary to change attitudes in order to obtain a sufficient and understanding response. A few refer to 'poor quality members', although more often it is traditional culture that is blamed. They identified as a major necessity the task of 'educating' the members about the implications of the new demands on them from the centre even more than in the earlier part of the decade. If leadership failed to come from the members some felt constrained to take an overt lead themselves. This was expressed as 'giving direction and leadership', 'trying to create entrepreneurial and customer orientated climate', and 'achieving political change within the authority'. But such a role was not always practicable. One London chief executive in fact defined his major opportunity as 'implementing things of which the council heartily disapproves'.

Difficulties are often taken as challenges which translate into major opportunities such as 'to achieve changes in culture and ethos', 'to adapt and change and look for new ways of doing things', 'to reflect the "commercial" approach to competition' and 'to tackle many of the old and unwarranted perceptions of local government'. Personal convictions are shown in responses referring to the need for change derived partly from practical experience and partly from management training and reading.

The negative responses given above are balanced by those cases where chief executives found a strongly supportive political leadership - particularly regarding a competitive approach. Here the business ethic was a matter that appealed strongly to some (but not all) politicians on the right wing of the political spectrum. Leading members also found that the legislation opened the doors to changes in attitude and approaches which they regarded as wholly to the good. In fact competitive objectives could encourage them to see the chief executive as managing director, so that it should not be assumed that a chief executive's stated objective 'to drive the organisation in its response to change' was not in accordance with political perceptions of his ideal role, as comes out more clearly in the account of interview evidence given below. One effect that is appreciated by some chief executives is the success the policy had in breaking down restrictive practices within a workforce despite resistance from shop stewards.

Concepts in the responses include some important themes in articles and books that were being published at this time. One is that of the 'enabling authority' (eg Brooke, 1989; Jones and Stewart, 1989). One chief executive defined the major opportunity in 1988-89 as 'Establishing the perfect enabling authority'. The legislation on competition and the transfer of local government institutions to outside interests in housing, education and elsewhere was linked with this concept which contrasts so clearly with the traditional view of local government as principally a service provider. The idea is of local government enabling and to some extent guiding individuals, families and voluntary and private bodies to provide for community needs and demands with the hope that they would do so more directly, efficiently and sensitively than local authority departments have often done. The key question was 'Can it be done better than local government can do direct?' The answer will differ not only on grounds of judgments of the outcome but even more fundamentally on the values taken into account, that is on what is 'better'. If it is undertaken only for reasons of economy without taking account of the social implications the answer will bear little relationship to concepts of the public good. This is an area of debate bristling with differences in individual opinion and at the heart of the political process.

The challenge is seen by many respondents as one of the competitiveness of local authorities in the free market. Many see it as a great stimulus to change: as one chief executive writes, it is 'to maintain or improve services by the 'council' being an 'enabler' rather than an 'adviser'. This raises questions of policy objectives, setting standards of provision, responsiveness, control and others which are seen to demand a thorough review of a local authority's structure, policy framework and relationship with the community. Hence the responses include 'finding a new role for the authority' and 'introducing a change of culture in customer responsiveness and managements style', 'restructuring in order to meet demands of competition [which has] allowed a breakdown of entrenched working practices and a new willingness to adapt and change and look for new ways of doing things and the re-determination of resources'.

Many responses saw the legislation as enforcing the need for restructuring, eg 'The split of client and contractor functions, with a new committee and department to manage commercial functions under the Local Government Act of 1988'. References to restructuring or creating more effectiveness and efficiency are however fewer than for the earlier 1980s. Those who see the matter as a main difficulty fall from one in five to one in ten, and those who see it as a main area of opportunity from one in five to one in four. It could be that in many cases the ground for radical change was laid before 1988, or that the level of new problems crowded this out of the limited space there was on the form for giving items. The flood of legislative challenges confronting local authorities in these two years make the latter a not unlikely reason. (It should be borne in mind that the proportion, as in other cases, does not by any means represent the number of chief executives for whom a problem or an opportunity was a major one. The average number of responses to the question on opportunities was just over two, and it must be assumed that there would have been many other items under this head had time and space allowed.)

Changes in attitude, style and culture are arguably more important than structural or procedural change. There is a fall in the proportion who name opportunities for reforming policy and decision-making processes from 43 per cent in 1980-87 to 35 per cent in 1988-89: a fall perhaps accounted for by the short-term tasks necessitated by legislation crowding out longer-term considerations as well as future uncertainties about resources and powers.

An outstanding feature in the responses is the sharp increase in the proportion of chief executives who give the recruitment and retention of staff as a principal problem of the period. Eighteen per cent saw this as a main problem compared with three per cent in 1974-77 and 1980-87. The need for staff, as some chief executives indicated, was to some extent created by the demands of the new legislation but this was also the 'boom' period which led up to the rapid increase in unemployment in 1990 motivating private sector employers to compete with the public sector by offering higher rewards, especially to senior staff. A closely linked factor identified in fourteen of the responses was staff motivation and morale. The problem is cited by one in three of the London chief executives, with other replies scattered fairly evenly through Britain, excepting Scotland where it was not mentioned at all.

The problems described above hardly make it surprising that there were leadership problems. A little over one in five report such difficulties - a rise of about eight per cent on the earlier years of the decade. But perceived leadership opportunities have also risen. They are cited by one third compared with a quarter for the earlier period. Chief executives became, if they were not already so, main agents of change faced with the task of reforming their authorities to enable them to meet the challenges they faced.

It is of the nature of the questionnaire that the results highlight problems and opportunities and give little indication of how they were met in practice. This question will be taken up to some extent in the evidence from interviews given below. It may be said however that the picture presented in this chapter is one of a management revolution, although it differed widely in its extent from authority to authority. The key factor, to judge from the responses to the questionnaire, was the nature of the response to challenge. It could give chief executives who had previously believed in the need for major change the scope to carry it through. A common interest could be could developed between politicians and officers to develop a competitive stance - usually it seems in the interest of the staff of the authority in winning the authority's tenders for services. On the other hand the members' response could be confused and unsupportive, leaving chief executives with the task of persuading them that action was necessary or, failing that, largely leaving to the chief executives and their officer colleagues the task of fulfilling legal requirements: in fact of placing the officers in the position of the executive and of accepting their proposals when they understood that they had no alternative.

But it would be wrong to end this history on a negative note. The role had been tested and in many cases developed with great commitment, vigour, imagination and ingenuity. Part B considers the nature and conditions of its achievements and their implications.

PART B

THE REALITIES OF THE ROLE

Chapter 3

INTRODUCTION: ON THE THRESHOLD OF THE 1990s

The evidence described in Part A showed that the redefinition of the executive role in the 1970s was often little more than an overlay on the role of the traditional clerk. There was no general shift to the corporate executive model as conceived at the end of the 1960s and which was the inspiration of the Bains Report. But the ground had been laid: the theory and practice of the corporate approach had been developed in authorities where the political climate was favourable or where the persuasion of chief executives had been effective. The challenges of the 1980s produced a much wider acceptance of the need for corporate management, if not for corporate planning. The advocacy of a redeveloped and far-reaching interpretation of the corporate approach, especially by John Stewart of INLOGOV and Michael Clarke of the Local Government Training Board, had, in the words of one senior chief executive, been 'cataclysmic' in the sense of revolutionary or the washing away all that stood in its path. By the end of the decade the role of chief executive had become the means towards which the Local Government Audit Commission and others looked to implement a corporate response to strategic management, structural change and a reshaping of roles among councillors and departmental officers.

The chapters that follow paint the picture of the situations, problems and achievements across the wide spectrum of authorities as it stood at the end of the decade. They are arranged according to what emerged from the questionnaire analysis to be the primary and secondary situational factors which determined the nature of the chief executive's role, apart perhaps from what individual executives had brought to their own job themselves. The first factor is the type of political control, that is whether there is a majority group in control or not - Conservative or Labour (there is no case described of an authority under majority control by any other party although there were two Liberal Democrat cases among the questionnaire replies); or whether or not most councillors were organised in party groups but none had a majority; or whether independent or non-party members predominated. The secondary factor is the range of services for which the authority concerned was responsible, taking as the groups that had a similar range of functions: first the counties and Scottish regions together; second the most purpose authorities - the London boroughs and metropolitan districts; and third the English, Welsh and Scottish districts. I was sorry that time pressure prevented a visit to one of the all purpose authorities, those for Scottish isles, although two of the three cases were covered in the questionnaire response.

A note on the interview programme

Dry statistics tell little of the nature of the job, its challenges and how it has been interpreted. All cases are unique and change with time. As Heraclitus put it, 'you cannot step into the same river twice'. The river of the 1980s moved the landmarks away faster perhaps than any other decade excepting the 1970s during the re-organisation. Uncertainties about what the role implies have been so much greater than for the chief executives' predecessors, the clerks.

To gain an appreciation of the challenges and relationships involved we relied mainly on interviews in individual authorities and 'open-ended' responses by chief executives in the questionnaire. In 15 of the 17 authorities chosen for the first round of interviews both chief executives and leading elected members were interviewed. The choice of authority was uninfluenced by personal knowledge of those interviewed or by special recommendations, so that there was no bias relating to the reputations or personal characteristics of those interviewed other than that arising from the aim to give a representative balance of the professional backgrounds of the chief executives and the characteristics of the authorities they served as far as was possible in a relatively small number of cases. The selection was also designed to represent all types of authority (excluding with the three Scottish island authorities), roughly related to their numbers, form of political control, socio-economic background, country and region and to some extent their size. The sizes of the authorities varied widely, although the largest and smallest groups were excluded with one or two exceptions on the ground that they were the least typical. An additional reason for not including the largest urban authorities was that they were known to vary so much among themselves that although each is of great interest in itself, any one case gives little idea of the relevant aspects of the others.

Additional interviews were arranged with six other chief executives from a list of suggestions by members of the advisory panel for the project. In order to give a balance between types of authorities two profiles are included based on questionnaire responses only. In certain cases interviews were held with chief executives who had not completed questionnaires. For these and other reasons it was not possible to cover all types of information given in the profiles that follow in every case.

Chapter 4

THE POLITICAL DIMENSION OF THE ROLE

To Whom is the Chief Executive Responsible?

Where do the chief executive's responsibilities lie? By tradition and in law he or she is the servant of the council, appointed by and subject to its control. But the council as a decision-maker is something of an abstraction: the majority present exercises its power, so that its chief executive is responsible for carrying out decisions which may in an extreme case be taken by only half the council members present plus the casting vote of the chairman, providing that they act within the law.

Chief executives' behaviour will be conditioned by whether they see their main responsibilities for policy advice and implementation as to the party majority or to the council as a whole. When asked about this in the research questionnaire replies were divided. Half of the respondents (49.8 per cent) said to the council only; a little under a third (30 per cent) to both the council *and* to the majority party, and over 14 per cent (14.3%) to the majority group. If we exclude from the total chief executives in authorities which lacked a majority party because they were hung and those that did not work on a party system, we find that 48 per cent saw their responsibility as to both council and the majority party and 23 per cent to the majority party rather than the council. Taking together authorities with Conservative and with Labour majority control (162 out of the 259 replies to this question), 57 per cent saw the main responsibility as being to the majority group: 49 per cent in Conservative controlled authorities believed this and 66 per cent in Labour controlled authorities.

The pattern of relationships can be fundamentally upset if party majority control is lost as a result of an election or a vacant seat. In two hung authorities visited in the interview programme and in another where the majority had gained control only shortly before the interviews, the chief executives were looking forward hopefully towards a situation where they would be able to work directly to a majority group again. It seemed clear from these and other cases that a special relationship with the party in power is not only a widely accepted convention but one which greatly simplifies the chief executive's pattern of working relationships and day-to-day responsibilities.

The references to obligations in the responses in the questionnaire as a whole show a wide and varied interpretation of responsibilities. Chief executives saw themselves serving the community and its representatives at various levels. There were the general public: phrases such as 'serving the community' and 'public service' are among those given as a motivation by some. In recent years 'the public service orientation' and 'customer consciousness' have come to be accepted as values which chief executives may justifiably propagate among council staff. Chief executives are much more than bureaucrats working to the rule of the council: it is accepted that they can exercise a wide range of discretion provided that in so doing they do not transgress the council's intentions, which is often in practice that of the leading members.

Within the council there are different levels to which the chief executive may work: the council chairman, the majority party members, a committee, the leader and other group officers, committee chairmen and individual councillors. The majority group is itself a corporate organisation at member level within the organisation as a whole. It may claim a political mandate in its election manifesto, giving it the argument that it is acting for the majority vote, but such an approach is disruptive if it is inconsistent with financial, legal or political feasibility. Developments outside the group's power are likely to upset its assumptions on what can be achieved. This has been particularly the case at the end of the late 1980s. Moreover priorities are rarely explicit and other influences from within the group are likely to raise new issues to which the manifesto lacks relevance.

Policy and strategy have to be constructed in the light of a changing reality. Judgments of feasibility and the means to maximise achievement will rely largely on information and advice from officers, some of it direct to committees but, often more important, that which is channelled informally through the leading members.

The officers can exercise great influence through their control of such advice and information. If the chief executive in particular fails to ensure that the majority group is informed and advised to such an extent and in such a manner as to maintain its confidence he or she will lose credibility. The fact that information and advice influence and determine the decisions of the council impels the chief executive to develop a special relationship with the majority party, and particularly with the leader and others who carry its main responsibilities in the council.

However in a democratic institution and under the principles of the British adversarial system of politics the opposition to the political administration also needs to be well-equipped to criticise and challenge the majority's proposals. It can be argued that ideally information and advice to opposition groups and even to individual members should be available to the same degree as to the majority. But the mountain of information that is available or could be made available on an issue is commonly such that the ideal model is impracticable. The primary objective must be to ensure that issues that come before the council are clearly understood and that advice on possible courses of action is given fairly and without bias to all parties.

Where a party sees itself as voted in with a mandate to implement a manifesto designed to form the basis of their policies, a dialogue between members and officers on the practical implications may legitimately start from that point, as in national government. But maintaining public support is ultimately the main consideration that faces the majority party, and increasingly so as it approaches the next election. Policies must keep within the bounds of the possible, meet mandatory legislative requirements and respond to a changing environment. The definition of policy in practical terms and its embodiment in programmes demands a close and continuing dialogue with the officers who bear the main responsibility for the design and management of services and their implementation.

At what point the opposition should be involved in the process of decision-making before the committee stage is a matter of local convention. Certainly the political administration is likely to wish to guard against premature disclosure of intentions. The most sensitive areas are likely to be confidential matters that have not even reached the stage of being considered by the majority group but are under discussion by the majority group's inner circle. Some may be trivial and not intended for group or committee at all, such as certain executive matters with possible political repercussions.

The most intimate responsibility of a chief executive in decision formation is that to the council leader - normally but not always the leader of a majority group - who has in common with the chief executive that he is concerned mainly with the corporate matters of the council. For a party leader the biggest embarrassment can be the leakage to others in his own group of matters under consideration with the chief executive. In a non-political council also its chairmen may expect strict confidentiality on proposals before they are opened up for wider discussion, and allegations of a breach of confidence by an officer can have serious consequences.

The involvement of council chairmen and leaders in executive matters, especially policy development and implementation, is a matter of convention, since they lack special status in law. This is a situation peculiar to the British and some other local government systems derived from British practice. In most other national systems there is a legally defined executive arm of the council, be it one person or a small corporate body. It may be popularly elected or elected or appointed by the elected assembly. Details are given in Part C below. The nearest that Britain comes to such a concept is in the non-statutory partnership between the council leader and the chief executive.

Both group leaders and chief executives normally head teams of colleagues to ensure that decisions are as well-informed and acceptable as possible. Political policy needs as far as possible to be moulded into decisions that possess the 'ownership' of those who have to live with them. Some chief executives reject the concept of consensual decision-making in favour of what they believe to be 'what is right', and many if not most leaders would probably do the same. There may of course be no achievable consensus, or the consensus may be biased by self-interest, or the overall view of leader and/or chief executive may be essential to the understanding of an issue. But there is a continuum here between those who regard consensus as a primary goal and those who have little confidence in it and rely on their personal authority to override opposition.

Decision-making may be seen as a process which seeks a progressive reduction of uncertainty about what should be done up to the point where measures are given operational definition. It is at the leader-chief executive stage that the general mandate for officer action on corporate matters is often confirmed, subject to confirmation or amendment by committee and council. The duo of political leader and officer leader is the executive core of the authority. If the relationship fails the system is in disarray. The two must be in gear with each other if the machinery of decision-making and implementation is to function well.

The chief executive is in some respects immeasurably better equipped to contribute to policy and programme development than the leader. He or she is head of a staff which may number thousands and be drawn on for a wider range of relevant expertise, information and experience than anyone else can command. Chief executives are appointed for their understanding, high ability and management capability, and can give themselves full-time to council work. In comparison a local political leader is in most cases part-time and otherwise disadvantaged, with little staff support beyond a secretary and possibly a research officer or two. But emergence as leader is likely to be due to the recognition of political skill and ability to hold the group together as well perhaps as ambition. The leader is dependent on the votes of volatile politicians and subject in some cases to attacks by group members who may not share the same point of view or values and who may not appreciate the limitations on what can be achieved. Nevertheless the leader carries political responsibility for ensuring that the officers 'deliver' political commitments which must be achieved largely through the chief executive and other chief officers.

The council leader has become increasingly dependent on the resources and ability of the chief executive in recent years. The heavier and more demanding new legislation becomes, the more that dependence grows. It seemed that a climax had been reached around 1989. Where there was no leader supported by a majority political group these demands placed a heavy and unprecedented challenge on the chief executive to reach a position in dialogue with members of more than one party to reach a viable position on key decisions which had to involve compromise.

The Pattern and Quality of Chief Executives' Working Relationships

Chief executives' working relationships can be classified as those with members of the council, those with the council's other employees as their head, and those with a great diversity of organised and unorganised interests within the general community. The pattern of contacts among these groups varies widely from chief executive to chief executive.

The response to the questionnaire explored patterns of relationship by asking about frequency of meetings and quality of working relationships. Chief executives were asked to state how often they met with those with whom they might be expected to work: whether daily, two to four times a week, weekly, fortnightly, monthly or more than monthly; and whether they rated the relationships very good, good, neither good nor poor, poor or very poor.

Taking all types of authority together two relationships were closest: those with the council leader and the chief finance officer (tables 4-1, 4-2). Over two-thirds (69 per cent) of the chief executives out of the 229 who replied to this question met the leader at least twice a week, and more than one in five met him or her at least daily. Seventy-one per cent described the relationship as a very good one. It was second only to that with the chief finance officer whom 83 per cent of 252 who gave details met at least daily, including 31 per cent who saw him every day. In terms of quality the relationship with the leader scored a little better than that with the finance officer: 71 per cent against the finance officer's 67 per cent. In both cases under five per cent described the relationships as less than good.

Meetings were less frequent with mayors and council chairmen who were not also leaders: more often than weekly in 49 per cent of 246 cases and daily in 4.5 per cent. The next closest relationships with politicians were with chairmen of the main policy committees who were not leaders (86 cases): in 28 per cent of these cases they met two to four times a week and in five per cent of cases daily. Weekly meetings were commonest at 34 per cent.

As observed above, relationships with leaders of minority parties should contribute to the effectiveness of the opposition and therefore be relevant to the quality of local democracy. Ideally the opposition leaders need a good understanding of the corporate

TABLE 4-1 PERCENTAGE OF CHIEF EXECUTIVES MEETING WITH COUNCIL MEMBERS MORE OFTEN THAN WEEKLY

Note: Percentages given in brackets are of the number of responses under each head. In most cases the differences between total questionnaire response and response on particular heads are attributable to the non-existence of the political office concerned in the chief executive's authority or a combination of offices, e.g. of leader and chair of policy committee. The response is counted against the first officer listed in the table. In some other cases respondents declined making estimates on particular heads because of unwillingness to generalise.

	Shire county	Shire district	Met district	London borough	Scottish region	Scottish district	All LAs
Members:	(30)	(173)	(22)	(15)	(6)	(17)	(263)
Leader of council	73 (26)	67 (147)	100 (21)	67 (15)	100 (4)	81 (16)	69 (229)
Council chair/mayor	55 (29)	52 (163)	15 (20)	7 (15)	100 (4)	80 (15)	49 (246)
Chair main policy committee	88 (8)	13 (60)	50 (4)	25 (4)	100 (3)	43 (7)	28 (86)
Leader(s) minority parties	8 (26)	3 (143)	42 (19)	0 (15)	0 (3)	8 (13)	4 (219)
Chairs other committees	7 (28)	3 (160)	0 (19)	0 (15)	0 (5)	24 (17)	4 (244)
Average member	0 (28)	3 (161)	0 (19)	0 (15)	0 (6)	12 (17)	2 (246)

TABLE 4-2 PERCENTAGE OF CHIEF EXECUTIVES MEETING WITH SENIOR OFFICERS MORE THAN WEEKLY

Note: As in Table 4-1, figures in brackets represent total response on particular head. The main reasons for non-responses are that chief executive is head of finance, and refusal to generalise.

	Shire county	Shire district	Met district	London borough	Scottish region	Scottish district	All LAs
Officers:	(29)	(176)	(22)	(15)	(6)	(16)	(264)
Treasurer/director finance	75 (28)	73 (167)	81 (21)	84 (13)	100 (6)	82 (17)	82 (252)
Other chief officers	59 (28)	70 (171)	38 (21)	40 (15)	40 (5)	71 (17)	64 (257)
Other senior officers	35 (26)	36 (156)	9 (20)	7 (14)	20 (5)	31 (16)	32 (237)

issues that the authority faces. They need to be well informed, formally or informally, on matters of policy and implementation and so be able to inform their group members whose views might otherwise be almost exclusively derived from experience on service committees.

Chief executives were a little less likely to be in weekly contact with opposition party leaders than with committee chairmen (policy committee chairmen apart): 20 per cent with leaders as against 24 per cent with chairmen. In 26 per cent of the cases the chief executive saw them less than monthly, compared with 17 per cent in the case of the chairmen.

It is commonly chairmen who are expected to guide debate on key issues within service areas in group, committee and council, supported where appropriate by specialist officers. Arguably they need to be closely involved in the determination of corporate policy since otherwise they may possess blinkered points of view which undermine corporate policy-making.

Practice appears to range from well-informed 'cabinet meetings' of committee chairmen with the chief executive and other officers present at one extreme to a remote relationship between chairmen and officers excepting the service officers responsible for services reporting to the committee concerned at the other extreme. Remote relationships between committee chairmen and chief executives suggest a serious problem in developing and maintaining an understanding of corporate as opposed to service interests. Where policy committees include the committee chairmen or there is a chairmen's forum which the chief executive attends, this may help: especially in the latter case where confidentiality on policy ideas can be maintained. Otherwise chief executives may have to rely on the indirect briefing of chairmen through leaders and the chief officers to whom they relate, which may often be inadequate. There were indications in the interviews that some chief executives are looking for ways to bridge the gap.

There is much less contact between chief executives and other members: out of 246 responses 12 per cent reported weekly or more frequent meetings, 20 per cent fortnightly, 30 per cent monthly and 39 per cent less often. Here the chief executive may be something of a mystery person and incur unfair blame.

Some variations between types and conditions of authorities are of interest - a subject to be expanded on in the chapters that follow. Close relationships between chief executive and council leader are notably more common in the metropolitan districts than elsewhere. All 21 respondents from these authorities met their leaders at least twice a week and 15 daily. The next closest relationship was found in Scotland where all chief executives of the regions who replied met their leaders at least twice a week, as did 81 per cent of those in the districts. On the other hand only ten out of 15 London chief executives had such meetings more than once a week and only one daily. Shire counties follow, 73 per cent having meetings more than once a week, followed by shire districts at 61 per cent. Taking all authorities together six per cent of the chief executives met their leaders no more than monthly or less often.

There is a strong connection between frequency of meetings with the council leader and the degree of urbanisation or 'built-upness' of the area served. In the authorities with the lowest population density - under 2.5 people per hectare - 53 per cent of chief executives met the leaders more than once a week and 14 per cent met them daily. Excepting that level, the higher the population density the more likely there were to be frequent meetings. They met more than weekly in 80 per cent of authorities with over 10 persons per hectare (the population density for example of Chesterfield, Birmingham and Glasgow).

There were no striking differences in the pattern of relationships in terms of chief executives' professional background or other variables tested.

Chapter 5

RELATIONSHIPS WITH ELECTED MEMBERS IN AUTHORITIES UNDER MAJORITY GROUP CONTROL

Counties and Regions

English and Welsh county and Scottish region councils are alike in carrying responsibility for the largest of the local government services - education, social services, structure planning, highways, fire and in some cases the police. They present a special challenge to corporate management ambitions because of their independent statutory basis, size and complexity, which result in their tending to behave more like federal bodies or holding companies than corporate entities. The legislation of the 1980s resulted in new needs for structural and procedural reforms that demanded a corporate approach as never before while also building new rigidities into the organisation.

Where do their chief executives see their responsibilities to lie? Amongst the chief executives of Conservative controlled counties two answered that they saw themselves answerable to the council as a whole, two to the majority group and four to both. One noted that a balance was needed according to subject and, interestingly, another that on policy matters he acted as responsible to a group of committee chairmen. In Labour authorities the replies were similarly mixed: one said his responsibility was to the council, three to the majority party and two to both.

All county chief executives who were in the same job in the mid-1970s gave the creation of their new authorities as one of their greatest opportunities and achievements. The financial and legislative demands of the 1980s also stood out in all their replies, however long or short their service in the role.

The difficulties arising from government policies in this period were to the fore as much in Conservative as in Labour controlled counties. A chief executive in a Conservative county gave 'more forceful political control' as one of the main problems of the first eight or nine years of Thatcher government, but it was in Labour controlled authorities that the political tensions were greatest. In explaining the implications of the Conservative legislation to Labour group members chief executives ran the hazard of appearing to be more the servants of Whitehall than of local government. On the other hand the legislation was a challenge to emphasise some positive opportunities it contained that were not always obvious to controlling groups. A chief executive in this situation could also point to how the party group might be able to meet their manifesto promises to some extent despite the heavy financial and legal constraints imposed by the government.

In most of these cases chief executives faced reluctance from members to abandon day by day involvement in minor management decisions that the new requirements implied. These were the activities which they had found the most interesting part of their role and which had to a large extent constituted the meaning of local democracy as they understood it.

Patterns of Relationship:

All sixteen chief executives in the survey met the leader more often than weekly and daily in three of them and the relationship was rated as 'good'. Meetings with the council chairman were only a little less frequent and in only one case less than weekly. All reported that their relationships with their council leaders were very good (14 cases) or good (one case), with the exception of one where the relationship was described as neither good nor poor. Relations with council chairmen were almost equally warm. There was very little difference between Conservative and Labour controlled authorities in this respect. The group of the leader, council chairman and chief executive appeared to be well established generally as the nucleus for the county or regional political control and for executive decisions on corporate matters.

Contact with minority leaders is one area in which there was much variation, ranging from weekly down to less than monthly. Some differences may be due to the shorter committee cycles in some Welsh county councils and Scottish regional councils which meet every one or two months as against the quarterly meetings that are normal in England. Interviews showed that some opposition leaders were handicapped by their lack of information about the new business of the authority.

There is a big contrast between the frequency of meetings with the council leader and chairman and those with committee chairmen. The latter were monthly or less often, influenced it may assumed by committee cycles. These exclude three cases of policy committee chairmen, who may be presumed to be an 'inner group' who saw the chief executive two to four times a week.

One related matter on which there is great variation between individuals is the average number of hours a week spent by chief executives in meetings with members. In the fourteen cases where the data is available hours of contact varied between three and sixteen hours a week. The responses fall into two widely separated groups. Six gave an average of 6.2 hours or less to contact with members, while eight give ten hours or more. If the two replies nearest to the average are omitted the contrast is much sharper: five giving between three and five hours and seven between twelve and over fifteen. These big differences in time spent with members do not vary with party control, by whether the chief executive heads a department or by the frequency or infrequency of contacts with leader and chairman, excepting two Conservative cases where contacts were weekly or less. Obviously the chief executive is dependent on the behaviour of the leader and of other leading politicians in this matter. If the leader treats the job as one amongst a number of business commitments then the closeness with the chief executives that is shown in most of the other authorities can hardly be possible.

Variations in Political Style

In the authorities visited the political style of the majority groups varied. In all three

Conservative counties it might be described as traditionally conservative with a small 'c'. In one case councillors towards the radical right wing of the party had been influential for a few years but the group as a whole had, in the words of the chief executive, 'moved in recent years from dry to fairly damp'. In the case of the county with the strongest majority the leader maintained a daily working relationship with the chief executive and the relationship was reported 'very good'. In the 'fairly damp' case the chief executive met the leader and also the council chairman two to four times a week and the relationship was rated as 'good'. In a third case meetings with leader and chairman were no more than weekly and relationships with both were rated as 'neither good nor poor'. The impression was that the relationship with the two senior politicians on the council was comparatively remote, as though their commitment to the support of the chief executive in the very innovative approach he was undertaking was an uninvolved one.

Two cases where the Labour group was in control afford an interesting contrast. Besides the political hegemony of Labour they shared a history of sharp decline in the main local industries from which the councillors had largely been recruited. In both cases the chief executive was in daily touch with the leader and the relationships were rated very good.

Three Conservative controlled counties

Profile A

This authority, controlled continuously by Conservative groups since it was set up, provided for an extensive and mostly rural area with medium-sized commercial and industrial centres. The chief executive described the political situation between parties as 'a healthy balance' and the Conservative group as having moved towards a more liberal policy stance. He carried responsibility for a large department and saw his responsibility in policy advice and implementation as to the council as a whole and also to an informal group of committee chairmen from the majority party.

The former chief executive had been a radical innovator, strong on corporate control and full of initiatives which tended to over-ride professional advice and the traditional autonomy of committees. This produced antagonisms in some cases. In succeeding him the new chief executive, with many years experience in the authority behind him, saw his main opportunity in the job as to improve relationships and corporate attitudes. He felt that in doing so he had established a level of confidence from which he could more effectively give influential advice and lead the authority in the new phase opening with the provisions of the 1988 Local Government Act.

He enjoyed off the record meetings with committee chairmen where they could talk freely about what was happening in the party group. Similar meetings with senior officers had ended the former tradition of 'washing dirty linen in public'. He believed his predecessor's ideas had 'been too advanced for members' and he had found it not difficult to overcome the mistrust that had grown up among and between officers and elected members. He thought members liked to listen to professionals rather than generalists.

For decision-making at officer level he thought it was important to listen to chief officers carefully and then come to a quick decision as to what he should do and where appropriate incorporate his conclusions in a report. The listening role was very important when combined with political 'nous' and a fair presentation of issues.

As well as fostering good relationships and carrying out well what was set out in his Bains-type job description, his most important personal objectives had been to retain the confidence of members, officers and clients and to improve the image of the authority.

The chief executive met the leader and council chairman two or three times a week, the committee chairmen monthly and the leaders of the minority parties and the 'average member' less than monthly. He rated his relationships good in all cases, with the exception of the leader of the largest minority party with whom he described his relationship as 'neither good nor poor'. In a typical week he worked about fifty hours out of which some twelve and a half hours were spent with members.

The leader saw the chief executive as a link between members and officers, responsible for communication 'between both sides' and for motivation generally. Councillors, he thought, needed promptings by the chief executive through their leader.

The leader of the largest opposition party seemed at a psychological distance from the chief executive and felt that the lack of contact handicapped the opposition in the extent to which it could make well-informed and well-argued cases against the ruling group's proposals. He thought that there was need for the opposition leaders to see more of officers in order to improve their general understanding of matters that came before the council; and if they wished, to discuss their problems with them.

This case contrasts with those of the two following Conservative controlled authorities which were not visited but where the profiles are based on written information by the chief executives.

Profile B

This council had a similar political balance to that described above. It was responsible for a rich agricultural area including prosperous towns and new industries. The chief executive, appointed a few years before, had previous experience in a wide range of types of authority, including one that differed sharply from his present council in its political complexion, balance of control and almost every other respect. He headed a relatively small department without most of the traditional clerk's functions. He saw his task in the post as 'to attempt a managerial revolution - for the second time in a new authority'. His personal objectives were to install 'real management processes and systems' and an officer culture which is 'flexible, looks forward, responds to customers and builds on real management information, preparing members for a new future for local government and a more clearly defined role'. He had pressed the need for radical devolution of management responsibilities within departments as well as to departments along with related values such as ensuring equity within the services. He rated his best past achievements as building very good officer teams twice and achieving effective officer/member working with real results.

In the previous authority he had had day-to-day relationships with the leading politicians. Here by contrast the relationships with the leader and council chair were no more than weekly. He rated the quality of his relationships as neither good nor poor in one case and very good in the other. He met the leaders of the minority parties every two to four weeks, with whom relationships were good with one and neither good nor poor with the other; and the committee chairmen monthly, with whom his relations were good. Meetings with committee chairmen and average members were less than monthly but rated good. Out of a fifty hour week he estimated that he spent about five hours with members.

He faced the highly challenging task of achieving radical reform in an environment in which he was handicapped by the comparative remoteness of the political machinery from his daily work.

Profile C

This large authority under strong but not overwhelming one party control served an extensive area which included major agricultural, industrial and residential districts. The chief executive had no departmental responsibilities and had been in his post for several years. He had seen the main initial problems and opportunities to lie in 'the need to radically reorganise, restructure and reorientate a service business' with a great expenditure and workforce 'in no time at all'. A subsequent aim had been 'to develop a devolved business style of management'. He rated the fulfilment of these objectives as his best achievements.

In pursuance of his aims he had launched a number of management initiatives which brought fundamental changes in the way services were operated. These were in accordance with principles recommended by him and adopted by the council of 'the devolution of responsibility and accountability from central departments to the service departments'; 'the transition from administration to management'; and 'the emphasis on service to the customer'. He had also actively pursued benefits from relationships with Europe and the European Community.

He met the leader daily, the council chairman weekly and the leaders of the minority parties and committee chairmen monthly. All these relationships were reported to be good or very good. Meetings with the 'average member' were less than monthly and he rated these as neither good nor poor.

Out of a typical sixty hour week he spent about three hours in council and other meetings with members, but also about fifteen hours a week in strategic thinking and discussion with the leader and officer colleagues.

Two Labour controlled counties

Profile D

This authority was responsible for large areas of heavy industry which had significantly declined, together with mixed and hill farming districts. Labour had been in power for a considerable period and had acquired a particularly strong leadership in recent years. The minority groups were small but by no means negligible.

When the chief executive took up his post a few years before the interview he had been convinced that a complete and radical reorganisation of the authority's structure was needed - in his own words 'to ensure that the authority worked corporately, to tackle deep-rooted departmentalism' and 'to try to make the authority work as a happy family providing a basket of services to the county'. He had seen it as necessary to set aims and objectives, instal the mechanisms to put these into effect, and to 'bring together chief officers and leading members working in partnership'. The implications of the new competitive tendering and other innovative legislation had by then become clear. There had also been a change in the majority party leadership and the new leader had given him strong and understanding support. The management team had been remodelled and some chief officers took early retirement.

Together with leading members and all-party support he was caught up in the wish 'to push the authority along'. He believed that the relationship with the leader of the council was critical: 'If any chief executive cannot get on with the leader of the majority party he's lost'. The leader was extremely capable and 'high profile, which is just what you want. If you don't have partnership you're lost'. In conjunction with the leader, senior members and chief officers he had prepared a list of major policy items, innovative subjects and keytasks which was continually revised and updated. Progress was monitored weekly.

He said, 'There's been a tremendous change in the thinking of members, who supported the need for a corporate approach, partnership, strong leadership, aims and objectives and getting value for money.' The members had always had a great deal of common sense - they are 'the salt of the earth'.

A new corporate planning committee had been set up and had proved very successful in sorting out priorities. Policies were very close to the party manifesto. All chief officers were genuinely apolitical, 'but there's no need for party appointments: the council won't appoint party advisers'. He felt well-informed about what was happening in committee and amongst the members generally. The management team was working well and corporately. He had an open door policy with the members, who came to see him regularly from all political parties. He said 'It's right relationships that matter'.

He worked with the leader and the council chairman daily and met other senior members several times a week. He met other chairmen and the leaders of the minority parties frequently, and had regular formal and informal contacts with all members. He rated his relationships with the majority and minority party leaders and senior members as very good and considered that he had a good relationship with other members. Out of about a 52 hour week he spent in all about 16 hours in meetings with members. He attended group meetings to present issues, but left before discussion.

The council leader saw the authority as having moved recently away from 'personality politics' with priorities determined according to the strengths of chairmen and chief officers. The chief executive had played a key role in shifting them to a corporate basis in which the leader was able to deliver the political support for reforming structure and system. He said 'a new chief executive who does not change the work of the council in the first three years of office is not doing his job. He must be prepared to negotiate change. From the members' point of view he has to be human and not aloof.' He 'has to make the members feel that their opinions are respected'. 'Professional men are sometimes academic and arrogant', causing 'conflict between the professional and political machines'. The chief executive 'must be very close to the political team with understanding of members' aims and aspirations. He would encourage him to have a wider perception of his own authority - linking with other tiers, regional bodies, tourism and sports committees... to be a leader in regional and national issues'.

In this case the leader had undoubtedly been the main force behind the great shift in style that had taken place, but otherwise the chief executive had been the principal instrument. There was a close partnership in which the leader was able to deliver the political support to effect change. Concepts of partnership informed relationships throughout.

Profile E

This authority had faced the challenge of large areas of obsolescent industry, but large-scale renovation had been achieved in the last twenty years. The leading elected members had come mostly from the traditional culture with which it was associated. The Labour group had held control from 1973 against a small and divided opposition whose effectiveness had declined in recent years. In the majority group itself the main power was held by twelve group officers and chairmen who were normally re-elected annually. The members came from areas that were geographically separated, each with its own strong identity and competing for services. The politics tended to revolve around this competition.

The chief executive, who also carried the responsibilities of a traditional clerk, had been appointed from another authority a number of years before. He worked in a close relationship with the political leadership group. He commented that it was essential for the chief executive to have the confidence of the leader. There had been a problem in the remoteness of the previous holder of the leader's office due to his involvement in outside business on other public bodies. It was possible to work with the new leader and his deputy on a daily basis.

He believed that a chief executive should be 'creative and innovative, developing a set of policies in co-operation with fellow chief officers; and pragmatic, taking account of the character of officers'. He aimed at a loose role in delegation: sensitive, realistic but firm. At his own level he felt that he could share responsibility but believed that there were limits to full delegation. There would always be a problem of the unforeseen long-term repercussions of a problem. 'You are right in the boiler-room' and 'have to stand up and be counted'. You must make the councillors believe that they are taking the decisions themselves. A chief executive, he said, 'needs to be a man-manager - you are as good as the team around you'. He also needs 'the ability to maintain constructive relations with a wide range of people: MEPs, senior civil servants, a multiplicity of agencies, and reasonable relations with the media - the ability to sell one's wares'. And a 'totally flexible approach to all problems'.

The views of politicians in this authority were of particular interest in showing the reaction to government policies. The leader saw the 1989 legislation for a designated 'head of paid service' as 'rightly defining the chief executive's responsibility' and 'making him more authoritative'. But he had to 'carry the other officers along with him'. He was a great believer in professional advice. The chief executive, treasurer and other officers made presentations in group and members accepted this. 'The chief executive has to be a first class communicator with positive relations with the press.'

Politics appeared to be open and frank. In general there seemed to be a high sense of dependence on the chief executive which had been severely aggravated by the members' interpretation of the new legislation. This latter had produced feelings of impotence and a questioning about the meaning of local government in the future.

Most-Purpose Authorities: London Boroughs and Metropolitan Districts

London boroughs and metropolitan districts share the widest range of functions of all local authorities. They have relatively compact but often somewhat arbitrary areas and a population range that with the exception of relatively few cases runs between those of the non-metropolitan district councils and the counties. The scale and variety of their services put their management problems in a class on their own. The case for corporate management to attack disadvantagement and other problems and to achieve social and economic development is at its strongest. It is also most challenging because of the size and complexity of their areas.

Of the metropolitan districts only two were under Conservative control at the time of the survey. Twenty-six were Labour controlled, one Liberal and seven hung. Within Greater London 15 were under Labour control, nine Conservative and eight hung or balanced evenly. In most cases they served areas that suffered from a high level of deprivation.

Five Conservative controlled most-purpose boroughs and districts

The information on this small group is taken from questionnaires returned by five chief executives. Three of the authorities were controlled by firm majorities; the other two were on a political knife-edge. Of the chief executives three were heads of departments which included traditional functions; the other two possessed strategic planning staffs.

Only one saw his main responsibility for policy advice and implementation as to the council alone without qualification. One saw it as to the council and the majority party; one to the council and to council policies 'which usually reflect the majority party's views'; one to the party by itself and one, uniquely, for advising the opposition party in addition to the council as a whole and implementing the policies of the majority party.

They identified their major opportunities during the previous year in contrasting ways. One experienced his main difficulty in the short time available to achieve necessary structural change. By contrast he gave his main opportunities as 'facilitating the articulation of the vision of the borough for the future' and 'setting the officer machine to achieving that vision'. Others were concerned with 'increasing competitiveness and productivity whilst retaining public sector values', 'team-building with chief officer colleagues' and planning for the take-over of new functions. Another in a much more disadvantaged area than the others gave 'squeezing resources out of government, Europe and the private sector to improve local conditions'.

In all cases they met the leader two to four times a week; in four cases the relationship was very good and in the fifth problematic. Otherwise member relationships conformed with the general pattern except that in four cases those with minority leaders and committee chairmen were more frequent than the average: fortnightly, weekly and in a case on a political 'knife-edge' two or more times a week.

The most important personal objectives of the chief executives related in all but one case to effecting change within the authority: obtaining speedy agreement on a reorganised management structure and implementing it; driving through managerial changes and adjusting structure to accommodate them; developing an effective management team; providing organisational leadership and stability in an environment of constant internal and external change, maintaining morale and, the only reference to policy processes, 'to develop and implement a coherent policy and budget process. By contrast one whose authority was exceptionally stable politically gave the enabling of voluntary bodies, resourcing and maintaining external links as his main objectives.

The working hours the chief executives spent with elected members were abnormally high in these five cases. They ranged from twelve to over seventeen and a half hours a week. The highest figures were recorded in the most stable situations.

Labour controlled London boroughs and metropolitan districts

There were 26 responses to the postal questionnaires from chief executives in authorities where Labour majority groups formed the political administration. Eight were from London boroughs and 18 from metropolitan districts. They showed interesting differences in the patterns of relationship by type of authority. In all but two instances the chief executive met the leader more than once a week. However, whereas in all but one of the London boroughs meetings were two to four times a week, in most of the districts they occurred five times a week or more. The quality of the relationship however was reported to be very good in most cases in London and elsewhere: five of the eight London boroughs and twelve out of 18 metropolitan districts. Contacts with the mayor were weekly in seven London boroughs and in ten of the 18 metropolitan districts, the remainder in both cases being fortnightly or monthly. The quality of the relationship was in all instances given as good or very good.

The greater frequency of meetings in the metropolitan districts than in London occurs in other relationships. In London boroughs meetings with opposition leaders are fortnightly (3 cases) or less than monthly (5 cases). In the metropolitan districts however they occurred weekly or more often in eight out of 18 cases; fortnightly or thereabouts in five; and less often than monthly in only two. They were reported to be very good in eight of the metropolitan districts but in only two of the boroughs. None is rated poor in either case.

Meetings with committee chairmen were weekly or monthly in five of the boroughs and 14 of the metropolitan districts. In two cases of London boroughs however they were less often than monthly. In all but four of the districts and two of the London boroughs the quality of the relationships was reported good or very good.

There is a smaller contrast in the case of frequency of relationships with the 'average member': probably because these relate predominantly to council and committee cycles. In both types of authority the frequency ranges from weekly (only one in each case) to less often than monthly (two boroughs and six districts).

The difference in the frequency of contacts with leading members between the two types of authority may arise from differences in the local way of life. In particular the extent to which work on the council is full-time as opposed to part-time seems to be higher on average in the provincial urban authorities. Connected with this is the extent to which the council rooms are the centre of daily social involvement. Certainly in most provincial town halls of which I have experience there is a much greater sense of being part of a community than in London borough accommodation.

Objectives of chief executives in Labour controlled most-purpose authorities and what they believe members most expect from them.

Of the main personal work objectives given by chief executives in most-purpose authorities, seven related directly to achieving or maintaining good member-officer relationships. Two of the seven who gave this objective also considered it to be a main objective expected of them by councillors. Other expectations of members occurred more frequently however. In twelve chief executives saw members as expecting from them major policy inputs or commitments: for example to 'deliver manifesto commitments' and in another instance 'group policies'; to 'implement on time, as many council policies as possible to maintain the confidence of the community'; and 'to give them 'maximum scope for developing the group's agenda for change within imposed constraints'.

Members' expectations of the chief executive's role in defining policy were expressed with less clarity. One chief executive saw the situation as one where members 'vaguely expect leadership of the (management) team to develop overall objectives'; others 'to take part in setting key priorities' and to articulate policies to fulfil political objectives (for example to 'recognise and develop achievable policies to bridge the gap between ^haves and have-nots`').

Economic development is a field where chief executives' personal objectives are perhaps most likely to coincide with those of the members. Two chief executives of cities in the North East of England laid emphasis on the 'enabling' role of working closely with the private sector (and in one case with academics) to revitalise the local economy. Looking back on what they considered to be their best achievements a large proportion of the metropolitan district chief executives gave specific developments: major investments by international industry in their areas, 'a series of related developments', creating an Economic Development Unit, constructing a broad-based community forum which had been instrumental in channelling effort into the rejuvenation of the town' and 'giving impetus to economic regeneration in tackling a number of redevelopment matters that had been allowed to drift for many years'. One mentioned in particular developing economic strategies which led to excellent developments.

Some chief executives put at the head of their objectives the improvement of morale and motivation, sometimes explicitly including elected members as well as officers. One refers to maintaining interest in the workings of the council in the last year of an administration.

Particularly in Labour authorities chief executives include amongst the main objectives departmental reorganisation and coping with compulsory competitive tendering and other government requirements of the late 1980s. These are implied in some cases to be problems that need to be sorted out by the officers themselves, particularly by the chief executive, in ways that would keep the provision of services as close to the authority as possible.

Chief executives here as in other types of authority expect to take the lead in increasing 'consumer consciousness and public access'. Some also look to a role in the promotion of their areas. They tend to see longer term and strategic planning approaches as being their concern rather than that of the members.

Matters with which chief executives appear to identify most closely emerge clearly in what they see as their best achievements. As well as those mentioned above they include 'providing unpalatable advice on legality', 'developing a culture which challenges previously accepted spending norms and historical practices', 'gaining acceptance from a traditionally socialist council that full partnership in economic regeneration embraces all aspects of business and industrial sectors, developing and maintaining corporate planning and budget processes', 'making a reasonable job of coping with often unsought rapid change and developing a more 'service-led rather than finance-led culture'.

If they are to fulfil the objectives they set themselves chief executives of most-purpose authorities need a general understanding of the highly complex social and economic problems which beset our main commercial and industrial areas in times of rapid change, identifying not only the main problems but also the related opportunities. They need to tune into the best thinking on establishing standards and quality in the conditions of life as far as the resources of their local authorities permit, working and stimulating others to do the same. In doing so some at least see a duty to play what is essentially an educational role in bringing the best out of their elected members. They see themselves as educators, guides, innovators and leaders, as well as facilitators and executives.

Three Labour controlled most-purpose boroughs and districts

The following profiles show three contrasting situations: one with weak political input, one with strong leader input, and one with high level of member solidarity.

Profile F

This authority's responsibilities were divided between well-to-do middle class districts and others suffering from decay and disadvantagement. Much of its former industrial and commercial base had gone, leaving large areas of dereliction. The requirements of the rundown areas were central to the concern of the majority party. The group had been in control for over twenty years and had a reputation for fractious internal politics. Cross-party positions were limited to social services and to some aspects of housing. The chief executive met the leader two to four times a week and rated the relationship as neither good nor poor. Meetings with minority party leaders and committee chairmen were less frequent than monthly but rated good. Meetings with 'average members' were similarly infrequent and rated as neither good nor poor.

Due to changes within the group not long before the interview the Labour leadership was new and inexperienced. The leader had problems in establishing an effective role. The chairmen tended to be relatively strong but government financial restrictions had made it impossible for them to deliver their manifesto promises.

The chief officers in the authority had aimed at more corporate direction and objective-setting but had failed to win the support of the committee chairmen in the matter. It seemed that they did not want a leader. While members might support corporate approaches in theory they also talked about stemming centralist action and wanted the areas in which they were involved to be left alone.

The controlling group was elected on a manifesto which could not be implemented because of resource problems. A basis for corporate direction was lacking because the group had won control on a manifesto of growth that was financially impracticable. Members appeared to see a programming or strategic approach as a threat. 'Value for money' was criticised as an argument for making cuts. Performance review procedures had failed to win the members' support. The leader was walking a tightrope between legal requirements on compulsory competitive tendering and the stance of the members against it.

Members could be unrealistic about what a chief executive could achieve - for example how quickly staff changes could be realised and public facilities closed down. They could fail to address themselves to what was involved in running public multi-service organisations. It might be possible to change the authority's culture by changing the structure, but 'it was immensely difficult to change structures in authorities of this kind unless you can throw money at it. You can't pay people to change - there is no money to do it': otherwise unions could undermine local support.

Failure to accept the chief officers' advice engendered feelings of stress and impotence. There was a failure by members to work through the problems they faced jointly with a determination to find a course which delivered the best in the circumstances. The officers had to be involved in the decision-making so that they felt that they had some ownership of the strategies adopted. But without a determination on the part of members to work in partnership with officers, create a strategy and accept some unpleasant realities, it was hard to see how a chief executive could resolve the problems faced. The dilemma lay in an unintegrated political process.

Profile G

This authority was also responsible for an area in a great conurbation which contained a mixture of disadvantaged and relatively prosperous residential areas. It had large suburbs with high ethnic elements and poor housing occupied by low income residents. It had traditionally been a Labour stronghold but contained a substantial Conservative minority.

The chief executive's appointment was recent but from within the authority, so that he was well able to anticipate the problems involved in the position. At his interview he had argued to the members the need for a change in role and style, which they had accepted and expected him to implement. The leaders had said that the chief executive should have a free hand in the development of the structure and not depend on the results of political dialogue in matters of structural reform. There were grey areas in the management of the authority between the officers and the members, but in general he believed that aims should be consciously articulated and the officers expected to work broadly in agreed directions.

He thought that a chief executive must have a vision of where the council was going beside that of the members. The reputation of the authority should and could be raised to that of one of the foremost in the country, with decent quality services, a caring and committed workforce and a full orientation to customer care. His action plan would be designed to take them there.

He had submitted a report containing his proposals for reform to the leaders' conference and obtained its general support for the underlying principles. At the time of the interview he was taking the proposals to a meeting of the minority group and hoped to gain their support also. His approach did not mean that members would not act in a managerial capacity, but he expected that this would be after they had received advice from the officers.

Profile H

This authority controlled a large area containing communities with mixed levels of wealth and styles of living. It centred on a historic town but had no single dominant centre. The council had a Labour majority but had been under Conservative control for periods in the preceding two decades. Interparty relations were described by the chief executive as 'very civilised'. Members of different parties sat together before meetings. Many decisions had cross-party support. The two party leaders got on together 'extraordinarily well'.

The chief executive had served in two other most purpose authorities. Although the last was similar in some ways to that he now served its politics were very different - volatile and full of sharp cleavages between parties and within the Labour group.

An Audit Commission report had provided a stimulus to the definition of what the council required managerially, arguing for a strong chief executive. His present council had included in the particulars of the post sent to candidates a statement of key areas of responsibility. These included translating members' ideas and perspectives into major policy options with realistic targets and implications so that their desire to implement progressive programmes to give maximum service delivery can be realised.' It went on, 'Much will be achieved by bringing members and officers closer together to foster joint and co-operative working'. The council had held a number of events away from work in which chief officers and chairmen came together to map the way forward and share ideas. It expected these events to continue. 'Team building will be a priority if strong objectives are to emerge in tandem with exciting service delivery plans. The skill here will be to develop widespread commitment to key corporate objectives such as the Council's image, developing tourism and "customer care" whilst at the same time encouraging departments to take initiatives which will have the full support of the organisation as a whole. The Controlling Group want to see the Council's image changed from what they see as an over-emphasis on economy at the expense of service delivery... The chief executive himself will need to give a positive lead on the image front by providing a driving force and a climate for change with a new shared vision and style of operation.'

The chief executive felt that he had a good understanding of members' broad priorities. The council approved innovative proposals set out in a review of the chief executive's department and its future role, which put forward values and orientations for implementation in progressive programmes aimed at the best possible service delivery. In doing this he was fulfilling the council's expectations that the chief executive should play the key role in ensuring that it responded to legislative challenges and that services were fully maintained. The process proposed would, he argued, bring members and officers closer together to foster joint co-operative working.

He was persuading other chief officers to raise their expectations about what the politicians would accept, and that if they put up a reasoned case for innovations the members were likely to go along with it.

He met the leader on average every two to four days and the mayor, committee chairmen and other members weekly or at least fortnightly, and rated all these relationships as good.

Comparisons

The authorities in profiles F and G both worked on the adversarial House of Commons model of two-party politics. In the volatile politics of their areas neither could ignore a possible dramatic swing that would take them out of power. The main contrast between them lay in the differences in their controlling groups. In the first case the group lacked unity and the will to adapt its policies to financial reality. The ambitions of some of its politicians undermined the ability of the centre to develop a management strategy and realistic policies. In profile G however the group had accepted the need for a restructuring of the authority and a realistic strategy that would bring its acute financial problems under control. The council had appointed a chief executive with clear ideas and the promise that he could develop reforms that should enable them to fulfil their aspirations as well as could be in the current political circumstances. He was expected to carry out a review of the issues involved and had the support of the leader and group in implementing an agreed approach. He hoped that he could carry along some support from the opposition in this as well. Here as in some other cases described the vision of a new approach arose first in the political sphere, and an officer was appointed who seemed best able to fulfil it.

Authority H enjoyed a contrasting culture, including a tradition of strong collaboration. There was cohesion within the group and within the organisation as a whole, along with a receptiveness to new ideas. A harmony appeared to have been established between the members and the new chief executive which promised a satisfying and innovative period for both sides.

SHIRE AND SCOTTISH DISTRICTS

The variety of the districts

The shire and Scottish districts are the most varied among types of British local authority. They cover the widest range of populations - from not much more than 10,000 inhabitants to over 700,000, and a similarly wide range of areas - from compact towns up to expanses of nearly half a million hectares. Socially they range from highly homogeneous to extremely heterogeneous: from one compact community to an assembly of towns and villages aggressively asserting their own identities. Their political style ranges from non-party to party dominated. They do not carry responsibilities for the great national educational, social and physical infrastructure systems and therefore have relative freedom from national obligations and a scope for discretion over the range of their services which other types of authority may envy. They are the closest of all authorities to their publics, and the town authorities in particular are most likely to be aware of their individual historical traditions. On the other hand many contain idiosyncratic and culturally conflicting elements due to the amalgamations of the 1970s. Here the relationship between the chief executive and council may be expected to be at its most diverse and unpredictable.

Despite the variety their chief executives' perceptions of their personal difficulties and opportunities in serving their districts were found to have much in common. Their responses were shaped to a large extent by the impact of national policies on local government on the one hand and by the influence of academic writers on local government matters, national bodies such as the Local Government Training Board and the Audit Commission, leading local government politicians and other chief executives on the other. But they also showed great individuality.

In this and the following sections we shall look for characteristics common to substantial numbers before giving a number of profiles drawn mainly from those near the middle size range. Near the end of the 1980s the greatest number (144) were controlled by Conservative administrations, due largely to the concentration of Conservative support in the south of England. There was a somewhat smaller number of Labour-controlled authorities (81), preponderantly in the North of England, the Scottish middle belt and South Wales, along with cities and towns with a strong working-class vote elsewhere. Somewhat over a third of all the districts had no majority party administrations, being mostly 'hung' in the towns and non-party in the rural areas. These last are dealt with in the following chapter.

We received responses to questionnaires from chief executives of 72 of the district councils controlled by Conservative administrations, 47 by Labour, one by Liberal Democrats and 70 without majority party control.

Chief executives' difficulties and opportunities

Most responses from Labour districts reflected the problems of working with members in areas where traditional mining and other heavy industries had collapsed. The councillors had seen their role as one of doing good for people - helping individuals to overcome their problems, with the clerk or chief executive and other officers assisting them in their responsibilities. The amalgamations of the 1970s took them further away from their community roots, resulting in councils with wider rivalry between areas, and in some cases introduced party politics for the first time in their modern form. The Labour Party continued to be dominant however because of the social and political solidarity of most of their areas.

As their traditional economic base shifted they faced the problems of rebuilding their economic infrastructure and way of life. Many of their councillors were retired or unemployed through redundancy and had looked for a more or less full-time service in local government. Political leadership tended to be dominated by seniority. The regeneration of their areas required the development of approaches that needed strong officer input and so increased their dependence.

The 'new local government' of the 1980s conflicted with ideas of what local government service was about. Members had been accustomed to exercising close control of matters relating to the personal interests of individual constituents, such as appointments to manual jobs and housing rental. They were 'neighbour-conscious' rather than 'consumer-conscious'. In some cases the decade brought a new political approach locally, with manifesto politics and, to quote chief executives, an advent of 'strong-willed inexperienced members' and 'overbold action'.

As in other types of authority the government legislation of the 1980s was seen by some chief executives as a means for converting attitudes and organisation, and by implication the members' role in local government. One chief executive counted himself lucky that he was able to obtain the strong support of a leader and deputy leader in undertaking action that he saw as imperative. Another saw the new demands as a means of demonstrating his ability to undertake a thorough reorganisation. A new basis for member-officer understanding had to be forged. It meant providing 'a new role for council and councillors as they feel so depressed about their future'.

If the council leader was unable or unwilling to take the lead it seemed to chief executives that they had to lead the council into the new era themselves. Such leadership ideally involved achieving clarity of purpose and an agreed definition of feasible objectives; and, as one chief executive put it, 'obtaining an acceptance of a new role for members which complemented that of the officers'. Some chief executives referred to 'changing the culture of the organisation' in their responses, but it is often difficult to know whether they meant changing the members' culture or that of the employees, or both. It may also mean changing the culture of the community, as might be necessary to inject new life into the local economy after the collapse of large-scale industry. In any event a change in the officer culture implied a change in the members' role, and to achieve that required a new set of assumptions on the part of the members.

Chief executives in Conservative authorities had problems that could be at least as difficult to solve as those in such Labour authorities, especially in default of imaginative political leadership. One chief executive described his major difficulty as 'making members understand that local government was really under stress'. Another gave 'keeping the local government ship afloat'. In some cases there was the opportunity to establish a much more powerful role, to become 'the boss' or to stamp 'my own style of leadership on the Authority'. The political leadership often realised that they needed an assertive chief executive but were sometimes working against feelings in their groups on this matter, and in Labour authorities especially, against political resistance to government policies.

Physical and economic planning needs as well as government legislation created what chief executives saw as the need for a new role structure. One chief executive saw his task as 'persuading members to face up to the challenges of big development pressures'. Some gave objectives relating to a perspective beyond that dominated by competition and other recent legislation; and others not only the almost universal themes of efficiency or effectiveness but also 'defining and agreeing medium term strategy', 'planning for the area's future', 'improving customer satisfaction' and preserving the responsibility of local authorities 'to retain local democracy'.

Labour chief executives' personal objectives are often more assertive - for example 'to provide leadership' to lead the council successfully', to 'lead the council in coping with the changed character of the borough', 'to anticipate the future', 'to inculcate a clear sense of purpose and direction', to attain 'cohesion of member and officer relations', 'member development', 'to deal with community economic problems' and 'a better response to the many challenges and opportunities for' the city. In one case a city chief executive was conscious of the extent to which the officers had taken over leadership and gave as one of his three objectives, 'delivering the "control" of the council to the elected members'.

And how do the chief executives see what their members expect of them? In Conservative authorities they generally see their members as sharing their own aims of good management. Some in Labour authorities see themselves expected to provide ways of achieving the council's objectives within present and forthcoming legislation, 'to secure survival of Direct Labour Organisation', 'to find a way round the constraints'; but also more negatively 'to keep them out of trouble from the law and government', 'to support the prevailing political view', 'to be more the Town Clerk and less the chief executive', 'to keep everything on the straight and narrow, but unobtrusively'; and more positively 'regeneration of the District' and 'promoting the City and its achievements'. Promotion of the authority's image is a frequently occurring objective of both Conservative and Labour chief executives.

Views on where their policy advice and implementation responsibilities lie

As in other types of authority views on where responsibilities lie were very mixed. Opinion were divided similarly irrespective of which party was in control. Out of 189 responses, 54 per cent believed their responsibility should be to the council, ten per cent to the majority party and from 13 to 30 per cent to both. Some chief executives sought to clarify where a distinction lay between responsibility to the council and to the majority. One who replied that it was mainly to the council added that he nevertheless must give priority to implementing the policies of the majority party. There were three cases where the question was said to be difficult to answer because they were virtually one-party states. Two distinguished between responsibility to the council for policy advice and to the majority group for implementation.

Meetings with members

Contacts with members are most frequent in the North of England and Scotland, where half the chief executives saw leaders at least daily and in all cases at least weekly. The frequency of meetings is a little lower in Wales, the Midlands and East Anglia and lower still in the South, but even here there was only one case, a Conservative authority, where contact was less than weekly. Contacts with mayors and council chairmen were somewhat less frequent. In 18 out of 31 cases they are at least weekly; in six monthly and in one less often still. The frequency of meetings between the chief executive and the chairman decreases again from north to south, but there is little difference between Labour and Conservative authorities in this respect.

Few minority party leaders were seen by chief executives more than once a month except in Scotland, where they mostly met weekly. One chief executive of a Midland authority gives as a main objective 'to see the minority leaders more often', the only reference to minority interests in this set of responses.

In the big majority of cases committee chairmen are met monthly and 'average members' less often except in Scotland, where none in our sample was seen less than fortnightly and most were met at least weekly.

Chief executives of Welsh and Scottish districts spent most time with members - an average of 16 and 15 hours a week respectively. In England those in Labour districts spent on average about two to three hours a week more with members than those in Conservative districts. There is little difference between parts of England, but the range between individual cases is very wide, rising from four and a half hours a week in a Conservative authority in the North to 20 hours in a Conservative one in the South and also a Labour one in Wales. As we found with other types of authority, there is no relationship between time spent with members and direct responsibility for a department; neither was there a relationship with the size of the authority or the committee cycle. It seems likely that the reasons for the range of differences lie chiefly in the characteristics of individual members and chief executives.

Conservative Controlled Districts

Profile I

This was a district authority for an affluent area of small towns and countryside, controlled by a Conservative group with a seemingly safe majority. It came under party control for the first time in 1979. Political initiatives were said to have been held back until 1982 by 'a repressive treasurer' who 'who wouldn't spend a penny if he could help it'. In 1983 the council set up a general review of policies, objectives and strategies, and 'everyone worked as a team on this'. The council had accepted a proposal to set up review groups for different service areas and this had helped to bring forward innovative ideas for future developments. The main problems in decision-making were understood to be related to the future arrangements for the management and development of leisure services (an area in which the chief executive headed a mixed policy study group), and the attitudes of councillors who were also members of town councils fighting for their own towns' interests.

There had been an acceleration in capital expenditure after housing had been transferred to a housing association, resulting in a capital gain of £8 million, much of which was spent on land. The housing association was the agent for statutory housing services and the council maintained its client role through the environmental services committee. Four members sat on the housing association to ensure that it followed the objectives of the council.

The chief executive was directly responsible for the secretarial department although for more than a year he had had a deputy who managed the department under his direction. He went through the post with the deputy for about twenty minutes every morning. He said that the main difficulties encountered in his work in recent years had arisen from 'the too philosophical approach by government and politicians in respect of many fields' - particularly compulsory tendering where 'experienced competitors to the council did not exist'. The main opportunities he saw in his job were implementing performance appraisal and rewards and the development of leisure projects.

He put among his objectives maintaining good relations between senior staff and between them and the councillors, and guidance on balancing the council's overall objectives. One of his most valued achievements he saw as 'enhancing a corporate image by the performance and publications of the council as a whole and overcoming non-corporate attitudes'.

He met the council chairman two to four times in a normal week and the leader weekly. He rated his relations with them as very good and good respectively. He saw the minority party leader and committee chairmen fortnightly and the 'average member' about once a month and considered all these relations to be good ones. Altogether he spent about four and a half to five hours a week with members of the council.

The leader defined the chief executive job in terms of liaison between departments and mediation in conjunction with the council. The division of responsibility between the council chairman and the council leader was still uncertain and could cause problems. Both leaders however felt that they would be happy for a more assertive role to be exercised by the next chief executive. In general the authority appeared to be firmly in the hands of the members and satisfied with itself on policy matters.

Profile J

This authority governs a large holiday resort with extensive leisure facilities. The Conservative group held a comfortable majority on the council although the opposition was stronger than in the case above.

The chief executive had been in office for little more than a year. Confronted with the special characteristics of the authority and responsibility for a department which he believed needed considerable development, he had found it difficult to make as much progress as he wished because of the combination of his departmental responsibilities and leading the managerial team.

He described the group as conservative with a small 'c' as well as a large 'C'. Politics were 'more obscure' than in his previous authority. Overall it lacked purpose and drive in key areas. It was not possible to effect change satisfactorily without taking councillors along with him, but the councillors 'didn't want to be pushed'. 'The council is in a time-warp'. They looked to the officers to sort out any difficult problems.

His main current objectives were to increase the managerial competence, self-reliance and initiative of the staff, prepare services for the 1990s and develop effective links with all the members of the council. After a short period of office he felt that he had succeeded in developing new perspectives for the chief officers and was making headway with fostering the skills and self-confidence of the staff to enable them to 'shape the future of their services to meet future challenges'.

Developing effective links with the council was more difficult. He had a good constructive relationship with the leader whom he saw twice a week. Relations with the council chairman, whom he saw about once a week, were 'neither good nor poor', as were those with the committee chairmen, whom he saw monthly. He saw the opposition leaders and the 'average member' less often than monthly and saw scope for improvement here. In all he spent four and a half to five hours a week with members.

The council leader liked the idea of a chief executive as 'city manager' or 'chief administrative officer' who could 'bring down to basic sense what may otherwise be couched in highbrow or professional terms, so that members can go forward with the advice of the professional officers'. In working closely with the chief executive the leader should 'exercise his 'logical sense' to 'keep management firmly on the ground - preferably with constant concern for the costs to the community'. Chief executives needed 'to show flair and enthusiasm to implement within the law the policies laid down by their councils and achieve the existence of a will to implement'.

The picture of the authority as a whole was of strong dependence for change on the central dynamic force of the chief executive backed by the leader. The chief executive faced the problem of a council anxious to protect local institutions and without a clear vision of long-term objectives. With the support of the leader he had been able to pursue innovative policies against resistance in the council, often with difficulty.

Profile K

This district council provides for a prosperous rural and residential area, not dissimilar from that in Profile G in many respects. The Conservative Party had a strong and as far as could be foreseen permanent hold on the council. Despite this the chief executive described the overt political situation as 'chaotic'. The authority was notable for rejecting formal political leadership, having no leader as such. The majority party politics were collegiate and while there was 'a very Conservative four year manifesto', steps were taken to involve the minority groups where possible.

The chief executive's responsibilities included those of a traditional clerk. When he took up his post several years before he had been faced with the necessity of slimming down staff. He then saw his main challenges as overcoming staff motivation problems and forging a good member-chief officer partnership. He was now seeking to help the authority adapt to a greater emphasis on 'enabling'. His general aim had been to challenge the orthodox thinking that had been typical of the authority in the past, but not from any particular point of view. He worked by means of 'putting forward provocative ideas and giving details of innovations in other areas, but without expecting an automatic response'. He said, 'You have to justify yourself every month'. He encapsulated his present aims as 'keeping services right through massive change, getting benefits from planning gain and preparing future plans and budgets after the problems arising from the community charge were overcome.

He met members of the council two to four times a week and described the relationship as very good. His relationship with the chairman of the policy committee was necessarily close - some members occasionally thought too close. On average he spent about six hours a week with members, especially chairmen. Despite their close involvement he had great managerial freedom. Contracts with pre-set financial limits were let by officers, with chairmen coming in 'to see fair play'. More than half the planning applications were decided without going to committee.

He believed that many chief executives were now appointed where the members were looking for 'change and re-direction of the whole ship' and expecting the onus for achieving this to fall on the chief executive. He had found a lack of clear thinking by councillors; but their collegiate approach was better than a 'one-man one-leader system'.

Labour Controlled Districts

The six Labour controlled districts visited ranged from a little below the middle of the rank order of populations of the 386 shire and Scottish districts to one in the top twenty-five. Their economies varied from mixtures of small industry, farming and tourism to important regional centres of commerce and industry. They included three with longstanding Labour majorities, two where Labour had fairly recently gained control and one under Labour during the 1980s by a narrow margin. Only two could be described as having two or three party politics of a Westminster style. In these cases there was an element of the 'far left', but the leaders had succeeded in maintaining their authority.

Under Majority Party Control

Profile M

This authority covers an industrial area which has suffered badly from the decline of traditional industries, together with a rural hinterland. The Labour group had always held control of the council by a strong majority. Its political life had sharpened as a result of the Conservative government's policies.

The election manifesto had in recent years provided the basis for the policies and evaluations developed in the policy committee and council. By and large the opposition accepted that in a reversal of roles the same commitment would be given, although feelings of unease were sometimes expressed by some members of the group. Policy was in practice a mixture of political and chief officer inputs. The chief executive customarily addressed the group on important issues. He reserved the right to address opposition groups as required. Ideas were fed in at policy committee meetings. Neighbourhood councils, set up from 1985, were now commenting on policies and this had had a big impact.

The chief executive believed that it was his duty to ensure that the policy-making process worked. The manifesto incorporated promises to the electorate. He would work with the leader towards their implementation. The system would not function properly if he had to go to the party secretary or any other party officer. He had his personal agenda, consistent with council policy. At present it included a new approach to housing, the implications of direct services, 'putting people first', 'green issues', the future of the area and service and customer care.

The new leader had brought a stronger political stance on policy but would accept officer advice and modify policies pragmatically. The chief executive saw the leadership as growing in importance in comparison with the past when styles were more authoritarian or sometimes more consensual.

According to the chief executive, 'In a council such as ours where political direction is central to most activity then a clear and strong working relationship between the Leader and the chief executive is required. That must be balanced with chief executive corporate responsibility to the council.'

The council leader confirmed much of what the chief executive said about styles, relationships and approach to policy development. He laid emphasis on the use of member seminars and in particular on frequent informal majority party discussion groups of selected members which gave him political support and direction.

Profile N

In this authority the Labour Party had maintained control throughout the 1980s by a small majority. The division reflected two cultures: that of the urban centre and that of the outlying agricultural and tourist areas. Despite this split it appeared that a high level of solidarity had been achieved that was based on joint achievement. The chief executive counted himself fortunate in having a small council which enabled him to maintain intimate relationships with all its members, including the opposition. There were close member-officer working relationships at service levels and credit was publicly attached to the politicians for the authority's successes. It was clear nevertheless that the chief executive had himself been the origin and driving force behind many of the highly innovative and varied policies undertaken in the previous few years.

Very soon after his appointment in the mid-1980s he had launched proposals which he believed would meet the government's developing requirements on competitive tendering in the best interests of the authority and its workforce. His philosophy was that it was in the best interests of the council and the community that the council should be maintained as a collegiate entity within which direct services were provided of a quality higher than could be achieved by outside interests. There had been no political division on the subject and it was with the support of the whole council that he had taken measures to develop the capabilities of the employees to ensure that they could win the contracts. This in itself had demanded not only rapid organisational change in structures and procedures but also investment in the development of competitive and contracting skills. The chief executive had chaired an officer management group which had planned implementation. A member-officer group supervised and ensured that the client/contractor relationship was effective. Corporate issues went to the chief officer group. Authority for implementation was delegated to chief officers.

He saw the strategic management function as being at the heart of his role, working with the council to ensure that the political objectives were realistic. The last Labour manifesto had been prepared by committee chairmen with help from departments to ensure that service commitments were based not only on political aspirations but also on financial realities.

The chief executive had worked with interests outside the council to develop imaginative approaches to joint action with public and private bodies to fulfil the ideal of an 'enabling authority'.

Profile O

During the 1980s this large commercial and industrial city had come under strong Labour control and leadership, but the council still contained an effective opposition. The groups had full-time secretaries and Labour an assistant secretary. The Labour group's electoral manifesto was modelled on national Labour policy.

Chief officers attended group meetings. Since 1976 agendas had been discussed by chief officers' meetings and then submitted to meetings with chairmen. Leaders confirmed that there were good, easy relations with officers.

The chief executive did not head a department and worked through three executive assistants. He met the leader daily and the council chairman more than once a week. He rated his relations as very good with both of them. He had on average fortnightly contacts with other members and rated them generally good except in the case of those with opposition leaders which he graded as neither good nor poor. He spent about 14 hours out of a typical 46 hour week with councillors.

He had seen his main opportunities in the job as using his skills to maximise urban and European aids for developing the local economy, improving personnel and management services and establishing a real equal opportunities programme. Amongst the most important skills required by a chief officer, he believed, were those of a good listener and a good persuader, referring in particular to proposals on the tenants' campaign and the community charge issues.

The leader believed him to be an officer 'in the traditional mould' who knew that it was his responsibility to carry out the group's policy on competitive tendering and other issues. The chief executive's role, as he saw it, was to ensure coordination and cohesion, get out and talk to departments and ensure that grievances were not allowed to fester. The opposition leader had similar views. The chief executive should override departmental views when he thought it desirable, giving an independent report. He should give guidance to elected members collectively and when necessary individually, and be able to interrupt council meetings on points of law and standing orders.

If, as suggested in one interview, the chief executive was 'in the traditional mould', he certainly appeared to be playing a non-traditional role, closely involved in the development of policy and with equal opportunities and economic development units reporting to him. The strength of the majority party leadership was such that it would have been inappropriate for him to have played the forward role illustrated in some other profiles. His role had been more to associate himself with developments in areas where he was backed by the council as a whole and to argue out realistic policies where strategies had been suggested by the group which might run foul of the law.

Profile P

The authority serves an industrial town with a large and sparsely populated hinterland. It had suffered severely from unemployment in recent years due to the loss of the basis of its former economy. The council was under predominant Labour control.

The chief executive had served the council from its establishment and had been the clerk of one of its constituent authorities before that. He identified closely with its problems, seeing himself and his members virtually as one family. Together they saw the early 1980s as characterised by 'the clear contraction of local government'. He viewed the period as one of 'determination of the government to slowly discredit us and strip us of assets and totally inhibit growth' - challenges which had 'bred innumerable initiatives and an expansion of thinking to secure funding from agencies and the private sector. We are forced to do things in which in all honesty we ought to have done of our own volition in preceding years'. From 1988 there had been a further and 'far greater demand on initiative and intuition'.

When he took up his present post the traditional industry of the area had largely collapsed and the collapse was continuing. A bold planning strategy was required for environmental as well as economic reasons to convert and relocate much of the industrial base of the main town. Member-officer relationships had at times been difficult due to the reluctance of a few members to understand and adopt measures which the officers were convinced were in the essential interests of the community, but had now much improved. Members had had understandable difficulty in coming to terms with the need for dramatic change. The corporate estate of the authority has been used to good effect and the new development carried out as a team under excellent senior officers.

He himself had long seen his main mission as the completion of the economic and physical regeneration of the area, improvement of service quality and recently 'maintaining the employment of colleagues within the Authority' with reference to the direct services organisation and similar issues. From the 1970s he had been 'recommending policies and persuading members of their realism in re-establishing the economic fortunes, so giving the council the confidence of the community', and helping to bring employment down from nearly 21 per cent to under ten. Recently he had taken the initiative in reshaping the workforce to enable the council to win borough services.

He had 'powered' annual estimates through the council. They had normally been approved within an hour. A leading councillor said that nearly all members found the accounts completely baffling, but they did not feel 'rail-roaded'. One said that 'The chief executive puts the alternatives before us, and we have to decide'. Their concern was mainly with the extent to which government measures had negated what they saw as their legitimate role.

The chief executive met daily with the leader, weekly with committee chairmen on an informal basis, and fortnightly with other members. He rated all these relationships as very good. Out of a typical 46 hour week he spent about 14 hours with the elected members.

He felt that ideally a chief executive should be a managing director. He had been able to lead the authority strongly along the path to being an 'enabling authority' with close business and government relationships. His philosophy was, 'I just feel that something's right, so I do it'.

The picture was confirmed in interviews with leading politicians in the authority. A group officer commented that the chief executive was very approachable and an all-rounder. He complained however that they possessed limited discretion now on housing allocations: the group was frustrated by lack of effective power on these and on appointments up to senior officer level. One said 'We have a need for professional councillors so that we have an understanding of management'.

This was an authority that had long been a community within itself. Yet as well as being part of the community the chief executive was able to be a member of wider communities: closely involved in bodies outside the council and also with higher levels of government. To a large extent he was able to compensate for the lack of the opportunity and ability of the councillors to participate in this wider world.

Profile Q

In this case the council is responsible for an area of mixed agriculture and small-town commerce and industries. The Labour Party had recently won a council majority after several years as the largest minority group, forming the political administration but dependent on support from other members. In practice political conflict over policy had been muted and only about a third of the council members voted on party lines. The Labour members were mostly housewives and unemployed. The second largest party included retired professionals.

The chief executive had no traditional department but a small staff for personnel matters, management services, corporate policy and employment training. When he came to the post in the mid-1980s he found services badly in need of development because of ineptitude. He took on the task of 'revamping' what he saw as an antiquated authority with an organisation and culture unsuited to the 1980s. The structure was reorganised and a new emphasis placed on the development of the services. A further reorganisation was being carried out in 1989. He gave as what he felt to be his best achievements in the post the change in the culture of the authority and the two reorganisations. He believed that his personal objectives - to manage change effectively as the council moved into the 1990s, to improve service to the customer and to translate policy into action - were in harmony with those of the members.

The chief executive remarked that Labour's victory had simplified relationships in that he no longer needed to carry the second largest group with him to gain support for his proposals. In the words of the council chairman the chief executive had formerly 'written a consensus paper and the proposals were accepted'. In the case of a major report such as that he had prepared on restructuring he discussed the contents with the chairman and leader to achieve 'some kind of backing', and this usually secured its acceptance.

He met the leader daily, the council chairman two to four times a week, the leaders of the opposition parties fortnightly, committee chairmen monthly and the 'average member' less than monthly on average; and rated all the relationships as good or very good. Out of an estimated working week of some 55 hours about eleven were spent with members.

Two of the leading members of the Labour group believed that the chief executive's job should be that of managing director for the authority. The leader said that they wanted 'someone who could look ahead, was completely down-to-earth, kept a firm grip on what was happening in the authority and was a good co-ordinator'. 'It was necessary for there to be two-way dialogue between the chief executive and the group. He might be invited to address the group and leave before discussion'. Another leading politician also emphasised the need for very good direct relations with the group. Readiness to listen was a quality emphasised both by the politicians and by the chief executive himself.

The leader of the main opposition party, a former company director, disagreed with the concept of the chief executive's role as that of managing director. He believed that as well as an 'efficiency role' the chief executive should have a 'democratic community serving role'. The chief executive was the link between the members acting as 'non-executive directors' and the directors of service, possessed of the knowledge 'to keep fingers on all the buttons'. But the local authority must be well-integrated and act corporately. Each department should have a corporate plan and the chief executive's role should revolve around the fitting of the business plans to a general plan. He should have strong powers subject to answerability to the council.

Here was a chief executive working in a close relationship with his members and respected for major contributions to the rehabilitation and continuing progress of the authority.

Profile R

This district council provided for a large and prosperous commercial centre with a wide range of traditional and modern industries. Its recent problems had arisen from speed of growth and the resulting mix of social affluence and social problems. Political control had swung between parties and for several years there had been no absolute majority. A few years before the interviews Labour had won an election by a small majority and had significantly increased its majority since then. On regaining power the new council leader, with an exceptionally united Labour group behind him, was determined to change both the structure and management processes of the council and to improve services while reducing expenditure.

There were initial problems when chief officers failed to deliver group objectives. The new chief executive was appointed to overcome these difficulties and bring a new approach to the management of the authority. Within months he had prepared a series of papers setting out a strategy to overcome the problems involved in achieving both economy and better services. They examined the opportunities and challenges facing the authority and defined general aims (which he termed 'values') to inform the strategy.

The leader had what the chief executive termed a 'a philosophy of delegation', and gave him the scope to carry out the group's intentions. He was given the leader's support in carrying out restructuring, including reduction in numbers. A thorough reorganisation of staff was achieved within four months after taking over.

In accordance with the leader's philosophy a procedure was set in motion whereby the key strategic documents gained all-party support. Policy proposals were routed through the management team to the chairmen's group and on to committee and council. The chief executive met the opposition leaders monthly to tell them 'what he thought they ought to know'. He admitted that these procedures limited the opportunities for opposition but he regarded support for member cohesion as an important part of his job. Committees usually completed their agenda within two hours.

The chief executive met the leader about twice a week and the leaders of the minority parties, the committee chairmen and the mayor once a fortnight. He was in touch with the 'average member' about once a month. Altogether out of a 65 to 70 hour working week he spent on average about six and a half to seven hours a week with councillors.

The council leader said that he had been influenced in his approach to the reforms required in the authority by a Brunel (BIOSS) brochure on the separation of roles. He had insisted on a 'very political leadership' together with a strong executive leadership; the political leadership being very much the directors behind the chief executive. He contrasted this with an earlier situation in the authority when a chief executive who was very strong in both character and political skill had dominated the council. He was the 'ring-master': leaders told him their secrets and he made the plan, dominating the chief officers. The leader wanted a strong chief executive but one who carried out the wishes of the controlling group. The chief executive and the leadership must be in harmony.

He saw the key institution as the chairmen's group, which consisted of the Labour members on the policy and resources committee meeting with the chief officers. Options from the officers were taken back to the group. There was also a shadow chairmens' group which he briefed in parallel. Roughly speaking the group determined philosophy and objectives and the chief officers' team put the options.

The chief executive had been given full responsibility for the implementation of compulsory competitive tendering. For the politicians to step in to try to sort out problems or a breakdown would, he believed, subtract from executive responsibility and be a waste of time.

An opposition leader saw his general role as to ask for and get as much information as possible. The key problem for the chief executive was to give as much relevant information as he could without breaking confidentiality. He had been impressed by the matters put forward by the chief executive under the new approach. He hoped that the authority would develop the equivalent of a business plan.

Although the chief executive had been only a short time in office there were no indications of failure in objectives. Both members and the chief executive gave stress to securing 'solidarity' between the parties and the officers, and this appeared to have been achieved to an unusual extent. The chief executive was happy with a description of his role as that of 'managing director', but he thought that British local government legislation militated against this as a general panacea.

Comments and Comparisons

It is obviously of fundamental importance to chief executives, and also to party leaders, that party commitments are well-informed and realistic. In practical terms this is most important in the case of the party in power and, where the practice is to set out commitments in party manifestos, of parties which may possibly hold power. Since it is the officers who are usually best equipped to advise on what is feasible and on the consequences of alternatives, member-officer dialogue on proposed political commitments is surely desirable. Moreover it may be agreed that officers should not be expected to implement policies that are impracticable. The distinction which is sometimes made between 'political policy' and 'operational policy' is dubious if only because both relate to the quality of intended outputs.

The evidence is that much generally commended innovation in local government has been the result of officer proposals. Chief executives stand at the peak of a pyramid of idea formation. They and their management teams are in a position to encourage the contribution of ideas from everywhere within the officer organisation, to evaluate their corporate implications and to advance them to the political leadership for their consideration and, if acceptable, embodiment in policies. The role of chief adviser to the council is inseparable in principle from that to its parties, not only on matters for immediate action but also, and perhaps more importantly, through the entire process of policy definition.

Differences in the degree to which the advice of chief executives was taken into account at manifesto and other decision-making levels emerged more clearly in this group of Labour authorities than in any other. Profile M describes a situation of joint involvement in innovation. In N, P and R at least the chief executives were at the centre of policy formulation. There was no question in these cases, as in the previous one, that much of the vision that inspired their councils came to a large extent from their chief executives. In two of the authorities based on important towns at the centre of sub-regions (N and P) the chief executives had been given wide scope to implement their own concepts. It seemed clear that in all three authorities policies were accepted in general by the whole council irrespective of party - not least because they came from the comparatively neutral ground of consensus-seeking chief executives exercising a role that was supported or fostered by council leaders.

N, Q and R identify chief executives exercising their influence towards consensus formation. The same tendency was also seen in Conservative controlled district L as well as the multi-purpose authority cases G and H. It may well be significant that in these cases there was a relatively fine political balance and that political control had changed in recent years.

There is no case here that fits well into the mould of parliamentary two-party politics. This is as true of those cases where parties have as far as can be foreseen a permanent majority (I, J, K, M and P) as it is in those with elements of consensual agreement.

All these cases tend to confirm what may have been concluded from the examination of relationships with elected members in other types of authority: that a high level of innovation is linked closely with close relations with council leaders and a more than averagely close relationship with other members. They also bring out strongly the degree to which leaders may be dependent on a chief executive for the achievement of innovation and the re-orientation of thinking in an authority.

Could the fact be significant that in two of the Labour-controlled districts (N and R) and in Conservative district L the authorities were centred on towns or cities for which it was possible to envisage true civic policies, identified with the future of clearly understood geographical and social entities? There could be a sense amongst the councillors at least of a 'civic mission' that transcended the party interests. For various reasons the solidarity they showed would be difficult in some other cases due to lack of a strong civic core or the nature of the local political culture. The authorities in Profiles I and K at least were artificial creations without a core, in which the concept of a 'vision of the future community' was more difficult to apply than in the case of a town or city. Perhaps the style epitomised in K of a fountain of particular eclectic and pragmatic suggestions on what can be done for the benefit of communities is more appropriate than the concept of an overall vision. The nature of the situation which confronts each council determines perhaps more than anything else the best kind of contribution to the development of a council's work that a chief executive can make.

Chapter 6

RELATIONSHIPS WITH ELECTED MEMBERS IN AUTHORITIES WITHOUT A MAJORITY

If all local authorities are unique, those without party majorities to take control are exceptionally so. The types of political balance, styles and uncertainties that need to be taken into account by the officers who serve them defy classification. Nevertheless for the purpose of this chapter they are divided into three categories. One is of those where a minority group - usually the largest - undertakes the political administration. One group takes the political offices but without the power they normally carry. If it is committed to a manifesto it may assume that its aim is to implement its promises as far as possible with what help it can get from members outside the group and perhaps compromises to win support that would otherwise not be available.

In other cases the hung situation results in a new system of political decision-making in which each party seeks to secure the best outcomes it can in a bargaining process. In some cases such a situation permits the election of one party as leader in the necessary negotiations. In others there is no council leader but a joint institution of leaders carries the central burden of decision-making with or without a formal coalition. In some instances key decisions are undetermined until committees meet, when even the choice of chairman for the meeting may be left to the last moment.

A third situation is where a party political system has never matured, mainly because of the strength of non-party members. Here and in cases of the former kind where there is no council leader it is the council chairman who is usually the main point of reference for the chief executive on matters of procedure, policy etc; but the chairmen of the various committees often dominate policy control in the services for which their committees are responsible.

(This classification roughly corresponds with the categories of minority, no administration, coalition and low partisanship cases in Leach and Stewart (1988) which should be referred to for a wide review of hung authority arrangements. It was not used here because one or two cases did not seem to fall clearly into one of its categories.)

Counties and Scottish Regions

During the 1980s a number of counties saw the end of longstanding one-party or Conservative with non-party member controlled regimes when the rise of the 'Alliance parties' brought about hung situations. The number of the latter rose from eight in 1981 to 25 by 1985 and dropped again to eleven in 1989. The hung situation usually demanded a novel major contribution from chief executives in order to overcome the uncertainty about the fate of proposals and recommendations from one day to the next. Similar changes affected three of the Scottish regions during the decade.

Among the respondents to our questionnaire there were eight chief executives of authorities with minority administrations at the time of the survey and six others who had worked under minority administrations before the 1989 elections. There were also three in authorities with forms of multi-party administration and three where independents and small parties held the balance. In the last situation no leader or minority party leaders were formally recognised but the council chairman was advised by the chief executive on corporate matters. There were no council leaders in five other authorities, but here the chief executive worked to the minority party leaders as a group.

Chief executives' patterns of relationship in these cases differed from those in other types of political situation; among other ways in that minority party leaders were three times more likely to be seen weekly or more often.

Writing about the major difficulties and opportunities in their role during the 1980s three quarters of chief executives in hung or recently hung authorities referred to the political situation as a main difficulty or opportunity in their jobs. The situation was represented as one of disintegration, instability or uncertainty. On the other hand two chief executives stressed that they found no major difficulties in the hung situation, and another whose authority returned to majority control in 1989 saw the change back to majority control as a major problem.

The great majority of responses relating to these situations were on the opportunities they created for making much needed change. One saw a hung situation as a major opportunity to 'introduce policies based on rational argument rather than political dogma', and another 'to achieve a medium-term planning process acceptable to all groups'. Others wrote of it as a major opportunity to use the situation as an 'instrument of change', to facilitate the exploration of funding alternatives and effective ways of getting things done and 'persuading all parties of the need to plan services and introduce new systems', to 'create a more business-like, corporately minded approach and to 'force action in a number of important but neglected areas'.

It is clear that the change to a hung situation in these cases had a liberating effect, enabling chief executives with the skills and sufficiently tractable members to overcome resistance to major innovation by long-established majority groups. It enabled them to realise latent political skills and to argue on policy to the whole council free from the inhibitions that had previously been essential for retaining the confidence of the majority group. They were able to concentrate on issues which made sense across party lines. The evidence is that this 'liberating effect' was stronger in authorities where groups were working together than those with minority administrations. In the latter case there was a need for the chief executive not only to act as a neutral arbitrator between the parties but also for the parties to be dependent on him for finding the common ground among the parties and the independents. The political situation had in itself resulted in a change in attitudes.

Chief executives in authorities dominated by independents and small parties had a much more difficult job in persuading members that there was a need for radical change. They could see their task as continuing a process of slow persuasion to adapt to conditions beyond the members' control. One chief executive in an authority of this kind commented that 'it was extremely difficult for councillors to carry out policy formulation in a meaningful way. Policy tends to be initiated by chief officers, and members are more interested in detail. On the other hand the difficulties have enabled chief officers to use advisory skills and take initiatives not available in tightly political councils'.

Some chief executives clearly enjoyed the demands on their skills made in such situations. A chief executive with exceptionally long experience as a senior officer in a county gave as one of his three main personal objectives in the role as 'managing a delicate political balance'. Among the best achievements cited in hung situations were 'getting the council to specify its vision, aims, working objectives etc', 'fostering a lively, vigorous council within political and executive spheres' and 'laying foundations for a "performance culture"'.

In the following section we look at three contrasting authorities in which no party held a majority. In the first two, administrations had been formed by the largest of the party groups: one Conservative and one Labour. In the third independents and small parties formed most or all of the council, preventing the development of an integrated pattern of leadership and representation.

Profile S

This council served a wide and complex area of great diversity. It was controlled by a Conservative group with slightly under a majority on the council. The opposition consisted mainly of two substantial party groups. The chief executive said that there was broad agreement on policies within the council and that it would be unpopular for the administration to produce statements likely to be used as targets by the opposition parties. By and large Conservative policies prevailed. The Labour leader focused on matters where he believed that he could obtain concessions from the Conservatives. The Alliance approach was 'hit or miss'. The main question was 'how far, how fast'.

The chief executive had no departmental responsibilities. He had a small personal support staff and a corporate planning unit reporting to him. He saw the council leader and the chairman two to four times a week and rated his relations with them as very good. Meetings with the chairman of the main policy committee and the leaders of the minority parties tended to be monthly and were described as neither good nor poor. Those with committee chairmen and other members were less frequent but good in quality. They were less often than monthly with committee chairs and the 'average' council member and were graded as good. In all the chief executive spent an average of about nine hours a week with members out of a 45 hour week.

His line of communication with the majority group was predominantly through the leader, who was very able and experienced and ready to deliver support on matters on which he agreed. His contacts with opposition members were in general only at committee meetings, but occasionally he also saw them on procedural and personal issues. In the case of a major departmental restructuring a meeting of the three leaders was held which gave the proposals cross-party support. He liked to maintain a degree of detachment from the political world. A chief executive, he believed, must have a certain independence because he served the council as a whole.

It had been agreed recently that significant policy issues would go to the chief officers' group and that all chief officers would contribute to the agenda. The majority of items were put forward by the three senior officers: the chief executive, the treasurer and the secretary. He thought it inconceivable that he should have his finger on everything. He had to live with that. In practice he did not have enough time to see what was going on and tended not to hear of things until they went wrong.

He had found no major difficulties in his work since becoming chief executive after moving from an authority of the same type a few years before. He had seen working in a hung authority as a major opportunity, along with the need to adapt to change caused by events in the previous year including the Education Reform Act, competitive tendering and the retirement of long serving chief officers. He considered his three best achievements to be 'managing a "hung" authority for several years without too many alarms and excursions'; leading a total restructuring of the largest department of the authority in face of new legislation and with the unanimous support of colleagues and elected members; and 'introducing participative and accountable management on the basis of an individual's responsibilities'. His three most important personal objectives were 'leading colleagues and myself to higher standards of performance', 'securing the continued survival of the authority in a time of change' and 'delivering standards of service to the public'.

Since being appointed to his present post he had designed, in cooperation with his officer colleagues, a major reform of departmental structure aimed to make the best possible use of the opportunity for separating and clarifying the roles of client and contractor organisations and their relationships. The nature of the restructuring evolved from discussion with those concerned, but it was clear that only the chief executive had been in a position to identify the common factors and to advance a solution that would best meet the shared goals of service quality and other key criteria.

But he was much more interested in policy-planning than in structural matters. 'There must be a top that can do policy-planning and maintain the services in terms of setting standards and how well they are kept'. He saw the reforms as a means to an end. His job was conducting the orchestra, taking a general view of policies and resource problems but mainly ensuring the fulfilment of what the council was trying to do.

He would have liked to have involved the members in the departmental restructuring but this would have been very difficult in a hung council. The members would be involved in any case in the determination of policy and resources. The setting of key areas of achievement would be taken on by the committees.

To complement these changes he had worked on the development of a system of achievement targets set by the chief officers and a process of monitoring which had stimulated more self-criticism and frankness about failures.

He made major contributions to policy on some matters. The strategy for an extremely large industrial facility was basically his own, developed in close collaboration with the local district council, although the policy committee and consultants had also been involved.

He had found the demands of the job very exacting on time and energy. 'You never knew when you might be required to make a decision and need to be quite clear on your next course of action. It needed a great variety of understanding to see things in the round and not be caught by surprise.' He was not an autocrat but rather a diplomat, and in general he felt that he could see the common ground on issues quickly. But he was not a consensus manager: he aimed at the most appropriate solution. Anything else was an abdication of responsibility. However he looked for the right solution to come from other people if possible.

Profile T

This authority was an amalgamation of levels of government in a rich agricultural area with mixed industries. The Labour group had assumed administrative responsibility as the largest of three main groups although short of a majority. The Conservative group had held power until the middle years of the 1980s.

When the present chief executive was appointed from a post within the authority several years before he had served a strong majority admnistration that was suspicious of officers and continually pressing for economies. He was expected to line up with them against the 'high spending' services. He could however be certain that any of his proposals agreed by the group would be implemented. The minority Labour administration depended on the unreliable support of a third party and this created a climate of uncertainty. It was however a dynamic authority and its policies were highly innovative. Implementing their policies involved a rapid increase in spending.

The workload involved was greatly increased by the spate of new legislation at the end of the decade. In view of this he was devolving his legal and administrative duties to a new department, giving him the opportunity to concentrate on corporate activities, including planning, budgetting and policy and performance review. He was aware that loss of direct involvement in committee administration and the legal advisory function would make him reliant on crucial information being passed up to him by colleagues. The problem was that 'the buck arrives at the last minute'.

He was relinquishing the departmental responsibilities he had kept on appointment in order to give more time to corporate affairs. He met the leader and the council chairman two to four times a week and described his relations with them as good and very good respectively. He usually met the the leaders of the minority parties weekly and the committee chairmen and other members monthly, and had good working relationships with all of them. He spent in all about eight hours a week in meetings with members out of an estimated 52 hour week.

His most important personal objectives included influence on policy and decision-making, ensuring effective performance, promoting good public relations and good staff relations. He felt that his best achievements had been instituting a system of policy review, setting up an economic development agency and a twinning link with a French *département*.

After taking over the administration the Labour group had expected the officers to follow them in 'shaking off the Conservative shackles', to use their own words. But new legislation had required them to comply with procedures designed to implement Conservative policy. They had resented especially the requirements for contract awards under the compulsory competitive tendering system. It had been difficult to persuade some members that the 'ultra vires' argument was not a plot by officers to frustrate their ambitions. Another problem was the reluctance of the politicians to delegate implementational responsibility to management.

The additional skills he had needed in recent years had been mainly personal qualities: to be able to think like a politician and to anticipate future actions by the political leadership. The senior members of the group had developed closer working relationships among themselves and had begun to work like a cabinet government. 'They expected to get results and to crack heads together if necessary'. It was necessary to have 'patience, tact and a sense of realism about what can be achieved: when to fight and when to run away'.

The statutory posts required by the 1989 legislation had raised new issues about the 'shadowy areas between officers and committees, occupied by party political machinery'. It appeared that the new officers with statutory status would be able to exercise considerable discretion and power, but the provisions just scratched the surface of the reality.

Leading members of the Labour administration confirmed the chief executive's description of their unease about the power of the officers. Since they had no overall majority they were continually uncertain whether they could enforce their wishes against officer advice and there was a feeling that the officers were presenting a united front against them. An incident in the implementation of corporate competitive tendering was quoted which rankled deeply. The council had wanted to test the law on their ability to award a contract to their workforce against an outside bid. They took independent legal advice but failed to obtain support for a challenge that went against the advice of the officers.

The council leader felt that a chief executive who worked for one political party for a long period tended to work to their ideology. He had serious doubts about the concept of professional integrity and how it related to the authority of the members served. Members in his opinion must put forward the policies they are elected on. The chief executive's main contribution was securing corporate implementation - 'delivering the goods'. The job was largely an administrative one.

Another of the leading politicians believed that the officers made much of the running pace of the authority. There was a clear belief that the political administration should be managing the authority and that the members' intentions were being frustrated. He said that they gave their chief officers copies of their manifesto and in some instances the officers threw it aside. He spoke of a session at a conference he had attended with the treasurer where four chief executives had spoken to a meeting largely of officers which revealed very clearly the attitude, 'We know what's wanted and can handle things without elected members'. There was no doubt in this case that the group wanted a political chief executive who would be willing to fight their political case in spite of the fact that they did not hold a majority. An opposition leader acknowedged the great change that had occurred in the way chief executives had operated and indicated that this was against his conception of the role. He saw the chief executive's job as to ensure that the authority was working in an efficient manner through the management team. A chief executive needed political sensitivity and the ability to smooth the way for the council's decisions. He should ensure that no department was acting in a non-corporate manner, as a general manager did in a large business. He appreciated however the way the chief executive attended their group meetings to ensure that the members had the best expert information before they reached any position.

He would have liked the chief executive to be known more as a public figure, as in the case of the council chairman, but a chief executive must ensure that neither he nor other officers wear political colours on their sleeves.

The stresses were very apparent in this case, both on the members and the officers, arising from a conflict of expectations and constant uncertainty about outcomes because the political administration did not hold majority control.

Profile U

This authority resulted from an amalgamation of different elements, each with a strong sense of its own identity. The economy of the area is sharply divided between agricultural and recreational activities on the one hand and manufacturing on the other, and its politics reflect that division. Its natural heritage was a matter of common interest between these two strands and has helped to bring them together. Political control was finely balanced. Failing consensus the power to determine decisions fell to the third party and independents. In the chief executive's words, 'Manifesto politics were clearly impossible'. In practice the 'hung situation had not been the source of any difficulty, major or minor'.

Committee meetings were held in different centres. Some services were geographically decentralised and had divisional offices for operations, but general management was centralised.

The chief executive, who was free of departmental responsibilities and had no support staff, saw his main opportunities when appointed to his post as to give credibility to his the role and its fulfilment, to reduce 'the Bureaucratic Tendency which afflicted the operating style of the council', and to begin changing the culture towards one which was more business-like, more product-conscious, more client/consumer oriented, more corporately minded'.

He defined his main objectives as reshaping the executive culture, promoting a 'long-term focus - in all things' and 'fostering a healthy injection of the political dimension'; all three aims being interdependent. The 'hung-council situation' he saw as an instrument of change and a means to fulfil these aims. One of his best achievements he thought was to succeed in using the authority of his position in the 'hung situation' to foster 'a lively and vigorous council - in both the political and the executive spheres'. He had launched major initiatives to bring many of the senior officers below chief officer level together with leading politicians in the authority to discuss and thresh out major issues. He met the council chairman and the three group leaders weekly and the committee chairmen and other members monthly or less often. He rated all these relationships as very good. Altogether he spent about six hours of an estimated 60 hour week with members.

The emphasis in this chief executive's approach was primarily on relationships and creating solidarity between parties and members and officers.

London Boroughs and Metropolitan Districts

Six chief executives sent information from authorities without majority control. In the great conurbations hung situations, once rather rare, had risen to nearly one in four at the time of the research. In two cases a party had missed control by the narrowest majority but the questionnaires did not reflect a hung situation at all. In two cases the political situation was more complex but the forms of council leader and a one-party administration were maintained. In the final two there were no council leaders and the chief executives worked to three party leaders.

The chief executive of one of the first two authorities gave his main responsibility for policy advice and implementation as to the majority party. He accepted the risk of allegations of over-close identification with the current administration such as described in Profile T above if it lost power. The second gave it as to the council. In the second pair the chief executives appeared to have a difficulty in saying where the main responsibility lay. One omitted to answer the question; the other commented that the minority administration was a very strong one and that he saw his responsibility as lying between the party that maintained it and the council as a whole. The third pair had no difficulty in saying that it was to the council as a whole.

The pattern of meetings varied in the same way as that for the group of counties and regions. Meetings with leaders in the first two pairs were daily but in the two where responsibility was seen as unambiguously to the council two to four times a week. Minority group leaders were met fortnightly in four cases. Where there was no council leader there were meetings at least weekly.

The time given by the chief executives to meetings with members in these authorities ranged from six hours a week to over twenty-two. There is no strong relationship with the nature of the political situation, but it may be noted that of the two chief executives in authorities without council leaders one gave the highest estimate of time spent with members (22 hours) while the second gave the fourth highest (11). The quality of the relationships was in all cases rated as good or very good.

On their difficulties and opportunities in these situations one in an authority with a minority administration referred to a particularly checkered history of relationships and frustrations among councillors. Coming to the authority in the mid-1980s the main opportunity he saw in the post was to overcome problems that no one yet had 'managed to crack'. He rated the establishment of good relationships and trust and respect with the elected members there as one of his best achievements as chief executive. In a similar situation the other looked to creating among the members a shared vision of the authority's performance for the 1990s, and rated as his best achievements, along with a new accountable management structure, solving major structural issues regarding the services despite the hung situation.

In a case without a one-party administration the chief executive gave as two of his three main objective remaining abreast of member/officer relationships and maintaining working relationships between the political parties. He included the latter as an objective expected by members along with giving advice whenever requested. His two best personal achievements as chief executive were he thought maintaining stability of operation in the authority in a potentially very unstable political environment and securing the members' approval for organisational change - 'especially where a ^change` of chief officer is concerned'. The situation shares characteristics with the second case which is outlined in more detail below.

Compared with the cases of minority party administrations in county and regional councils the party lines appeared to be harder and the parties to work less like all-party coalitions. Hence there appeared to be less possibility of using the situation to promote open, rational discussion about policies instead of focusing on manifesto commitments. In these cases establishing a common vision is an ambition more against the odds. In organisational matters however pressures and necessities can be an aid to radical restructuring. Moreover the strong pursuit by chief executives of solutions to external problems can deliver successes in matters which would be intractable without the chief executive's strong leadership.

Profile V

This large metropolitan authority covers areas of mixed industry, residential development and open land. It lacks a natural centre and the inhabitants still identify with the areas of the local authorities that preceded reorganisation.

Until the time of the interviews the authority had moved sharply from strong Labour to strong Conservative majorities within a two-party system. The successes of the Alliance parties in the mid-1980s ended this tradition, bringing about a hung situation with no formal party administration. The Labour group's policies were described as far-left. Labour had been short of an absolute majority by one or two seats but nevertheless set about exploiting their position with zeal. To quote the chief executive, 'There was 'violence in the air, especially when Conservatives and Alliance voted together'. The Democrats emerged as power-brokers and tended to vote with the Conservatives on financial matters but not on others. In these circumstances an attempt at a Labour administration was short-lived. To be chairman of a committee became devoid of the possibilities of leadership. A high level of polarisation between the parties and the tradition of adversarial politics continued, resulting in *impasses* which proved extremely time-absorbing for all involved.

The chief executive thought that despite the stress and frustrations the council had nevertheless ended up on the whole with well-argued decisions. When he took up his present post he found dispirited officers but also the opportunity to create an effective management team. The financial outlook was bleak and he set about overcoming the problems by presenting policy options to officers and launching value for money exercises. The welter of legislation from the third Thatcher government and its rigidly imposed timetable brought the opportunity to use this challenge as a means for introducing much-needed radical change. He saw the hung situation as creating the possibility for fostering more open government and evenhandedness. He rated his most important personal objectives and achievements as the management of change; harnessing the latent resources of the officers; and, of a very different type, leading a public/private partnership development team to create a large scale science park with leisure facilities.

There was no pre-committee decision-making, so that for example the elements of the budget had to come straight to the policy committee for determination. The chief executive attempted with very little success to hold a liaison committee of the leaders. Each party group made its own arrangements with the chief financial officer for financial briefings.

He had tried to interest the leaders in concepts of medium-term policy planning in order to enable them to take control of the agenda, but they argued that with expenditure 30 per cent above the Department of the Environment's grant-related expenditure assessment they were in a hand-to-mouth situation which made such procedures futile. Nevertheless he felt that he must make them face forward planning issues in order to press them to judge priorities. This was largely unsuccessful because for two groups to agree on a priority meant that they ran an unacceptable risk of being identified with each other and then being pilloried by the third group in the eyes of the electorate.

One of the party group leaders said that the major factor in the control of the authority was the interface between the political leadership and the officers. A chief executive needed listening skills: he needed to recognise disguised consensus between the groups. He did not think the concept of the chief executive being 'managing director' was useful in terms of his need and ability to pursue a broad mandate. Much depended on the leader. He could be powerful, making it possible for the chief executive to act backed by the leader's authority, but this might make it extraordinarily difficult for the chief executive to work well with the next political administration.

One leader thought that the most effective approach by the chief executive had been to tackle leaders and chairmen separately, mediating on policy. He had to become a kind of 'policy-broker', but he recognised that this could be a very time-consuming process. On the other hand he criticised the chief executive for lack of decisiveness in that he had tried not to upset the Labour group. Another said that whatever the officers put up was bound to be interpreted in political terms. If they proposed to close three schools it would be a political decision which schools they were. They had to tread a line which offended the least. If the officers failed to set policy there would be chaos. Dictatorship was forced on the chief executive. The officers 'take stick from all the parties'.

The chief executive said that he had suffered one 'deep experience' while serving the 'hung' council. He had persuaded the three leaders to agree on a study examining the officer structure in relation to compulsory competitive tendering and the need to establish a director of commercial services. As a result the Labour leader had been badly mauled by his group. (It can be a fundamental problem for an officer in this situation that to obtain what he sees as essential concessions from the leader is likely to alienate the leader from elements in his group and thereby undermine his leadership). The chief executive had in the end achieved agreement between management and the unions, leading to an agreed way forward. But he was now very wary of consensus politics on the subject of competitive tendering.

The 'hung' situation had presented a challenge to the management team to develop a corporate approach and to address the key issues. They had launched far more initiatives and proposals than they would have done under a majority administration. A leader confirmed that although at first the members had been anxious not to see the officers as running the council, they now complained if they received a report without recommendations in it. Officers had to argue a case vigorously in order to satisfy all three groups. In the chief executive's words they had been acting 'in trust' as it were for an eventual political administration. As a result political accountability had been frustrated.

The leaders confirmed that they saw the officers as a 'fourth party' who had to deliver policy. All the members considered themselves to be in the opposition. As one put it, 'the chief executive has acted more as a chairman of the board than as a managing director'. He saw this as inherent in a situation in which members pushed the officers to put forward positive proposals.

At the time the chief executive was seeing the three leaders on the council weekly, the mayor fortnightly, the committee chairmen monthly and other members less frequently. Out of a typical working week of 45 hours he gave eleven to twelve hours to meetings with members. One effect of the situation was that although the chief executive was outward-looking in his conception of his role the decision-making problems within the authority had much limited the time he could give to important external matters.

Without Majority Control

District Councils without Majority Control

At the time of the survey some 130 districts in Britain were not controlled by a majority party group: 30 per cent of English non-metropolitan districts and about 60 per cent of Scottish and Welsh districts. Of these about 90 had various combinations of minority party groups (some unorganised and very small), independents, non-party members and others whose political status was undeclared. The remaining 40 councils consisted entirely or predominantly of non-party councillors. We received responses to the research questionnaire from 49 of combined administrations and 22 of non-party.

The following analysis of chief executives' relationships is based on a random sampling of returns from twenty English, seven Welsh and five Scottish authorities with these types of control. The two profiles that follow are from authorities not included in the number. The populations of the authorities drawn on come from those with populations of between fourteen thousand and three hundred thousand.

A 'hung situation' close to that described in most-purpose authorities was found to be typical of medium-sized towns and cities ranging from 85 thousand population upwards. Eleven of the English authorities in our sample fall into this category. They possess traditions of majority party government and in nearly all cases appoint council leaders, normally from the leaders of the largest party group. The other cases are of mixed areas of countryside and small towns where the council contains a major independent or non-party element. In four English, one Welsh and one Scottish case the members not belonging to the Scottish National Party or Plaid Cymru are balanced against two or more party groups. In other cases the non-party element predominates.

In all instances there is a clearly defined problem of the legitimacy of political leadership: a power vacuum which may be filled by a leader who can maintain credibility with enough members - a possibility where there are enough independents willing to support most of the policies of a Conservative group in divisions in council, or more rarely where in a marginal situation the largest minority party agrees to run the administration with the help of whatever support it can rally for particular decisions. The leader's relationship with the chief executive in these cases is usually a very close one, meetings between them occurring at least weekly and in half the cases more often. There is also usually a close relationship between the chief executive and the minority group leaders, with meetings in most of our sample at weekly intervals and in others, with one exception, fortnightly.

In the largely non-party political authorities (13 of the 20) members normally look to the council chairman and possibly to a policy committee chairman to represent them as a whole on procedural and policy matters. The chairmen thus provide the main point of reference for the chief executive on policy issues and all or most other corporate matters. In seven of the authorities the chief executive met the chairman at least twice a week and in the others weekly. Like working relationships with leaders in this category of local authorities they were all described as good or very good. Meetings with the chairman of the policy committee, where one existed, all took place fortnightly. In these respects there was a remarkable sameness about these authorities.

In all these situations a large vacuum remains to be filled in decision-making in the absence of a majority group. Policy on organisation, priorities, resource allocation and the many other corporate matters that have to be dealt with at the centre need to be resolved in ways that carry the support of the council. In the 1960s the essential matters were generally within the comprehension of leading members, who might direct the clerk in detail and leave little for him to determine; on the other hand a clerk by force of character could use his position to lead the council himself. In the 1980s the rapidity of legislative change affecting all councils and the pressure on resources made a passive role impossible. The officers had to steer the council in most central matters.

The chief executive found himself in a position where essential decision-making needed communication skills and political judgment not only in determining what was feasible but in building up a framework of objectives, procedures and action which the members would agree. Moreover he had the full officer resources to draw on directly to achieve this end. If he could sell his solutions on challenging problems to the council, he could, given the backing of the council chairman and other leading politicians, become its informal leader, willy-nilly.

A management team of chief officers could carry the responsibility on their backs, although there could be obvious problems in the face of the structural issues of compulsory competitive tendering where chief officers' views and interests might conflict. The chief executive might have to take virtually full informal responsibility for the solutions adopted.

In a rapidly changing situation where traditional behaviour is inadequate, coping with problems of morale and confidence of members as well as of officers may be just as important. Party groups provide members with rules of a game, the equivalent of which does not exist in a council of independents. The chief executive can provide purpose by propagating concepts which have been widely adopted in the 1980s - the themes that recur again and again in the responses to the questionnaires including consumer-consciousness, competitive services and the enabling approach. Chief executives had to translate them into a language which all members could appreciate as a means of rebuilding confidence in local government, linked with the generally appreciated theme of 'value for money'.

As in the case of most-purpose authorities some chief executives in authorities with minority administrations had difficulty in answering the question on whether their main responsibility in policy advice and implementation lay to the council, to the majority party or elsewhere. Some comments showed them wrestling with a matter that has no simple answer. One chief executive wrote that he saw responsibility as to the majority party 'but not so as to prejudice his duty to the council as a whole'; another that he did not think it inconsistent to blend the two responsibilities, giving greater priority to one or the other according to the nature of the issue. One in a large town authority without a leader commented that 'In present circumstances advice is general to all groups and the role is akin to that of an honest broker'.

In three 'party political' hung districts political conflicts were given as main difficulties, but in the majority of cases the hung situation was unmentioned. The stress that arose from it was not given the prominence it had in replies from the most-purpose authorities.

A common theme is the need for management reform and a change of culture. In all but one of the replies the opportunity to carry out reforms was set against the problems of an environment resistant to changes that the chief executive saw as necessary. Thus, to quote one chief executive, 'while the members are aware of the premises for change they are reluctant to face them'. Some chief executives who replied had moved from party authorities to authorities without traditional structures and had found that problems of adaptation were tied up with culture and structure: there was a need for the authority to accept innovation if the chief executive's role as they perceived it was to be fulfilled. One such case is described in more detail below. Another who had moved to a leaderless authority from one with strong political control saw in retrospect the main opportunities in his former job to have risen from the majority's overall political control, clear party directives and relatively easily defined objectives. In the new authority on the other hand he saw a main opportunity as 'management of a change of culture' and bringing in an 'up to date concept of what the authority exists for'. He needed to exercise if possible a profounder, more philosophical role.

The 'missionary' concept of the role is strongly expressed in some cases: for example 'There is a major opportunity to guide and influence direction in an uncertain political climate' and 'to tackle old and unwarranted perceptions of local government'. In another case 'the council's emphasis had been on restraint' and 'there was a tremendous potential and ambition built up and awaiting release... there is an opportunity to lead the way into a new culture'. The difficulties are seen as in so many other cases as opening up a revolutionary approach to the authority's work.

In writing about their objectives and achievements these chief executives place a special emphasis on establishing good relations, morale building, and 'realising the potential of the authority and the community'. They aim to produce a corporate structure and 'a strategy for the new decade'. The hung situation could make this more difficult or more possible according to the possibilities of producing cultural change.

In authorities without organised parties difficulties relating to the disunity of their councils are not remarked upon: in so far as they exist they have always existed as a fact of life. Chief executives identify the difficulties as arising from 'fixed attitudes', demoralisation and frustration resulting from constraints and the demands of new legislation. The main problem, not dissimilar from that in some of the hung authorities, is to make members more prepared to innovate, or 'to make the authority think corporately'. A Welsh chief executive coming from another type of authority saw the absence of party control as 'offering greater opportunity to participate in the formulation of policy'; and another in Scotland as 'developing defensive attitudes into positive approaches and challenges'.

These chief executives define a wide range of personal objectives: to develop or complete a corporate plan, to 'instil attitudes in favour of quality of service rather than saving at all costs' and 'to maintain a corporate approach to problems'.

The question about what it was thought councillors expected the main objectives of chief executives to be produced indications that members are not as resistant to change and corporate working as might be assumed from other sources. They are said to expect the chief executive to give clear, concise corporate advice on policy matters, to keep corporate planning under review, 'to provide guidelines in the formulation of policy', 'to run the council without appearing to', and 'to suggest imaginative and constructive options for the council's consideration'. (Most of the quotations in this paragraph come from replies by chief executives in Scotland and Wales).

There are some very pithy formulations of members' expectations from chief executives in English non-party authorities which provide a useful summary. One said that his members expected him 'to lead, to guide, to listen, and help to achieve corporate working'; another that they expect 'Leadership, Commitment, Action

Decisions'; yet another 'Leadership, policy advice, strategic planning'. These are very much in harmony with the chief executives' own stated objectives except that some of the latter would place an additional stress on innovation. It is striking that these views have in common the expectation that the chief executive should provide leadership in the authority.

Amongst what chief executives give as their best achievements are the development of a corporate attitude to the council's affairs, the 'final agreement of members to review all activities, policies and objectives after each election and set a realistic programme of action for the following four years', and ' encouraging a change of approach by elected members so as to produce a council which is less officer-led' and more 'member-led'. The problem may often be to find or even develop leadership potential amongst the members to propagate and meet the need for change.

The members' expectations in districts of this kind may be difficult for chief executives to read and understand, as several who had moved to them from party political and county authorities had found. Usually there were no articulated policy objectives and a need to weigh carefully the costs and benefits of decisions to different areas, population groups and not least individuals if the council was to avoid being the subject of intense criticism. In fact a form of 'customer-consciousness' - or clientelism - is rooted in tradition, although attenuated by the distancing of councils from small communities by the amalgamations of the 1970s. But this 'customer-consciousness' is very different from that implied in the commercial slogans that relate to the need for profitability and often to standardisation of product.

Particular local problems that stand in the way of otherwise desirable developments may be of their nature difficult or impossible to resolve without incurring hostility from those who are very close to them, and yet a thorough weighing of local representatives' knowledge and opinions is needed if they are to be resolved sensitively. The concepts of innovator, coordinator of resources, leader and others are rolled together in a role which only the chief executive can perform. The elected members are dependent on him and so are other officers responsible for plans and programmes who face political obstacles on particular issues.

The qualities involved in a small and close non-party authority are not necessarily less than those in a large party-motivated one, although they are likely to be required in a different balance. There is in fact a surprising similarity between the language in which chief executives express their objectives whatever the size of their authority. This may be partly a testament to the way in which government-driven change on the one hand and new ideas on organisation, management and local government objectives from the new local government literature on the other have penetrated everywhere.

The profiles which follow indicate some of the problems of relationships and opportunities considered above.

Profile W

This authority was formed out of an amalgamation of urban and rural districts. Agriculture predominated and industries were small scale. The council's offices were scattered and still in the course of centralisation. Conservative Party representation had grown over the years to a point about the same as the number of independents. There were also a small number of members from two other parties. The Conservative members had no group organisation and there was no way of predetermining committee and council decisions.

The chief executive had taken up his appointment not long before the interview. His previous experience was in authorities which he described as 'well-developed politically'. In his new authority he met with the council chairman two to four times a week and with the chairman of the main policy committee weekly. Relationships were sometimes difficult. Altogether he spent about ten hours a week with members out of a fifty hour week.

He described his accountability as in practice not to a group or to the council but to a small number of senior members who possessed effective control. They tended to be powerful and strong-willed and without any experience of authorities other than their own. There was virtually no delegation to the chief executive. Everything had to go to committee. Members were involved in interviewing for quite junior staff posts. In compulsory tendering for an activity they came close to refusing to allow the authority's own organisation to tender.

In general the members did not want to make policy, as this could clash with an ad hoc style of decision making. There was a lack of predictability on how things would go in committee and council.

The chief executive identified his own main difficulties as lack of knowledge of the geographical area; a council isolated from practices of authorities nationally and somewhat resistant to imported ideas; the insufficient width of experience of the staff of the council; lack of obvious political direction; and the depth of councillor involvement in day to day management. The opportunities he saw in the job were 'to create a customer-orientated, value for money organisation in line with a strong democratic and independent tradition, and with strong links with employers and other voluntary groups', and 'management on a team and involvement basis'. His most important personal objectives were to gain the respect of members and staff; to assist in identifying the role of the authority in the community; and to get the chief officers to think and work corporately.

The council chairman and leader both had doubts about whether a chief executive was necessary. If they had one they felt it should be a professional, partly because it was less expensive if he could also direct a department. They had wanted an administrator because they already had a good treasurer.

The leader's view was that decisiveness was very important in a chief executive. The council needed a chief executive who would put forward original thoughts and alternatives and provide a channel for feeding up ideas to the members from other officers. Some second-tier officers were full of ideas. They wanted someone who could put over a point of view firmly and with authority. But he must be totally loyal to the decisions of main committees.

It was clear in this authority that although there was a demand at the top for a strong role, such an approach would be very difficult to put into practice without effective influence over the council and especially over its leading members - something difficult to achieve in the circumstances. The challenge was to work out a relationship that would not compromise the status and authority of either side.

Profile X

This authority was formed out of several urban and rural districts. It is an area of countryside, villages and small towns with well-developed recreational and tourist facilities. The Conservative Party held much the largest representation on the council but was short of a majority. There was a large group of independents. A few members from two other parties held the balance.

The chief executive had been in office for several years. He met the chairman of the main policy committee daily, the council chairman two to four times a week, chairmen of other committees fortnightly and the 'average' council member monthly. All relations were reported good and those with the leader and council chairman very good. He was involved with members for about four and a half hours a week or so. He was exceptional amongst respondents in spending about 45 per cent of his time (18.5 hours upwards out of a more than 45 hour week) working for the authority on relations outside his the council offices. He said that he also spent about five per cent of his time in 'trying to think'.

Early in his work as chief executive to the council he saw the main difficulties he faced as injecting political direction into the authority and achieving corporate attitudes. He saw his main opportunity as the enhancement of the authority's performance and status. From 1988 one of his main difficulties was the hostile central government climate and controls. He gave his main recent opportunities as increasing the public's perception of the role of local government and motivating the workforce in unfavourable circumstances with the spirit of 'we can still do it'.

He saw one of his three best achievements as 'bringing the political process in an independent council to a state of relative sanity with help from a small number of elected members' and 'gaining media respect' for the authority.

The Aims and Achievements of Chief Executives with Regard to their Political Environments

The situations faced by chief executives in the profiles in chapters 5 and 6 relating to the implementation of organisational reform suggest a number of typical patterns. The ideal situation for prospective chief executives may be one in which they are able to obtain the warm agreement of those appointing them for their interpretation of what, if appointed, would be their own objectives in the post and their vision of how the authority should change to face the future. In some ten of the twenty-four authorities described in the profiles the situation approximated to that ideal. The political leadership expected the chief executives to implement radical change and gave them the scope and support to do so. In most cases there was a background of failure by members and officers to achieve their aims in the past. New chief executives were sought and appointed who were committed to major change backed by a philosophy of reform. They came to the management of their authorities with clear and agreed ideas on what they wanted to achieve. Managerial vision and proposals for decisive action were welcomed and sanctioned. This situation was found both in three authorities controlled by strong majorities (profiles C, D, and K) and seven in which majorities were marginal or, in two cases, the authority was hung but there was a significant tendency towards consensus on management and development issues (profiles G, H, L, N, R, S and U).

In two cases radical change was a well-established objective of the political leadership. Experienced chief executives worked with this situation, and their well-established chief executives were able to make major contributions themselves within the majority party's policy commitments and in some respects beyond it (profiles M and O).

In two other cases the chief executives brought an innovative approach which won the members' support and created a relationship which continued through the changes effected in the wake of the new legislation of the late 1980s (profiles Q and X). In the case of a more traditional authority the chief executive enjoyed a receptive environment in which there was a willingness for change and a stress on collaborative working to fulfil the service objectives (profile I).

In all these instances there was willingness among the members to accept management reform, and in most of them it was strongly welcomed. In one case there was no effective political leadership because of a hung situation and a failure or unwillingness among politicians to find common ground themselves. The chief executive and management team sought to find that common ground for the members - in effect negotiating and determining decisions with the three political leaders (profile V).

There remain four authorities where the implementation of change was seen as hindered by deep-rooted political cultures. In these situations the chief executives had to approach innovation cautiously since members were likely to be upset by proposals that were not consistent with their view of their political mandates. It was easy to cross the members in a situation where they believed they had to fight government imposed legislation that offended against their concepts of local government rights or of social justice (profiles B, J, T and W).

In another case strong differences on central issues of organisation and responses to resource problems existed, both amongst political leaders and between some of them and the officers. The chief executive saw his problem as converting members to feasible policies against the political commitments of leaders who were themselves sometimes in conflict within their party group (profile F).

In one case the problem was past history. A thrustful chief executive had undertaken innovations in a way that had upset members and broken down solidarity. The new chief executive took over when relationships had been to some extent disrupted. The chief executive's first objective had been to re-establish good relationships, cooperation and openness to new ideas, building the foundations for reforms that were 'owned' by committee members and chief officers (profile A).

Last were two authorities where the implementation of change was against deep-rooted political cultures, but the elected members had confidence in long-serving chief executives who in the past had played a leading role in halting the economic and social decline of their areas and, in the previous two years, had been able to guide the leadership into accepting necessities arising from new legislation (profiles E and P) .

It will be noted that most of these typical situations cut across local authority types and patterns of political control. They were also found in authorities of contrasting sizes. Apart from the chief executive's own character and abilities it is differences in the members' relationships, values and culture that appear to determine the nature of the relationship between the political leadership and the chief executive.

Without Majority Control

The cases where chief executives enjoyed a strong mandate from the political leadership outnumbered by fifteen to nine those where they worked against political problems. Those with strong political support were all except one appointed in the second half of the 1980s, the exception dating from 1982. In the cases where local authorities were being asked to take measures that went against their members' political culture and understanding of local government but were required under national legislation, chief executives who were fully acclimatised to the local culture of their regions were able to guide their authorities to accept their recommendations in ways that were accepted, although not always very willingly, without compromising the promotion of efficiency.

Three of four chief executives who faced other difficulties in overcoming local problems inherent in the local political situation were fairly new to their authorities. In two other cases the chief executives knew their authorities very well but were struggling with the problems of conflicts at political level which they had found no means to overcome.

The 18 authorities chosen to obtain a balanced sample of British authorities in terms of their geographical location, social composition, type, scale, political situation and backgrounds and experience of their chief executives may be taken tentatively to give a rough indication of the national situation and its variety. Extrapolation from this suggests that chief executives in about half of British authorities experienced problems of resistance to changes which the chief executives believed necessary or highly desirable. In around two-thirds there had been impressive achievements in adapting to new demands and values with or without resistance. In the remaining third the chief executives had faced difficult obstacles arising from the nature of the local political culture and politics in attempting to achieve the standards of organisation that they believed desirable.

It has been suggested to me that failure by a chief executive to overcome such problems might be due to his personal limitations. All I can say is that judgments on whether this is so in a particular case should not be made without a thorough appreciation of the situation. In certain authorities problems of this kind have defeated a succession of chief executives. One highly successful chief executive who had previously been a chief officer in a 'problem authority' was adamant that he could not have succeeded as chief executive there because it had been endemically lacking in the strong political backing which he was now enjoying. In one case where the problems arose from the political balance it is understood that constructive action backed by a majority became possible within the following year due to the results of a local election. In two cases a new leader from within the majority party had apparently transformed the possibilities for action by the chief executive. For a high level of performance that fulfils democratic criteria, both leading politicians and chief executives need to command good support and to share feasible objectives.

Chapter 7

THE CHIEF EXECUTIVE AND THE STAFF ORGANISATION

HEAD OF PAID SERVICE, LEADER OF STAFF OR GENERAL MANAGER?

The position, status and formal authority of the chief executive have normally been defined in terms of his or her relationship to the council's staff. As described in Part A, the Bains and Paterson Reports formulated the status as 'head of the council's paid service' with 'authority over all other officers so far as this is necessary for the efficient management and execution of the council's functions'. What may be 'necessary' remains subject to varied personal judgments. The Paterson Report added 'except where the discretion or judgment of the professional officers is concerned', but I have failed to find evidence that the qualification has in itself made any practical difference. The implications of the title are still open to debate.

The Housing and Local Government Act of 1989 created the mandatory role of 'head of paid service', a designation which councils were expected to confer on their chief executives. The statutory title carries with it the duties to report to the authority on the coordination of functions and the organisation of staffing. This does not in itself do more than confirm the right to report on matters which chief executives and their prececessors had reported on by convention for over a century and more.

In the consultative stages of the legislation discussion centred on the recommendations of the Widdicombe Report and what was termed the 'management officer' role. It was expected by some councillors interviewed in the research that the government would impose on them the requirement to delegate responsibility for appointments other than those of the higher grades of officer in accordance with the recommendations in the Widdicombe Report. At time of writing the outcome remains uncertain.

The existing job descriptions remain the starting point for the formal definition of the role, although by themselves they are a very inadequate guide to practice. Nearly nine out of ten of the 263 chief executives who replied to the research questionnaire reported that their job descriptions were wholly or substantially those recommended in the Bains or Paterson reports. They mostly define the chief executive's main duties within the officer organisation as the leadership of the 'officer management team in securing a corporate approach to the affairs of the authority generally...', 'the efficient and effective implementation of the council's programmes and policies' and securing that the resources of the authority are most effectively deployed towards those ends'.

The Audit Commission gave a managerially orientated definition to the chief executive's management role in a paper prepared during the consultation stage of the legislation. This related closely to an earlier paper advising local authorities on management practice (*Management Paper No 2, More Equal than Others: the Chief*

Executive in Local Government, 1989; and *Management Paper No 1, The Competitive Council*,1988). The Commission defined the chief executive as 'both the authority's centre of continuity and its agent of change'. In the earlier paper the Commission had defined the 'key success factors' of an authority as 'understanding customers', responding to the electorate, securing consistent and achievable objectives, defining clear responsibilities, training and motivating people, communicating effectively, monitoring results and adapting to change. They were to be pursued by the chief executive through key tasks defined as:

1. managing internal relationships
2. converting policy into strategy and strategy into action
3. developing processes, people and management skills to ensure that the authority is, and will continue to be, capable of delivering its strategy
4. reviewing performance against stated objectives
5. thinking and planning ahead.

These are management performance related functions, closely analogous to those of a general manager in business. They constitute check-lists relating to aspects of the management process but do not in themselves explain how established patterns of behaviour are to be changed so that the form becomes reality, or how they their performance is to relate to the will of the council and the prerogatives of its members. 'Models of management built for the purposes, conditions and tasks of the private sector do not encompass the purposes, conditions and tasks of the public domain' (Stewart and Ranson, *Management in the Public Domain*, 1988). They have little relevance to the nature of local government's management, budgetary process, accountabilities, the public and political demands made upon authorities and, most important of all perhaps, its values.

One obvious problem of the business analogy is the lack of a measure of performance that is at all comparable with that of a firm's financial balance sheet over the years. If local government is local democracy, then the criterion of the performance of a local authority chief executive, as the servant of the council, lies in the extent to which he or she meets the council's will within the limits of the law. The new legislation has not changed that position. In a way very typical of British government institutions expectations of the role have developed flexibly. They have evolved in response to the changing situations and interests, just as did those of the clerks before them. But unlike the clerk the chief executive has no traditional professional role from which to operate: each holder of the office has to recreate it according to his or her own concepts in a struggle with rapidly changing demands from with within and outside the authority.

In practice past role definitions, whether in the contract of employment or in statute, appear from the research to be of little relevance to the range of tasks performed by chief executives or to the authority they can exercise in performing them, although they may be influential in determining member and officer expectations of the role. They seem to be little more than reference points in hard cases.

In connection with the Paterson limitation regarding 'the discretion or judgment of the professional officers', chief executives stated in interviews that they would not intervene in a matter where they lacked the professional experience to make a judgment. In this respect there is little difference between the chief executive's position and that of a general manager in business who knows that he would challenge the professional opinion of a lawyer, accountant or engineer at his peril, and probably at the risk of damaging his personal authority. What matters much more are the expectations held by members and officers and not least by the chief executive him or herself about what a chief executive can and should be contributing to the performance of the council organisation, together with the support members are prepared to give to the holder of the office.

The research evidence described in more detail elsewhere in the book shows that the main shift in what political leaders expect of the role is towards seeing it as that of a general manager of its affairs within the special circumstances of a political organisation where success is not measurable in market terms, except perhaps in functions where the council is competing directly with the private sector. As such the job carries the responsibility for ensuring the organisation's effectiveness in fulfilling its purposes in accordance with the wishes of the politicians who exercise the power of the council, and especially in most cases those of the council leader. In so far as leading politicians control the vote in council they can determine the scope of the chief executive's influence. In practice however, on a day to day basis, the relationship needs to be one of a successful partnership between them and the chief executive.

Chief Executives, Chief Officers and the Management Team

The definition of the job put forward by many of the senior politicians interviewed in the research programme implied that it must be defined in large part as one of management leadership. Such a definition is wider than those set out in the Bains and Paterson specifications but it does not remove the relevance of the Bains and Paterson view that the chief executive's performance is dependent on that of the management team under his or her leadership, giving him a vital need to ensure its quality, effective functioning and corporateness. Only three of the 263 respondents to the questionnaire said they had no team or chief officer group.

Over 95 per cent of the 263 respondents to the research questionnaire believed that the appointment, leadership and appraisal of senior officer performance was essential to their role, confirming that these functions are seen above everything else as vital to a chief executive's performance. Chief executives would therefore seem to have a right not only to be involved in chief officers' appointments but also for advice to the council regarding chief officers' ability to manage and contribute effectively to the performance of the services. Accordingly therefore they have a right to be central to the appraisal of their performance.

Matters relating to management teams figured largest among chief executives' work objectives, excepting only organisational change. Typical responses were 'to run the management team efficiently', 'to lead the corporate management team setting the tone of the organisation' and, implying that the existing team had not reached its potential, 'developing an effective management team'.

The team also figured prominently among what chief executives regarded as their best achievements. One recently appointed chief executive wrote 'so far the establishment of properly constructed team meetings has improved communication with members and created a better atmosphere'. More established chief executives gave 'creating a harmonious and increasingly effective management team', 'maintaining the corporate enthusiasm in the chief officer group and their enthusiasm for the job', 'to have built a team that is slowly making council services popular' and 'to have created a superb and successful management team'. The responses confirmed that the management team was seen generally as the main and essential means through which chief executives had effected change within their authorities.

The questionnaire made a distinction between chief officer groups, defined as consisting of all chief officers for consultation and communication, and officer management teams of selected senior officers working with the chief executive 'in the overall direction and management of the authority', a definition which comes close to that of the Bains Committee. Sixty-five per cent of the chief executives reported the existence of chief officer groups and 51 per cent that they had officer management teams for direction and management instead of or in addition to chief officer groups. Sixteen per cent had groups which could not be described as either.

County and region chief executives were most likely to work with selected management teams in the overall direction and management of their authorities: 74 per cent possessed one. They were found most frequently otherwise in the London boroughs at 60 per cent. The figure for both the metropolitan districts and the shire and Scottish Districts combined was 48 per cent.

The responses to the questionnaire showed that the management team concept became firmly rooted in the 1980s. Pressures from the political leadership faced by financial stringencies and the demands of new legislation gave chief executives a mandate for rebuilding their teams, placing on them a much more challenging role which they would fail to fill at their peril. The nature and scale of the tasks that had to be undertaken and the extent to which everyone's interests were bound up in them created a situation where the managerial and corporate approaches were much more meaningful.

Many chief executives were able to rebuild their teams, partly through the luck of retirements and resignations of weak or uncooperative heads of department, partly through having the support of the political leadership behind them in persuading unsuitable officers to move or accept redundancy or in the last resort in forcing retirement, and partly through restructuring. The management team had begun to come of age in cases where it was previously peripheral.

Chief constables were members of most of the county groups. It appeared to be increasingly the rule that the head of personnel services was a member, whether or not he or she had chief officer status, as also not unusually the estates officer to complete the trio of resource officers for finance, manpower and property management. Flexibility was built in by providing for officers who were not the regular members of the team to be coopted when anything was under discussion of particular relevance to their work. Some authorities had wider meetings of senior officers, called less frequently than the team, and also special purpose senior officer meetings.

None of the teams in the authorities visited could be called 'an alternative political process' (to use a phrase coined by one chief executive). Two chief executives stressed that they were concerned that the business of the meeting should be 'possessed' by the chief officers rather than dominated by themselves, and one regarded the team as a means to ensure that common cultural values were owned by the officer group. To achieve this it was essential to encourage the managers of the authority to work corporately. The team concept appeared to be central to the shaping of a corporate approach in an authority and developing new perspectives. In many cases the management team appeared to had been a primary means of acclimatising new chief officers who had joined these teams in the previous few years to the chief executive's concept of corporate management.

The chief executive of one large borough appointed a lead chief officer for meetings who was required to consult his colleagues on its business. One county chief executive said that he preferred a management team without too heavy an agenda, 'driven by strategic business'. Another set up the agenda and used supporting groups and panels of officers, including inter-departmental teams for particular policy areas, to report to the team on specific subject areas and briefs. This 'dialogue' between a team and a second level team was sometimes a deputy chief officers group, which among its merits involved potential chief officers in a development process. In one case such a group researched matters referred to it by the team and referred up any issues which it considered needed attention. It was particularly concerned with policy review and research and information for decision-making.

In another county the team featured in a new plan for the organisational structure and principles of management. A newly founded management team had been established consisting of eight chief officers, including those for finance, property and personnel. Aims and objectives had been set out and the mechanisms put in place to facilitate collaborative implementation of policy. The team's primary role was to support and advise the chief executive in exercising his corporate and co-ordinating functions. It was to be concerned with efficient management and implementation, reviewing organisation and administration, 'considering what policies should be recommended to the authority for adoption, bearing in mind changing needs and circumstances, ensuring the carrying out of agreed policies and strategies, ensuring co-ordination, monitoring and progress chasing, problem solving and "major issues affecting a particular service"', with a proviso that it was concerned with the totality of functions and that otherwise 'its corporate role should not be restricted in any way'.

The team was 'to be regarded as the counterpart at officer level of the policy and resources committee, receiving instruction from the committee and reporting back through its chairman'. 'In the majority of cases reports from the management team were to be based on a consensus but at the end of the day' the chief executive 'will have the ultimate responsibility for determining what corporate advice, options and recommendations are to be submitted to the Council'.

Leadership of the team was an essential part of the concept of the role of most of the chief executives interviewed. One chief executive of a very large county without a team but with a meeting of all heads of departments each month was an exception. But forms and practice are very varied in all types of authority and it seemed that these were likely to differ more with the style and concepts of the chief executive than anything else.

The Pattern of Relationships

Information was collected on how often chief executives met chief finance officers, other chief officers and senior officers, formally or informally (see table 4-2). On average the closest contact was that with the head of finance: 82 per cent saw him more often than weekly including 31 per cent daily. For other chief officers the corresponding figures were 64 per cent including 16 per cent daily. Separate figures were not collected for meetings with secretaries or directors of administration but this relationship can be at least as close as that with the head of finance. Thirty-two per cent also had more than weekly contacts with 'senior officers'.

There is no significant difference in the frequency of meetings with heads of finance between types of authority, but in the case of those with other chief officers more than weekly meetings were on average less frequent in most purpose purpose and Scottish region authorities at 38-40 per cent against an average of 64 per cent across all authorities. The corresponding figures for meetings with senior officers are seven per cent for London boroughs, 15 per cent for metropolitan districts and 29 per cent for regions compared with a general average of 32 per cent. The main factor behind the differences in the case of the most purpose authorities may well be the complexity of their functions, the immediacy of the political and administrative demands made on departmental officers and often the separation of their offices.

According to chief executives' estimates they spent on average a little more than a quarter of their working hours in meetings with officer colleagues - about thirteen and a quarter hours a week (table 7-1). As in the case of contacts with elected members, there are wide divergences from the average. Chief executives figuring in the profiles spent ranged from five to 35 hours and about two-thirds of them between 11 and 14 hours a week, without any discernible differences relating to size of authority, region, political control or any other identifiable factor.

Chief executives of large authorities have the opportunity for personal contact with only a small number of officers. The task of 'communication with staff' was rated as essential by fewer than six out of ten of the respondents to the questionnaire (58 per cent - fewer than those who believed public relations to be an essential concern). Their means of influence on most of a large authority's employees otherwise are largely indirect except when they can address meetings.

TABLE 7-1: AVERAGE HOURS WORKED IN A TYPICAL WEEK

	(1) total		(2) with officers*		
	hours	mins	hours	mins	
London Boroughs	57	18	18	45	(15)
Metropolitan Districts	56	18	16	23	(22)
Scottish Regions & Island	54	30	15	24	(69)
Counties	52	12	12	23	(29)
Shire Districts	51	30	12	23	(167)
Scottish Districts	46	48	12	00	(17)
All authorities	52	06	13	23	(256)

*attending working parties/ other meetings with officer colleagues

The evidence from interviews and replies to the questionnaire gave no indication that anything but personal contact was regarded as significant, with the exceptions of bulletins or newsletters which were issued from the chief executive's office periodically, usually aimed primarily at the public but morale building in that they gave accounts of the authority's successes and so helped to create and maintain a good corporate spirit.

Changing Values

General management responsibility implies concern for behaviour in the authority as a whole. The survey evidence confirmed that most chief executives see and acknowledge that within their role they have essential tasks relating to staff behaviour in general.

As already mentioned in Part A, there is a new language for these tasks. Four out of five chief executives replying to the research questionnaire agreed that the promotion of the following values and behaviours is non-delegable and essential to their role:

1. commitment to collaboration at all levels
2. commitment to quality of service
3. commitment to output and efficiency
4. commitment to other council objectives
5. otherwise building organisational culture.

More chief executives consider the first three listed as essential than they do the review and appraisal of policies and programmes. Although collaboration, output and efficiency have long been generally applied watchwords, the concept that they and other characteristics are part of a culture of which the chief executive is the active promoter throughout the authority is a relatively new development.

This new orientation to management reflects a general return among leading writers on management theory to the fundamental importance of behavioural factors in business performance. It is a return in a new and more popular language to the insights of the 1950s on leadership which at that time barely penetrated the shell of local government or even, in Britain at least, that of private industry. The grandfather of modern theory on leadership was Chester Barnard (Barnard, 1938) who defined the art of the executive as securing commitment, actively managing the informal organisation, shaping and managing the shared values in an organisation, developing the system of communications, promoting 'the securing of essential efforts' and formulating and defining purpose.

Ideas of Barnard were reformulated by Philip Selznick, who has also been much quoted in the management literature of the 1980s and who defined the institutional leader as 'primarily an expert in the promotion and protection of values' (Selznick, 1957). *In Search of Excellence* (Peters and Waterman 1982) takes off from a more recent work, J.MacGregor Burns' *Leadership*, which posits two types of leadership. For one he uses the phrase 'transactional leadership', which involves a battery of activities, including 'shifting the attention of the institution through the mundane language of management systems', 'altering agendas so that new priorities get enough attention', 'being visible when things go awry, and invisible when they are working well', 'building a loyal team at the top that speaks more or less with one voice', 'listening carefully much of the time', 'frequently speaking with encouragement', and 'reinforcing words with believable action', 'being tough when necessary', 'the occasional naked use of power' and 'a hundred things done better'. The second form of leadership defined by Burns is 'transforming leadership'. This occurs when one or more persons engage with others in such a way that leaders and followers raise each other to higher levels of motivation and morality' (Burns, 1978).

These influences have created a new set of concepts which emerged repeatedly in interviews with some chief executives. They have permeated the executive culture, giving wider grounds for the justification of organisational change than the impact of recent government policies. The elements of the definition of 'transactional leadership' are clearly to the fore in their descriptions of active management, as are here and there those of 'transforming leadership'. This new approach is quite alien to the traditional 'keeping things correct' attitudes as well as to the sometimes autocratic style typical of some clerks and chief executives of local authorities in the past.

The credibility of adding these functions to the role of the chief executive depends on the extent to which they are practicable in an organisation with the scale and level of departmentalisation of a local authority. Assuming the intention to institute change in the organisation and the opportunity and political support to do so, the vital factor is the ability to communicate somehow to the organisation as a whole. The principal means must surely be through senior officers, notably the management team or chief officer group, and also through training initiatives.

Although some chief executives may 'short-circuit the system' to sample the performance, concerns and ideas of staff at any level, and although they may be able to replace old with new structures and systems which open up possibilities of deep reform including changes in motivation, they must ultimately depend on shaping and influencing the organisation through those who carry direct responsibilities. These are primarily the heads of departments, including their own if they have one.

According to the Bains Report chief executives should use the management team to undertake 'the long term strategic function of considering and advising on what policies the Council should be adopting to cope with changing needs and circumstances' and the overall management co-ordination and progress chasing role. The 1989 Act has enabled them to be appointed 'head of the paid service' with the duty of advising the council on the coordination of its functions and the organisation (including discipline) of its staffing. But it is primarily through the management group, working groups and other means that chief executives have to make an impact on the behaviour of the staff organisation as a whole.

Local authority chief executives head the staffs of their councils and depend on them for their authorities' success. Their success depends on how they affect their performance. They stand at the critical centre between the elected members and their employees. Their direct communication with all but a few staff is inevitably limited, and the larger the authority the more tenuous it may be expected to be. Yet in their response to our research inquiries many chief executives showed confidence that they could significantly influence the culture of the staff as a whole by their leadership. One purpose of this chapter is to throw light on the substance of this belief, the values chief executives seek to develop and the means they employ.

The inclusion amongst the chief executive's responsibilities of the performance of the authority's staff as a whole is a fairly recent development, closely related to the concept of the corporate authority. The replies to the research questionnaire showed that by the late 1980s the concept had gained wide acceptance among leading members as well as officers. It carried the implication that members and officers must work together towards shared goals. It is a behavioural concept, a concept of relationships between the parts and the whole, not to be secured by organisational means alone but by influencing people's values - that is, the way in which they define their working objectives and the means they adopt to achieve them. The extension of what chief executives demand of themselves in this respect - and what members are beginning to demand of them - shows a great change from what was expected of them and their predecessors the clerks in pre-reorganisation days.

One term that has recently come into common currency in describing the changes in behaviour sought has been the word 'culture'. Its meaning appears to be close to the definition by Elliott Jacques (1951), 'the customary and traditional way of thinking and of doing things, which is shared to a greater or lesser degree by all its (the firm's) members'. This could cover customs and habits of managerial behaviour, incentives and disincentives, organisational objectives, values placed on different kinds of work, degree and nature of communication and consultation amongst other things. The new local government situation had helped to make this a realistic area for effecting change. Restructuring can unfreeze habitual ways of working and give everyone concerned the challenge if not the necessity to rethink their assumptions about practice. The belief that they and their colleagues are in competition with other groups and that failure may mean redundancy can be a powerful motivation to change practice. But is it not expecting a kind of alchemy which seems to have been rare even in industry where the 'chief' may have unrestricted powers to hire and fire, to organise and reorganise, and personally to set and require the attainment of objectives which necessarily command the respect of employees?

The responses to our questionnaire show that a large proportion of chief executives believe that they do have a responsibility for behaviour within the authority as a whole and that they regard this as a reasonable expectation. They also indicate the means employed, especially in statements they gave of what they considered their best achievements. As indicated in previous chapters, chief executives' motivations are various, but one that recurs frequently is the conviction that there is a necessity for radical change in behaviour in their authorities in the face of central government's pressure and legislation. This response may reflect a conviction that a reformed service can establish a new degree of legitimacy and support for local services: something as much in the interest of the local government service as in that of the elected members.

Many replies on main objectives reflect morale problems and the need to maintain and improve morale - to achieve good motivation and commitment in a time of change and uncertainty. The commonest theme however is the objective of 'cultural change' - often using that phrase itself but also 'changing the ethos' and 'establishing shared values' - and expanded into 'developing a sound corporately orientated management culture'. Chief executives write of developing a new organisational culture of 'efficiency, effectiveness and accountability'; one that is 'flexible, looks forward and responds to the customer' and is 'closer to the public'. The main watchwords here are 'service quality' and 'customer consciousness'. There is a repeated emphasis on the need to develop or maintain the value of corporateness.

One new district chief executive who was interviewed said that changing the culture of the organisation meant making staff aware that the council had to be run as a business

- on value for money principles - with good staff communication and an 'image of quality'. Another said that in taking the job he had seen the challenge as to create a customer-orientated, value for money organisation with 'management on a team and involvement basis'. Another, about a year in office, said he believed that there was a need to shift attitudes in the departments rapidly: to create a change in the management culture throughout the staff. A more open managerial style was called for which, he believed, would take a year or so to achieve. A London borough chief executive said that his plans required the establishment of cultural values owned by the officer group. A county chief executive said that his primary aim was 'to convert the culture' - to move from bureaucratic to business-like, product-conscious, client/consumer and corporately oriented behaviour. Another spoke of part of his job as creating the right climate and environment for good committed management.

The strongest emphasis was on service to members of the public, usually described as 'customers'. One county chief executive said that he was seeking to take the authority towards customer choice. The use of the concept of community was exceptional, as in the case of a London borough chief executive who gave one of his main aims as 'making the council truly close to the community'. One long serving district chief executive, personally responsible for innovations in the geographical decentralisation of the administration, said that his present personal agenda included 'putting people first' and customer care initiatives, including in practice policies that brought together communication with local communities, listening to them and seeking to provide for individual wishes.

Next in the sets of values most frequently referred to was that relating to the concept of quality. One chief executive of a large urban authority put highest among his objectives enhancing services generally. The council had agreed to enable him to perform a service quality role across the departments as well as his strategy and performance review roles. His intention was that the roles should be developed as part of collaborative working across the council between members and officers. His current administrative services department was to be merged with his existing staff for information and customer service issues in a new department under his direct control which would be concerned amongst other things with service quality and performance review. He had got to know the senior people on the staff very quickly and laid great stress on achieving common values among them. He was giving special stress to customer orientation.

What quality means in practice others must attempt to define. Certainly in local government it is a matter where 'the best can be the enemy of the good'. Only two of those interviewed raised the key question of accessibility. One of these was a London borough chief executive who gave among the main opportunities he had seen in his job as 'providing quality services which are accessible to all irrespective of ability'.

One concept that subsumes consumer service, quality, value for money and other criteria is that of performance and performance standards. Several chief executives gave 'better performance' as one of their main current objectives. This is an issue raised by the legislation on compulsory contracting. Price is meaningless without a measure of what has to be provided: otherwise service and quality could be minimal. Hence renewed concern for standard setting so that a rational basis can be established as far as possible for choice between tenders. Monitoring of services has also acquired new importance due to the need to monitor the work of contractors. Whether the two direct parties in a contract are a client department and an external body or a department and a direct service provider, the chief executive is likely to be concerned in any dispute as the officer whose mediation may be required between the two parties. But concern with the evaluation of services is of course of much wider importance, as the stress given to it by the Bains Committee implies.

Some saw their best achievements as success in achieving better recruitment and/or motivation through better systems of reward, performance-related or otherwise. For example, 'to encourage staff at all management levels to participate more fully in the management process and to introduce the necessary staffing and grading proposals to bring this about' and, simply, 'performance appraisal for senior officers'.

To return to the reform or development of values generally in a local authority, chief executives number among their achievements acceptance of corporate strategy, creating a deeply embedded corporate approach', 'creating a customer-orientated philosophy' and 'developing a culture which is high-profile, high risk and well-known by public and staff alike'.

It is early at the time of writing to be sure of the lasting effect of such achievements but if the conviction of the chief executives is valid evidence, the combination of perceived external threat, structural change and the infusion of new values and work objectives worked much faster to create culture change in any cases worked much faster than might reasonably have been expected.

Principles, Aims and Means

Communication

Effective communication is the most fundamental necessity for a chief executive in any organisation - most of all in enabling it to adapt to external pressures such as those described above. Since the problems of communication in a large and complex local authority are difficult to overcome it was surprising that the subject came up rarely in the interviews. Where it was identified it could be given great stress. The problems may start with the political relationships. One chief executive, frustrated in this matter, spoke of 'the vital importance of understanding what the council want' - which can be very difficult if not meaningless in some apparently rare political situations. Otherwise references were to communication within the officer organisation. A county chief executive said, 'What matters is internal communication, upwards and downwards - proper briefing and proper understanding... people knowing where they are going and relating to the council.' Another chief executive of a large county said that it was inconceivable that he could have his finger on everything. He did not have enough time to see what was going on. He relied in general on the secretary to inform him when something went wrong. 'I have to live with that'.

This chief executive like eleven others described in the profiles had no department of his own. A principal argument against not having a department has been the lack of 'eyes and ears' within the authority, as for example learning about the concerns of committee chairmen and chief officers through servicing committees, whether directly or through assistant staff. In two instances, both from counties, the responsibility of keeping the chief executive informed about what was happening was placed on the secretary. In three cases the need was obviously met by formal or informal 'executive offices' of the kind described in the previous chapter, consisting of the chief executive, treasurer and secretary meeting about business day to day. Possibly the matter is less critical where the chief executive is in day to day contact with the leader, although the leader himself may not be aware of problems developing within the knowledge of group chairmen. Other avenues of information are necessary.

In many cases this problem had been lessened by bringing most of the departmental headquarters and their chief officers together in new central offices. Not surprisingly difficulties in achieving a joint view of priorities seemed to be at their highest in two cases where the accommodation was scattered and officer meetings less frequent than the average - as in one London borough with the chief officers and their departments in seven different locations. One district chief officer gave the centralisation of offices as one of his greatest achievements in his seven years of serving his authority. In a metropolitan district the chief executive visited each departmental management team at least twice a year and sometimes also when an important topic such as the implications of a national report were under consideration.

Purposeful informal inter-departmental communication and working between officers at other levels is essential to developing the full potentiality of a local authority. One county chief executive had arranged six-monthly two-day meetings of fifty senior officers from all parts of the organisation to study and discuss major issues. The meetings built up contacts, created a sense of unity and gave participants a chance to show their abilities. In the wake of their success a 'senior 100' meeting had been set up to spread the benefits of the approach more widely.

A chief executive of a fairly large authority met each chief officer every six months to agree the key elements in the latter's work programme in a discussion of up to around three hours where he raised issues from which he could benefit as well as the chief officer, such as how communication could be improved in the authority. He chief officers what they thought he, the chief executive himself, should be doing as well as what they should be doing - and had benefited a lot from the results.

The closely related issue of coordination, so long referred to as a main role and justification of the role of a chief executive, was hardly raised as such. Perhaps there is a danger that it is assumed to follow if sharing of ideas and corporate decision-making is achieved at chief officer level. One chief executive said that he was only concerned with departmental matters when clashes occurred. In some cases chief executives had fostered the growth of inter-departmental working groups and task forces, but there must be a danger that in some cases the need for collaboration in service delivery is overlooked - especially perhaps when services are being delivered on contracts between client departments and service providing bodies. These are of course matters that can be sorted out where there are regular face-to-face discussions between the chief executive and heads of the services or where inter-departmental groups have a brief to report on the subject.

Standing alone was one district authority where the chief executive placed communication with the lower-paid employees high among the activities which he had learnt to be of value to his job. He liked to spend plenty of time with 'the people who are weakest in the authority'. He met them in the lift or walking to the administrative block. They told him what he wanted to know about the white and blue collar areas. He said, 'It is important to be better informed than anyone else - not to be caught out'. He rated contact with blue-collar workers particularly high. Fundamental decisions on the reorganisation of the services had been suggested by them which had led to great improvements in working practices.

But the chief officer group or management team, as described in the previous chapter, has been unquestionably the main channel of communication with officers, upwards and downward to other staff.

Delegation

The importance of delegation to the chief executive by the council or political leadership acquired a new emphasis in the late 1980s with the need for fast and effective structural reform. The profiles in chapters 5 and 6 have shown the wide scope given to some chief executives in accordance with agreed proposals to change management structure and processes, improve service and hold expenditure. For example it was agreed in a London borough that a new chief executive should have a free hand in the development of the structure along with results proposed in a wide-ranging report that he had put before the members without being required to reach agreements with members on detail.

Giving wide delegated scope to chief executives, formally or informally, appeared to be particularly characteristic of the English counties visited in the research. One county chief executive named management delegation together with performance management as the vital approaches to success. A second gave 'the devolution of responsibility and accountability from central departments to the service departments' as fundamental to his approach. A third said that he delegated responsibility to chief officers as far as was consistent within his corporate responsibilities.

One factor making delegation or devolvement a matter of concern were the costs of central services if they were on-charged to local authority direct service organisations. They could make the difference between the success and failure of a bid for a contract by the authority itself. Chief executives directly responsible for departments had to bend backwards to show that they were not prejudiced in the matter. It will be seen from chapter 10 that the scope perceived for delegation of what are commonly accepted as central responsibilities is very wide indeed.

Structural change

It is clear from the evidence that the driving force for structural change had been the government legislation on competitive tendering. It appeared repeatedly in the research inquiries as a chief motivating force for action by chief executives, just as the setting up of new authorities would have been if similar research had been undertaken in the late 1970s. Just as decentralisation was the *grande affaire* of President Mitterand's first presidency in France in the early years of the decade, so the initiatives to reform the delivery of local government services were the 'grand affair' of the Thatcher governments in this field in the latter half of the 1980s.

Chief executives were bound to be the principal actors in the multi-departmental reorganisations that ensued. The reaction in the great majority of local authorities, Conservative as well as those under other political administrations, was to work to win the services in-house. The legislation was seen as an opportunity to unfreeze not only structures but also attitudes. It provided the opportunity to pursue a reform of services and incorporate not only efficiency but also the principle of responsiveness to what members of the public really wanted from local government.

One newly appointed chief executive gave 'a successful response to the compulsory tendering legislation' as one of the main purposes he brought to the job - and as in other cases this included the winning of tenders by the authority's own workforce. But it also provided the justification for reductions in labour force, staff development measures and performance orientated innovations amongst other things.

Another district chief executive appointed several years before was the first in his part of Britain to develop a strategy for the implementation of competitive tendering. He saw that rapid organisational change was necessary not only in structures and procedures but also in the development of competitive and contracting skills. He had chaired an officer management group for planning its implementation. A member-officer group supervised and ensured that the client/contractor relationship was effective. Corporate issues went to the chief officer group. Authority for implementation was delegated to a chief officer.

A county chief executive had put forward the key decisions in the total restructuring of the largest department of the authority and received unanimous support from colleagues and elected members. It had been undertaken in response to the challenge of the new Education Reform Act and the compulsory tendering requirements. He saw the restructuring not least as an opportunity to introduce 'participative and accountable management on the basis of an individual's responsibilities'. The general aim was to redesign the departmental structure so as to make the best possible use of the opportunities for separating and clarifying the roles of client and contractor organisations and their relationships'. Each body or department would care for the functions which it could best deliver. Everyone had accepted the principle and it had made it possible to ensure the best management for particular functions. The nature of the restructuring evolved from discussion with those concerned, but it was clear that only the chief executive was in a position to identify the common factors and advance a solution that would best meet common goals of service quality and other criteria.

The impact of the legislation led in some cases to a 'shake-out' of employees at senior as well as lower levels. As mentioned in the last chapter it was part of the reshaping of the management team 'to give it a sharper edge'.

Management functions

Performance evaluation and monitoring were subjects repeatedly given as central to the concerns of the chief executive along with other innovations involving initiation of management systems. In a district where a comprehensive approach was developed by a new chief executive a management reform programme had been implemented including annual plans, processes for the setting of standards by departments, policy and performance review procedures, financial monitoring, output targeting and staff development schemes. Under the new staff structure responsibility for implementation was placed on some 70 executive officers who were accountable for success or failure. Another chief executive had established systems of strategy and policy definition and review, linked with a performance budget with over a hundred cost centres under individual managers accountable to their managerial superiors.

Some authorities visited had initiated systems for setting up achievement targets for members of staff. In one large county chief officers had agreed with the chief executive to set achievement targets and to arrange for monitoring of the results within their departments. They discussed their own performances with the chief executive who found that as a result they had become much more critical about their work and frank about their failures.

Only a few chief executives amongst the 263 responses gave developing a wider management strategy as a main objective or achievement. In a large county visited the chief executive was doubtful if they would ever be able achieve a general corporate plan although targeting and monitoring at departmental level had become well-established. The need for effective strategic and financial planning systems was recognised and indeed obvious in London boroughs with acute financial problems, if only to ensure that the council would not be in deficit, but political divisions and the lack of enthusiasm by members had to be overcome, as shown in the case of the most-purpose authorities in the profiles in chapters 5 and 6.

Motivation

Research and common sense indicate that as in other types of organisation the work climate and motivation must be expected to vary between departments and work groups (Hinings and Greenwood 1973). Chief executives are naturally most concerned with morale amongst those with whom they are in frequent contact and dependent for their effectiveness - notably the chief and senior officers in the authority.

The political leadership situation is seen as very important if not the dominant factor here. Political agreement on objectives provided a strong foundation for developing positive attitudes to work and performance. Where there was a divided political will and uncertainty about political outcomes there were pessimism and signs of despondency. A hung situation however can in some cases be a great stimulus to officer initiative. In one large authority it was said to have resulted in more officer-led innovations than would have otherwise have been likely, and greater scope is patently a morale building factor to set against problems arising from deadlocks between parties.

In smaller authorities which lacked a tradition of strong majority party direction 'performance' could be equated with carrying out administrative tasks efficiently rather than managerial initiative. Expectations were relatively undemanding and feelings about the situation seemed to be introverted.

Infusing new and well appreciated values and shared purpose into the organisation may be expected to improve morale. In authorities that had been galvanised by a new approach chief executives spoke of keenness, enthusiasm and even excitement among staff. The picture given was that the improvement in motivation had exceeded expectations.

Conclusion

This chapter covers few of the matters which a chief executive deals with day by day. Anything can reach him which other officers are incompetent, unequipped, unwilling or lacking in authority to resolve, and elected members may expect many things of him which are not integral to the role. Many matters are deeply traditional, such as the association with the mayor or council chairman's role. Seventy-seven per cent of the chief executives who replied to the questionnaire believed that these remained essential or desirable parts of the job, but the remaining 23 per cent believed they could be delegated. These apart there are 23 internal tasks listed in chapter 10 which chief executives considered to be essential.

The matters internal to the authority which chief executives wrote into the questionnaire gave some idea of how they spent their time beyond hours given to paperwork and meetings with elected representatives or officers. These included advising, consulting and talking with staff, training and management development generally, specific projects and visiting offices and sites - including walking about to get a feel of what is happening and to give staff the feeling that the chief executive is concerned with them and their work. The potential tasks within the authority are legion and unpredictable. A great challenge of the job is to spot those matters which are vital to achievement and which only the chief executive can undertake. One of the greatest of these is delegation.

A Note on Departmental Responsibilities

The disadvantages of heading a traditional department vary widely from situation to situation. A chief executive who knows his authority intimately and has built up his own dependable staff can use it as a powerful resource for corporate work. Thus in a district with a population of under a hundred thousand where the chief executive had been in post since 1974 he headed a department that included library, theatre and entertainment and printing responsibilities. The borough solicitor, housing manager and environmental health section answered to him direct. It was an authority with a clear strategy although there was no doubt that the strategy was the officers' - and particularly the chief executive's - rather than that of the members. He was able to answer very directly for the services involved to the members, with whom he had daily contact, - 'managing' potential tensions such as those relating with the hot subject of the delegation of housing management functions. The situation could however have been extremely difficult if not impossible for a newly appointed officer from outside. The chief executive was well aware of the desirability of developing staff with high management potential within the authority whom he believed would be able to fulfil the chief executive post when he left, although it seemed unlikely that they could cover the same range of functions. His range of responsibilities did not stop him from being deeply involved in external activities in the local community and in regional and some national matters and still having plenty of time for peaceful recreation.

Perhaps the most difficult situation is where an officer appointed from outside enters an introverted authority lacking competent staff to whom to delegate managerial functions within his traditional department while having to learn, often painfully, about the nature of the situation within other departments - while being dependent on councillors for the approval of staff management decisions which he knows would be delegated elsewhere. His leadership role can be compromised within and outside his department. To relieve him of the departmental responsibilities would not necessarily solve the problem, although it could give him much more time to work on the problems of the authority as a whole.

In authorities with fully competent staff to head the central service departments the possibility arises of working with heads of the administrative and finance departments in a central management team, as described in cases above, and being able to exploit to the full all the advantages of having much more time to give to relationships, new developments, strategy formation and the other matters detailed in this part of the book without being tied to particular service interests. In authorities in which radical reform is needed to build a management strategy and attack poor standards the case for a department-free chief executive is clear, at least if he or she has good political backing.

Chapter 8

THE CHIEF EXECUTIVE AND THE OUTSIDE WORLD

The chief executive of a local authority carries overall responsibility for the officer organisation's dealings with the community, including both the public at large and the many private and voluntary organisations through which the community's interests are organised. As chief adviser to the council he or she may be expected to be knowledgeable and understanding about the community's needs and potential resources, how the council's purposes can be pursued through identifying external resources that can be mobilised and opportunities for collaboration. As its central channel of relationship with central government, the European Commission, the many public agencies through which government policies are implemented, other local authorities, regional associations and the national local authority associations and their agencies, he or she may be expected not only to ensure that the council is well informed about their policies and recommendations that are relevant to its interests, but also see that full advantage is taken of the opportunities they provide for furthering its work for local communities. As in the case of other aspects of the chief executive's role, it is impossible to say where the chief executive's responsibilities end in this field since he or she can be called upon to deal with all matters that do not fall into the field of particular heads of service.

The Bains Report is inadequate on the subject, as is John Boynton's 'Man at the Top'. The Bains job description refers only to the maintenance of good external relations. In arguing for what it terms 'a detached chief executive' in smaller districts it carries the matter further by referring to the desirability of his exercising 'a wider co-ordination, public relations and representative role than his counter-part in local government today finds possible'. The report is also subject to the criticism, due partly perhaps to its narrow terms of reference, in that it approaches the subject of relationships predominantly through recommendations on joint inter-authority machinery and without considering the implications for what it calls the 'community' approach and for officer and particularly chief executive roles.

John Boynton writes unambiguously that the chief executive 'should be the public relations officer for his authority' and 'recognise that one of his prime tasks is to foster good and personal relations with the world outside'. His definition of the role in public relations is 'ensuring that the authority's policies, objectives, problems and achievements are known and explained to those concerned' - for example in arranging meetings with representatives of commerce and industry for discussion of a more extensive nature than those required statutorily by the Rates Act 1984 (Boynton, 1986). There is no reference to the 'enabling' function, understandably in that the term was not in common currency although it had in fact been carried out widely in different directions in the past and became central in the discussion of the corporate role within two years of the book's publication.

Chief executives' relationships with the outside world cover an extremely wide range and vary greatly between individuals. As the head officers of a council they represent its interests both in their own area and at regional, national and international levels. They do this in an occasionally difficult relationship with elected members, particularly the chairman of their council, its leader and sometimes other local politicians who speak for the council locally, nationally and internationally. They stand at the central point of their authorities' web of relationship, carrying a special responsibility as spokespersons for the services and interests of their authorities as a whole. They would seem therefore to carry the chief responsibility for integrating the picture which the authority presents to the outside world: a picture above internal politics and vital to public understanding, its reputation and recruitment success that stands over and above the viewpoints and images of individual political groups and services, complementing the role of the mayor or council chairman at officer level.

It is not altogether clear where the boundary between role of the mayor or chairman and that of the chief executive lies in these matters, particularly regarding formal relations. Chapters 5 and 6 have shown that chief executives see themselves in many cases exercising responsibility to the majority group rather than to the council, but must reconcile this with a parallel responsibility to all its members. Some of the apparent difficulties in this field are described below.

The chief executive is regularly required to speak for the council and to act for it in its best interests. If he holds its trust, which must be assumed by the nature of the responsibilities placed on him, he can not only communicate and negotiate on behalf of the council but also build up relationships with the community, acting as the voice for the council as a whole in explaining where its interests lie in relationships with outside organisations and the joint benefits of working together. It follows that his confidence in doing so and in encouraging other officers to do so directly contributes to his or her ability to present the council's case in discussions and negotiations to the council's best advantage.

In this matter he is not of course acting alone amongst the officers: all members of the chief officer group and many others should be able to speak confidently on behalf of the council. But in leading the officers as well as leading members, he has the task of ensuring that they speak to the outside world; if not with one voice then with a clear idea of what will be supported politically and what will not, both through the management team or chief officer group team and otherwise.

How much importance do chief executives place on being involved directly in face-to-face representation of their authorities? In response to the survey question on essential, desirable and delegable tasks chief executives were widely divided on the matter (see tables 10-3 and 10-4). In all most weight was placed on representation on formal occasions, 67 per cent of the 255 respondents seeing this as essential and non-delegable. A further 31 per cent saw it as desirable but delegable. The following proportions of respondents saw the related tasks as essential and non-delegable, in descending order: 60 per cent public relations; 42 per cent relations with the media; 27 per cent with government agencies and private and mixed sector bodies; 26.5 per cent with other local authorities; and 13.5 per cent with other interests in the community.

Analysis by party control shows some wide differences in the stress given to representation on formal occasions. Seventy-six per cent in Conservative authorities saw this as essential against 55 per cent in those controlled by Labour - possibly because of a higher stress on tradition or formal social occasions in Conservative authorities. The position is reversed in the case of representation with private and mixed sector bodies, 30 per cent regarding this as essential in Labour authorities as against 22 per cent in Conservative ones - probably explained by Labour strength in urban authorities with concentrations of commercial and industrial interests.

There are also differences of view according to the type of authority. External relationships were more likely to be considered essential in metropolitan districts than in London boroughs: representation on formal occasions by 65 per cent to 53 per cent; government agencies by 35 to 13 per cent; other local authorities by 35 to 20 per cent; private and mixed sector bodies by 50 to 13 per cent; the media by 32 to 13 per cent; and other community interests by 24 per cent to nil. The metropolitan districts also place more weight on relationships with government departments and MPs and European Commission officials and MEPs than those in London boroughs, probably because far more are in areas eligible for economic and social aids. Another feature of the response is the difference between English and Welsh county chief executives on the one hand and Scottish region chief executives on the other, the latter being less likely to regard external representation as an essential role that should not be delegated.

Other differences emerge according to age groups. In general it appears that it is chief executives aged under 40, of whom 17 replied to the questionnaire, who place the least weight on external contacts, followed by the 12 respondents aged 60 or over. Only 12 per cent in the youngest group see relations with other local authorities as an essential task, compared with 34 per cent of those in their 50s. There is a much wider contrast between age groups on relations with private and mixed sector bodies. Only six per cent of the 17 under-40s saw this as an essential personal task as against nearly 32 per cent of those between 40 and 55. There is a similar difference between these age groups on contacts with other community interests. Analysis shows that this contrast is not explained by length of experience in office: there are no significant differences between those in their first year as chief executive and those who have been longer in the role.

Two other sets of responses give evidence of the weight attached to external contacts: the time chief executives spend on external matters and frequency of relationships. The data on the first do not differentiate between local community and national or international involvements. The response showed that in all about twelve per cent of chief executives' time was spent on outside representation of the authority. Using also the details of the hours spent on work in a typical week (table 8-1) we can estimate that an average of 6.4 hours a week is spent by chief executives on representation (12.3 per cent of an average of 52.1 hours worked). Again there is a sharp difference between metropolitan districts and London boroughs. Although the London borough chief executives work a slightly longer week (57.3 hours as against 56.3), the time they give to external representation is less (5.8 hours as against 7.9)

For all types of authority other than London boroughs and Scottish districts the time given averages between 6.3 and 7.9 hours. In the case of the Scottish districts it is lower at 5.2 hours a week (10.9 per cent of total working time).

Differences on this head vary widely within the same type of authority. Strikingly the London borough responses showed the time in a typical week given to external

TABLE 8-1 ABOUT HOW MANY HOURS DO YOU WORK IN A TYPICAL WEEK?

	mean number of hours	(no. responses)
County	52.1	(30)
Shire district	51.4	(169)
Metropolitan district	56.3	(22)
London borough	57.3	(15)
Scottish region/island	54.5	(6)
Scottish district	47.6	(17)
All authorities	52.1	(259)

relationships to range from half an hour to 18 hours. In the non-metropolitan districts the range was from two and a half hours to 18; in the counties and in the Scottish Regions from three to twelve; in the shire districts from nil (two cases) to 18 ; and in the Scottish districts from nil to twelve.

In some authorities visited chief executives placed a strong emphasis on external contacts. A Welsh county chief executive believed that he needed 'the ability to maintain constructive relations with a wide range of people: MEPs, senior civil servants, a multiplicity of agencies, and reasonable relations with the media - the ability to sell one's wares'. He believed that this had been crucial in the county's success in the development of the infrastructure of its area.

The chief executive of a Welsh district met civil servants and representatives of government agencies, voluntary agencies, local employers and other local interest groups, local business people and other members of the general public weekly and rated all these relationships as very good.

The chief executive of a large borough in the North-East of England had a very good relationship with the county council and found it essential in fighting for economic development to co-operate well with government agencies to achieve his authority's priorities. He held regular meetings with the chamber of commerce and their committees. He was a member of a general forum on the development of the area led by businessmen, an integrated operations steering group set up by the Department of the Environment regional controller, a regionally based development company and other regional organisations. Was it significant that these three executives were natives of the region in which they worked?

Many respondents wrote in details of external involvements other than representation which took up part of their time. These included, in declining order of frequency, meetings with developers, investors and consultants, with boards and other authorities, with the public, in connection with public relations, economic regeneration and visits to sites and offices. Some chief executives who were clerks to the lieutenancy stressed the importance of this role - a survival of a county or city role in which they were servants of the crown.

The Public Relations Role

The practice of 'public relations' has to some extent become professionalised in the second half of the twentieth century, drawing on private sector practices. Creating an 'image' for the authority appears among the main objectives of chief executives. A confidence inspiring image is clearly of great advantage to the morale and recruitment of both councillors and officers as well as to the authority's standing with the local community, nationally and even internationally.

But as mentioned above chief executives like other officers can be in an ambiguous position in representing and justifying the policy positions of the council. It may be seen as 'selling' the policies and achievements of the majority group and therefore liable to attack by the political opposition. The role can be difficult to play when there is a strong bias in the press against the controlling party, fuelled by opposition representatives. A chief executive can be on sensitive ground in presenting a picture of the council's achievements which the majority group sees as its own. The majority party may want achievements blazoned in its own name or in the names of its chairmen, while the minority party may feel that the chief executive in presenting them as the achievements of the council as a whole is glossing over their justified criticisms and so undermining the democratic process. In some instances such reasoning has led authorities to deny the chief executive anything but a limited public relations role. But if chief executives are heads of service they must take ultimate responsibility for the function.

Nevertheless 'image creation' was not mentioned either in the interviews or responses to the questionnaire as a matter that presented major difficulties. Chief executives along with other chief officers are protected by the convention that their role is apolitical and by the argument that they are describing and explaining rather than making political claims for the council's policies and its achievements. In many cases, as shown above, a large area of policy is supported by a wide consensus within the council - as for example values and objectives defined by chief executives and other officers in reports which have cross-party approval.

Clearly the quality and efficiency of information to the public is an appropriate and important area of officer responsibilities. The development of local authority news-sheets delivered or made available free for all has commonly been the responsibility of officers responsible for public relations who are able to integrate the interests of services, ensure a corporate view and maintain their non-political character. Chief executives are commonly seen as the most appropriate officers for the purpose. Specialised public relations units report to them direct, although the secretary or director of administration responsible for common services may equally meet the requirements. Excellent examples of public news-sheets or bulletins were seen during the research visits that had been prepared under the guidance of chief executives. They can include information about achievements in the form of statements attributed to committee chairmen without giving grounds for complaints of use for party political purposes.

When asked in the questionnaires for their three main objectives 24 chief executives out of the 263 gave enhancing the image or raising or maintaining the profile or public regard for their authority. Eight gave this as a main objective expected of them from within the council. Nineteen rated it as amongst their best past achievements in the job.

Information diffusion tasks are more likely to be seen as delegable than the 'image-building' function. Chief executives were asked three questions in the research questionnaire about the importance of public relations related activities in their role. One was on public relations generally, one on general information to the public and one on relations with the media. Sixty per cent regarded public relations generally as an essential part of their role compared with 42 per cent in the case of relations with the media and 22 per cent that of information to the public. Most others regarded these tasks as desirable but delegable, but a significant minority regarded them as non-essential: eight per cent in the case of public relations generally and 25 per cent in the case of both relations with the media and information to the public (see tables 9-3, 9-4 and 9-5).

With some exceptions responses did not vary greatly between the types or sizes of authority, political control or the age and length of service of the chief executives. When the response was analysed by type of authority the highest proportion seeing general public relations as essential was among chief executives in the Scottish districts (82.5 per cent); the lowest in the counties and the Scottish Regions (50 per cent in each case). There were also wide differences between the Scottish districts and the regions on information to the public but not on contacts with the media.

In Conservative authorities chief executives are more inclined to regard a relationship with the media as essential (47 per cent) than those in Labour authorities (38 per cent), probably reflecting greater political sensitivity in this matter in the latter. An analysis by the age of chief executives showed that the older chief executives tended to put more weight on the relationship with the media: 55 per cent of those over 55 years of age regarded this as an essential part of the job compared with 42 per cent of all chief executives. In general however it can be said that chief executives differ widely on the subject within all types of authority and within personal categories of chief executives such as age groups and professions, and that the differences may be worth further investigation.

Public relations acquire a specially high importance in authorities covering a wide area and without long historical traditions. For example in one large county consisting of amalgamated authorities with long historical traditions and slow road communications the identity and popular image was believed to need reinforcement despite over fifteen years of the new authority's existence, and it was not therefore surprising that this should be to the fore in the chief executive's concerns. He placed a high emphasis on external relationships and commented that 'a high profile and involvement is essential in these matters but the sheer weight of occasions and meetings means that delegation is necessary too'.

Relations in the Community

Rodney Brooke forecasts, 'as direct service provision contracts, so the local authority will seek a wider role of influence over its area though exercised through other agencies'. The 'enabling' concept puts in the centre of a local authority's role 'finding new ways of influencing other agencies to achieve a desirable result', finding ways to 'ensure local choice'. It requires establishing 'networks with agencies which are key to its plans' (Brooke, 1989).

If chief executives identify themselves with the role of the skilful helmsman they may see themselves as sharing the bridge with the political leadership, playing the pilot towards new directions. The connections in the community that political leaders can maintain are often haphazard and limited. The chief executive and his team may be expected to take the lead in surveying the range of possible contacts in the private and voluntary sector that are likely to offer possibilities for inter-sectoral collaboration and investment and for following them up.

The chief executive's enabling role is by no means a new one. Since the oil crisis of the 1970s many local authorities with officers' guidance have reacted creatively to financial pressures and government policies that have deeply affected their local authorities' abilities to meet community requirements. Many chief executives in disadvantaged urban areas took the lead in responding to government supported schemes. One London borough chief executive for example wrote that the main opportunities he had appreciated in the job before 1980 had been in developing work under inner cities legislation and in partnership arrangements with the private sector. The high level of interest in partnerships with the private sector continued from 1980 along with an added interest in forms of organisation, initiatives associated with the release of assets and other new approaches. This chief executive gave his main current objectives as enabling other institutions such as voluntary bodies to provide outputs in line with council objectives, developing new sources of funding and maintaining external linkages. He rated sponsorship and partnership for new projects and establishing and maintaining new community-based bodies as two of his three best achievements.

In certain cases spectacular developments have been undertaken involving many firms, agencies and sources of finance, often with assistance from the European Community structural funds. While the most dramatic developments have been in some of the great cities - most notably perhaps in Birmingham and Glasgow - there have been remarkable developments throughout the country. Some chief executives have taken the lead in raising the interest of the private sector in ways in which it can contribute to public purposes by means of discussion with leading businessmen facilitated by contacts with chambers of commerce and trade, membership of Rotary and other associations orientated towards community purposes.

The Enabling Role and Economic Development

Local government's role as an enabler of community achievement has been conceived in various ways. One starts from a narrow view of local authorities as simply planners and providers of services and then stresses the fact that they may be able to increase their efficiency by contracting out work to private sector firms. The competitive tendering legislation required them to open the opportunity to outside bodies to bid for contracts to provide certain specified services in competition with any tenders that might be made from within the authority's own organisation. Chapter 7 has described the impact this had on organisation and efficiency in some authorities.

Another concept was that described by government ministers as the role of coordinator - perhaps with the use of some financial aid from public funds - for filling in the gaps which are beyond the normal interest or capacity of the private sector and the means of the voluntary sector. On the other hand the enabling role may be seen much more boldly as the local authority acting with rather than for the community by providing the extra 'leverage' it needs to meet the reasonable aspirations of its members. This may involve the whole management process: identifying in consultation with a wide range of local interests the needs, ambitions and priorities of the area; planning and programming to fulfil those needs; and commissioning from potential service providers - including its own direct service organisations - what is needed in the way it can be best provided.

When considered broadly 'enabling' expresses the fundamental role of government in a free society: enabling individuals, families and private organisations to fulfil desirable economic and social purposes for the good of the community as a whole (Brooke, 1989). A review of the possibilities may be expected to show ways in which community bodies can provide some activities currently provided by the local authority more satisfactorily beyond the authority's capacity. This is by no means a new function. Authorities have been enabling community bodies to undertake to enrich the welfare, economy and culture of communities from long ago.

It is hard to see how the broader goals involved can be achieved satisfactorily except through good relations with interests within the community. One chief executive described the aims of his approach to 'enablement' as 'trying to develop some sense of civic pride in the business community by helping to set up a group which could express 'enlightened self-interest' on behalf of industry. Basically the concept is enabling the community to do things for themselves for the common welfare consistent with agreed aims.

Only fourteen chief executives named developing relations with the community as one of their three main objectives, and seven others either named creating an enabling authority as an objective in itself or described aims that may be construed as enabling. Seven gave enabling innovations as among their best achievements. In view of the prominence given to the concept in recent years the number might have been expected to be larger among the 263 respondents.

One large group of replies additional to these figures but clearly of an enabling character relates to those in the field of economic development. Over a quarter (27.5 per cent) of respondents saw this as an essential part of their job, and a further 47 per cent saw it as desirable but delegable. Analysed by type of authority the highest proportion considering it an essential part of their role came from the Welsh districts (33 per cent) followed by the Scottish districts (30 per cent). Looked at from the opposite direction the lowest was among the London Boroughs (seven per cent). The highest proportion believing that the function was neither essential nor desirable came from the shire counties (43 per cent), followed by the London boroughs (40 per cent), the metropolitan districts (18 per cent) and the Scottish regions and islands (17 per cent). The Welsh and Scottish district chief executives were least likely to see this as an undesirable part of their role (10 and 12.5 per cent respectively).

By personal characteristics the chief executives most likely to regard the economic development task as essential were the over-60s (33.3 per cent); those least likely the under 40s (18 per cent). An attempt to explain the differences by the distribution of these officers regionally or between types of authority was unsuccessful. It may be that the explanation lies in the level of experience of economic recession between the two categories, the younger chief executives having generally been recruited in the period 1986-90 when unemployment was declining.

Economic development was cited as one of their three main objectives by 26 chief executives out of all replies, and 46 gave successes in this area as among their best achievements. The achievements included for example 'obtaining a major commitment by members and officers to reverse the economic decline', being 'part of a team that has reduced unemployment from 15 per cent to 3.5 per cent' and attracting 'many 'high-tech' and other major industries to the area by aggressive promotion... and all the advantages of a vibrant economy that flow therefrom'. In some cases the emphasis is on attracting outside help, including a high level of European aids. In nine cases the redevelopment or regeneration of town centres was instanced; in six others major development projects and in four leisure and tourist facilities.

The development of 'arms-length' or inter-sectoral bodies to meet an authority's purposes has often been the result of a chief executive's initiative and has provided a direct bridge to community involvement. Chief executives had been directly involved in setting up enterprise trusts and companies and served them sometimes as board members along with representatives of industry and other local bodies. They had worked with their colleagues in setting up community service agencies, in one case running skill centres in association with large scale industry (a possibility open to shire districts, at least until the establishment of TECs by central government). One chief executive was playing an important informal role in the development of initiatives at the local college of technology and working with the Prince's Trust.

In a few cases chief executives show pride in their part in improving the environmental quality of their districts, as in the case of one in a Welsh district who gave as among his best achievements success in transforming the area from one characterised by industrial dereliction to one in which it had become very attractive to live, and another in an English district (an ex-planner) who had 'changed the physical face of the place dramatically'. It can be a matter of just as much pride to have played a leading part in the transformation of economic conditions. A good example is given in chapter 5 (profile P).

More Examples of the Enabling Role

Non-metropolitan district authorities have the advantage here in that they are relatively unhindered by statutory obligations and their demands on resources. They have relative freedom in what they provide and the manipulation of capital assets can give them significant means for new development. Outstanding examples tend to be found in fairly affluent areas, often with a special interest in leisure services - especially in authorities where chief executives are given strong support by their elected members.

In one case it was reported that when the members appointed their present chief executive they were looking for one who would 'change and redirect the whole ship'. After appointment he reduced the authority's own staff drastically, first by internal economies and then by moving the workforce into the private and voluntary sectors. A management buy-out had moved 180 employees in the public works function from direct control. Housing had been taken over by a housing association with an independent membership. The council was close to being a 'client authority' contracting with outside bodies for the provisions they decided to put to tender. Having slimmed down the staff the chief executive had found in the 'enabling authority' concept a satisfactory definition for his subsequent aims. In the summer of 1989 he was spending only about five per cent of his time on representing the authority externally but was giving 30 per cent to meetings with third parties such as parish councils, consultants and developers concerned with projects in which the authority had an interest. Three major local plans had been prepared with major financial spin-offs such as the provision of by-passes, recreation developments and commuter car-parking. Developers were paying for the new roadworks. The job he said 'was about working-parties and making things happen'. They had reached a situation in which he was optimistic about the value of longer term plans for housing and other developments for which sound financial backing was available.

One of the opportunities another chief executive had looked forward to on appointment was to develop the authority's relationship with the private sector and at the same time respond to the needs of disadvantaged groups in the community. He had sought to bring together the resources of both levels of local government with those of other sectors. He had put forward new ideas on action for community care, with service responsibilities split between county social services and the housing department. In these matters and others he had been able to lay strong emphasis on relationships with the community: with business, schools and other local organisations. He and his chief officers had found a great deal of untapped enthusiasm and gained greatly from the opportunity to listen to what people in other sectors had to say.

An overall economic development strategy had been developed which involved working with local business to devise and implement new initiatives and help achieve a rational relocation of industry. The authority had been instrumental jointly with a local development company in establishing a new business park on redundant public land, persuading major employers that they should stay and enabling them to expand.

Social objectives were not absent in the previous case but in this instance they were fundamental. Both these chief executives had prided themselves on their ability to stimulate their councils with ideas and to take the lead. Both were under Conservative control at the time of the interviews. The following two cases are examples of Labour controlled authorities and, like the ones above, relatively free from inter-party acrimony.

In one of these the 'competitive' and 'enabling' approaches had been pursued from the time of the chief executive's appointment. Enabling and collaborative relationships with forces within the community were seen as more fundamental to the role of local government than competitive tendering. The chief executive envisaged the district as the centre of a network of interests and local, regional and national resources, all of which had relevance to its economic and development strategies. These included government departments and agencies, the European Commission, other local authorities at different levels, the local authority association, housing associations, energy providers, the district's new enterprise trust, voluntary sector bodies, businesses and business groups, the trades unions, the voluntary sector, the local university, community councils, local groups and the general public.

Inspired by a model from a scheme in Massachusetts brought to the attention of key actors in the local community by the manager of the branch headquarters of an international firm, a seminar had been set up of heads of public and private interests in the area to consider and plan for the future. Within a limited and strictly controlled budget it had been found possible to underpin and develop a remarkably wide range of projects involving private and public sector interests, and in many cases to draw on financial and other resources of the businesses involved. Local development bodies had been established with the freedom to adopt bold policies outside the constraints of local government law. An ambitious scheme to establish close contact between local government and local communities down to village level had also been developed, with inter-departmental teams for sub-areas, local offices to ensure accessibility, and support for local communities to enable them to develop their own initiatives and services.

In the second Labour controlled authority the chief executive had stressed in an initial report to council after his appointment that in view of a political commitments to lower expenditures and providing increased service quality, full regard should be paid to the need to work in partnership with other agencies and the interdependence between actions by the council and those of other authorities within the sub-region. In this case the leader had taken a forward role in creating new relationships with external bodies, targeting key agencies and seeking to develop their contributions to civic aims. Jointly with the chief executive he was seeking to develop the partnership approach between bodies in all sectors in relation to the development of the geographical and economic region in which the town lay.

In four of the authorities visited it took new chief executives some time to relate to the possibility of developing a new network of relationships with bodies outside the local authority, particularly since they felt that it was essential for future achievement and credibility to give the major part of their time to dealing with the internal problems of their authorities. Some had been frustrated by political situations. For example one London borough chief executive who gave as one of his most important personal objectives 'to assist in identifying the role of the authority in the community' had been constrained by decision-making problems in his hung authority to an extent that had greatly limited the time he could give to external matters. He nevertheless gave one of his three best personal achievements as leading a public/private partnership development team to create a large science park with leisure facilities.

The information from the research questionnaire on contacts within the community showed the extent to which chief executives were directly involved in local matters. Working meetings with people outside the authority were much less frequent than with those within it. Few chief executives were involved in them more often than once a month on average. Chief executives of metropolitan districts proved much more likely to have regular meetings with employers' representatives than those in other authorities: 62 per cent met them at least monthly as compared with an average of 29 per cent in other types of authority. It seems likely here that the difference arises not a little from the extent to which business interests are organised in chambers of trade and commerce in the metropolitan centres. This is one factor explaining why Labour authorities have a higher proportion of chief executives who meet representatives of the business community at least once a month than those controlled by Conservatives: 43 per cent as against 32.5 per cent. Contacts with business people were also most frequent in metropolitan authorities, being at least monthly in 75 per cent of cases compared with an average for all local authorities of 66 per cent and as low as 46 per cent in the London boroughs represented.

Only eight of the 252 chief executives who answered the question on relationships with voluntary agency representatives had weekly or more frequent contacts, but 85 (33 per cent) had meetings with them at least monthly. There was little difference according to type of political control or urban density in this case, or by type of authority except that for reasons that are uncertain London borough chief executives were fifteen per cent more likely than average to have contacts at least monthly while those in metropolitan districts were less likely by 14 per cent. This reverses to some extent the relationship with business between these two types of most-purpose authority.

Meetings with representatives of other interest groups differed little in frequency. They were shown to be least frequent in the most sparsely populated areas (under 2.5 persons per hectare) and also in the most densely populated (50 or more persons per hectare). The quality of relationships was also at its lowest in these groups.

Parish, town and community councils can be seen as thorns in the flesh. When they were mentioned it was usually in connection with the problems they created for the authority. On the other hand in one authority the chief executive gave as a main current objective the development of relationships with them.

In so far as an authority needs an understanding of the needs, problems and opportunities for collaboration with the voluntary and private sectors the research evidence appears to indicate that most chief executives are not achieving this through direct personal contacts, excepting perhaps in the metropolitan districts and some mainly urban districts. One case of the latter was a district chief executive of an authority in a moderately sized town who stood out in his general involvement in community life, being chairman of local organisations, president of the operatic society and probably knowing the resources of the area better than anyone else.

In the broadest sense of the enabling authority - that is one that is enabling individuals and families as well as businesses to overcome obstacles, understand their opportunities and how the services can relate to their needs - it may be very helpful for the chief executive to ensure some regular contact with the general public. One well known example was that of Roger Paine when chief executive of Wrekin District Council who sat at the public enquiry desk of his offices for a time every week. Even if such contacts must inevitably be somewhat random they could at least be deep enough to gain some understanding of the factors behind statistical surveys. Many appear to lack such contacts: forty per cent of chief executives saw representatives of the general public less often than monthly. Only 40 per cent met them weekly or more often. Thirty-three per cent rated the quality of the relationship in meetings with members of the public as less than good, which gives rise to the speculation that they met them either in impersonal situations or when they were dealing with complaints or grievances.

Relations Outside the Local Community

Contacts at national level varied widely between individuals. Proximity to centres of government is an important factor in some cases but not in others. Chief executives in Scotland and Wales are much more likely to be in a close relationship with civil servants than those in England. When seniority as a chief executive, ability and proximity to government offices coincide there may be frequent contacts. John Boynton in his book on the chief executive emphasised the value of contacts with the civil service for the purpose of benefiting from the advice it could give - a point that did not emerge at all in the research survey (Boynton, 1986).

Meetings with representatives of national government and the European Community are less frequent than monthly in the great majority of cases. Over 60 per cent met civil servants or other government representatives less often than monthly. Twenty-seven per cent of chief executives reported meetings monthly or more frequently in this case: nine per cent fortnightly and two per cent more often. Twenty-nine per cent saw MPs monthly or more often; three per cent met MEPs as often as this and five per cent ministers.

The differences between metropolitan districts and London boroughs are very sharp in some respects. Whereas 74 per cent of metropolitan district chief executives saw civil servants or government representatives monthly or more, only 23 per cent did so from the London boroughs. (The case of Rodney Brooke when Chief Executive for Westminster and Honorary Secretary of the London Boroughs Association is an outstanding exception. He had more frequent contacts with Whitehall than any other known case in Great Britain). The situation is redressed a little in the case of meetings with MPs and government ministers. Thirty-six per cent of the London chief executives met MPs monthly or more against 23 per cent of those in the metropolitan districts.

Contacts with civil servants are most frequent in the North-East of England - a reflection of the close relations with government which were started at least as early as the regional development policies with which the Macmillan government of the 1960s was associated. The Welsh county chief executives have the most regular contacts with the civil service, due no doubt to the system of regular meetings in Cardiff and the closeness of the Welsh Counties Committee to the Welsh Department in Cathays Park. In general it seems that the further chief executives are from London the more they are likely to have regular relationships with civil servants.

There was an exceptional emphasis on national and regional contacts in three authorities visited during the research. A Welsh county chief executive believed that he needed 'the ability to maintain constructive relations with a wide range of people: MEPs, senior civil servants, a multiplicity of agencies, and reasonable relations with the media - the ability to sell one's wares'. He believed that this had been crucial in the county's success in the development of the infrastructure of its area. A Welsh district chief executive met Welsh Office servants and representatives of government agencies weekly.

In a large borough in the North-East of England the chief executive had a very good relationship with the county council and found it essential in fighting for assistance with economic development to co-operate well with government agencies to achieve his authority's priorities. He held regular meetings with the chamber of commerce and their committees. He was a member of the general forum on the development of the area led by businessmen, an integrated operations steering group set up by the Department of the Environment regional controller, a regionally based development company and other regional organisations.

Relations with other Authorities

Relations with other local authorities can be passed over more quickly, not because they are unimportant but because they appear from the research to be lacking in closeness in most cases, except through involvement in local government associations. As reported above, little more than one in four chief executives regarded representation in relations with other local authorities as essential. The strongest weight was placed on them by metropolitan district chief executives (35 per cent) followed by those in shire counties (32 per cent), shire districts (27 per cent), London boroughs (20 per cent), Scottish regions and islands (17) and Scottish districts (12).

In general the county joint committees set up after reorganisation have failed badly to meet original hopes. At interviews two county chief executive acknowledged that relations with districts were poor, but another reported them to be good. In the latter case the success was understood to be at officer rather than member levels. The greater closeness among metropolitan authorities seems likely to relate to the work of associations set up in England at least around 1974 to bring the county and districts together, followed in the mid-1980s by successor bodies to achieve continuity on their dissolution. Only one survived as an association, the Greater Manchester Association of Metropolitan Authorities, although four other metropolitan counties kept joint or coordinating committees.

That is not to say that contact between chief executives is poor. Networks are important: emphasis is placed on meetings with other chief executives as learning experiences. Chief executives participate in activities organised by SOLACE nationally and its regional branches, local authority association conferences and committees and Local Government Training Board and other national and regional meetings. But there was little evidence of local inter-authority collaboration. It may be that in this matter the chief executives are handicapped by the attitudes of members.

The main exception in England is the Northern Region Councils Association which aims 'to promote the economic aims and social wellbeing of the people of the region, provide a forum for discussion on matters concerning the region, promote liaison with government and other institutions and secure maximum inter-authority co-operation for these objectives'. It appoints to the board of the Northern Development Company on which, to use the European Community term, the social partners in commerce, industry and the trade unions are represented. It is perhaps a European region in embryo. Chief executives stressed the importance to their objectives of their work in this and some other inter-authority bodies. They provide a means for a 'common front' to be developed between county and district authorities in matters of importance both within their authorities, regionally and nationally.

Conclusions

The distancing of many senior officers from personal involvement in the community has been partly an effect of amalgamations and the consequent increase in areas and their complexity - something already stressed to me by chief officers in interviews on the Black Country reorganisation of the 1960s. Chief executives no longer appear to be an important part of an historic network except where there are survivals from the clerk's role, as in the case of county and some other chief executives in their involvement with the lieutenancy and courts administration. Changes in the structure of commerce and industry, the media, the mobility of elite groups and social culture have also had their effects. The speed of change and central impositions such as compulsory competitive tendering have not helped: priority has often had to be given to internal management. But some chief executives at least had put as much effort into building up new structures of relationships as other priorities allowed. Subject to outstanding exceptions chief executives appear to be valued much more for managerial competence than for understanding of the local community. Those promoted from within their own authorities undoubtedly have considerable advantages from their local experience, although some chief executives from without can no doubt often compensate with talents beyond those of any local candidates for the post.

The attitudes of elected members, and particularly of the political leadership, are a vital factor in the chief executive's ability to promote constructive relationships within the local community and beyond it. What chief executives themselves can achieve is limited unless the politicians support the development of external working relationships and identify themselves with the work that chief executives do to improve them.

The job is essentially one of challenges, and whatever the circumstances, the task remains of achieving an understanding of the needs and culture of the local community and using opportunities that exist or can be created not only to spread information and understanding about the local authority's work but also to achieve dialogue and working relationships within the community as a whole. This is at the centre of the 'enabling role'.

Chapter 9

THE TASKS OF THE CHIEF EXECUTIVE

The chief executive's role has no definable limits. He or she is the factotum of the local authority in the sense that anything that nobody else feels authorised or able to deal with is likely to land on his or her desk. He is likely to be expected to deal with any issue the council or leader considers important even if he feels that it is not. As the previous chapters have shown, the role has been shaped mainly by executives responding to the problems, challenges and opportunities of the situation. Much of it has been unpredicted and unpredictable to those entering the post, as for example overcoming the problems of a hung authority, critical financial situations and the challenges of the legislation of the late 1980s. It is essentially a role of response to the unpredictable, but it is also one of anticipation so that defences can be put up against future problems and new opportunities seized.

Research findings described in the preceding chapters have shown the variety of the role. Nevertheless there is a high level of agreement on its central elements although views are much divided on others. The main purpose of this chapter is to report the findings of the research on the role in more detail and to consider their implications. It introduces aspects which have not yet been considered, filling gaps in the knowledge of the job as it is perceived by chief executives.

A search was carried out before the research questionnaire was drafted to identify the individual tasks that chief executives saw as included in their responsibilities. Information was drawn from earlier inquiries, including that undertaken by Hay/MSL in collaboration with the Local Authorities Conditions of Service Advisory Board in 1987 (*A Profile of Chief Executives and their Jobs*, 1988). Fifty-four tasks were identified. Some of them were highly complex and could be broken up into sub-tasks, but for practical reasons the list had to be limited.

When combined with other sources used in the research the responses provide the foundation for a statement of the core responsibilities of chief executives at the beginning of the 1990s based on the replies of over half of those in office. The respondents reflected fairly closely the characteristics of chief executives as a whole, at least regarding those on which information on all is available from yearbooks, especially length of experience, profession, type of authority, population size, form of political control and countries and regions of their authorities.

Chief executives were asked to indicate how far they considered each of the tasks listed in the questionnaire was essential to their role; or desirable but delegable; or not essential. Nevertheless the 'desirable but delegable' category may be considered to overlap the 'non-essential category. Those consulted on the questionnaire however felt the distinction was meaningful, and those who replied since it was nowhere commented on adversely. It can be argued that delegation implies retaining responsibility for the outcome, so that delegated tasks remain in a sense essential. 'Non-essential' is therefore taken in the analysis to be exclusive of 'desirable but delegable'.

The Core of the Role

Our survey demonstrated that despite the lack of a uniform model of chief executives' duties certain tasks are seen as central to the role. As reported in chapter 7, almost all (98.9 per cent) considered the appointment of chief officers and the leadership of the management team or chief officer group to be an essential and non-delegable part of their role (table 9-1 below). In contrast a study in the year following reorganisation based on a questionnaire and interviews with senior officers led to the conclusion that 'it was not clear that the management team had been a success' (Greenwood et al, undated, *In Pursuit of Corporate Rationality*). It is now virtually the general rule that the chief executive role and some form of management group or team are inseparable. The task of performance appraisal of senior officers, including members of the team or group, is a closely related matter on which there is almost as much agreement that it is essential (95.4 per cent).

This combined with the range of other tasks detailed below relating to the quality of the services that are believed by a substantial proportion of chief executives to be essential show that chief executives tend to see themselves as responsible for the quality of the administration and its services as a whole, jointly with the management team but ultimately in person.

One task considered as essential by more than nineteen out of every twenty chief executives in the response was the promotion of constructive relationships between members and officers and also among the members themselves. During a period when the sharp ideological character of national leadership and legislation had provoked an adversarial stance, and when many councils were hung and the loyalty of officers strained by enforced cutbacks and restructuring of priorities and organisation, chief executives often played the central role in overcoming the negative effects on relationships which threatened to undermine effective decision-making. As described above, the chief executive is normally the one neutral figure in a position to mediate and attempt to remove *impasses* between parties. From interview evidence it appeared that it was not uncommon also for a chairman's relationship with a chief officer to become critical and for the committee chairman concerned or the leader of a group to seek the intervention of the chief executive to sort out the trouble. The ideal is of course for the chief executive to use his influence to develop a spirit and culture where such breakdowns are unlikely.

In line with the Bains Report and earlier definitions of the role of the clerk and chief executive officer, all our respondents regarded policy advice as essential or desirable: 93.9 per cent saw it as essential. A similar proportion classified 'translating political requirements into management action' as essential; as did over 90 per cent the closely related matters of strategy formulation and planning. Markedly fewer (83.5 per cent) classified the review and appraisal part of the policy-making cycle as an essential task (table 9-2).

Table 9-1: THE CORE OF THE ROLE: TASKS CONSIDERED BY OVER NINETY PER CENT OF CHIEF EXECUTIVES TO BE ESSENTIAL TO THE ROLE

	per cent classing task as:			
	essential	desirable but delegable	not essential	(base)
Appointment, leadership and appraisal of top management				
Appointment of chief officers	98.9	0.8	0.4	(263)
Leadership of management team or chief officer group	98.9	0.4	0.8	(261)
Appraisal of senior officer (particularly chief officer) performance	95.4	3.9	0.8	(260)
Promoting constructive relationships (between members, members & officers)	96.6	3.1	0.4	(261)
Policy and its implementation				
Policy advice generally	93.8	6.2	0.0	(261)
Translating political requirements into management action	94.6	4.3	1.2	(258)
Strategy formulation and planning	90.4	8.5	1.2	(260)

Note: the base refers to the number of respondents for each item.

The few chief executives who classified policy advice as no more than 'desirable but delegable' came from shire or from Scottish districts with relatively small populations. Those who did not think that 'translating political requirements into management action' warranted top priority came in general from rural rather than urban authorities. Otherwise the characteristics of their authorities, including political control, did not relate significantly to chief executives' views on these matters.

Promoting Values

Table 9-2 brings together a group of tasks which between 80 and 90 per cent of respondents classified as essential. With the exception of the last - protecting the interests of minority groups and individual members - they stress the promotion of commitment to values within the authority: in particular efficiency, quality of service to the public and other council objectives, and otherwise building organisational culture.

Emphasis on commitment to policy objectives was somewhat greater amongst chief executives serving Labour-controlled councils, while support for the development of organisational culture tended to come in particular from those under Conservative control.

Table 9-2: PROMOTING VALUES: TASKS CONSIDERED BY 80 TO 90 PER CENT TO BE ESSENTIAL TO THE ROLE

	per cent classing task as:			
	essential	desirable but delegable	not essential	(base)
Promoting collaboration at all levels	88.6	10.3	1.2	(262)
Promoting quality of service to public	86.6	11.9	1.5	(261)
Promoting commitment to output and efficiency	84.2	14.6	1.2	(260)
Promoting commitment to fulfil the council's other objectives	83.1	15.3	1.5	(263)
Building organisational culture otherwise	82.7	13.1	4.2	(260)
Review and appraisal of policies and programmes	83.5	16.9	0.0	(260)
Protecting rights of minority party groups and members	81.8	13.4	4.7	(253)

Other Major Tasks

Table 9-3 lists further tasks which a substantial majority of respondents classified as 'essential'. These fall under two main heads which have already been discussed in the text: innovation and organisational development in chapter 7 and relations with the public in chapter 8. We found that the promotion of innovation was more likely to be regarded as particularly important by chief executives in Scotland while the Inner London chief executives were unusual in that none of them thought that personal involvement with the local government ombudsman was essential for a chief executive. Direct involvement with the satisfaction of the public, other than concern with complaints, is given least support by chief executives located in East Anglia and Yorkshire and Humberside, while the greatest support for this task was found in the West Midlands and in Scotland.

Table 9-3: OTHER MAJOR TASKS CONSIDERED BY BETWEEN 50 AND 80 PER CENT TO BE ESSENTIAL (EXCLUDING REPRESENTATION OF AUTHORITY'S INTERESTS)

	per cent classing task as: essential	desirable but delegable	not essential	(base)
Organisational development and innovation				
Promotion of innovation in services	76.3	21.0	2.7	(258)
Organisational development	67.9	30.5	1.68	(249)
Communication to staff	57.8	31.4	10.9	(245)
Treatment of the public				
Complaints not met satisfactorily at department level	78.9	19.9	1.28	(261)
Complaints referred by the Ombudsman	65.8	31.2	3.1	(260)
Satisfaction of the public with treatment otherwise	54.1	40.5	5.4	(257)
Public relations generally	60.3	31.9	7.9	(257)

Tasks Most Likely to be Delegated

The findings on the representational role outside the authority (table 9-4) have been described in the previous chapter. The group of tasks in table 9-5 shows the greatest variety of opinion and therefore provides particularly wide scope for debate. Otherwise functions which a majority of chief executives saw as candidates for delegation fell into four broad areas - conduct and arbitration; information; various aspects of implementation (including responsibility for such areas of work as economic development and equal opportunities which are frequently run from units reporting directly to the chief executive); and a number of other functions, some of which are highly specialised.

As described above, the Widdicombe Report and the statutory requirements for the appointment of a monitoring officer and standing orders that ensued brought into prominence aspects of political behaviour which came to be generally referred to as issues of 'propriety and probity'. One in eight of chief executives believed that it was not essential or desirable to hold direct responsibility for these matters. Forty-seven per cent thought that ensuring probity was essential and 40.5 per cent that it was desirable but delegable. More (43 per cent) considered that direct concern with propriety matters was desirable but delegable.

More chief executives (22.6 per cent) believed that arbitration on standing orders, codes of conduct and similar matters was a non-essential task. Only ten per cent thought that they should be directly responsible for legal aspects of action and non-action. In all therefore it would seem that those who believed that these tasks could be delegated together with those who regarded them as non-essential were in a clear and in the case of legal opinion a strong majority.

When analysed by party the biggest proportion (over 70 per cent) of those who saw probity as most essential to their role was found in authorities controlled by Independents. As these were generally in small authorities this result probably reflected the lack of officer colleagues who were likely to be able to cope with these matters. After this came those in authorities with no overall control (46 per cent propriety and 41 per cent probity), followed by those in Conservative controlled authorities (41 per cent on both counts). In Labour controlled authorities there was a wide difference: probity matters

Table 9-4: REPRESENTATION OF THE AUTHORITY'S INTERESTS

	per cent classing task as: essential	desirable but delegable	not essential	(base)
Representation				
On formal occasions	67.1	30.6	4.4	(255)
With government departments and MPs	57.6	39.5	2.7	(256)
With EC officials and MEPs	49.2	44.9	5.9	(254)
With media	42.2	49.8	8.0	(249)
On delegations	40.9	55.9	3.2	(254)
With government agencies	26.9	64.8	8.3	(253)
With private/mixed sector bodies	26.8	61.6	11.6	(250)
With other local authorities	26.5	62.5	11.1	(253)
With other interests in the community	13.5	70.6	15.9	(245)

were seen as an essential task by a majority (54 per cent) while only 36 per cent regarded responsibility for propriety matters as essential. By region the need for personal involvement in propriety matters is felt most strongly in Yorkshire and Humberside. In general it is the chief executives in major urban areas who feel that it is desirable not to have direct or indirect responsibility for these matters for reasons discussed below where information from interviews is taken into account. It is striking that, excepting propriety matters, it is those under 40 and those with less than a year in post who were significantly more likely to regard these tasks as inessential than their older and more experienced colleagues.

Not unexpectedly perhaps, support for the task of providing services to the mayor or council chairman was highest in the least populous authorities. About 42 per cent of respondents from places with populations of less than 75,000 judged this an essential task.

Regarding the importance of the chief executive's involvement in economic development there did not appear to be any striking variations by type of authority, political control or region. However support for the task tends to decrease with the size of population. In the case of the London boroughs the chief executives split evenly between seeing economic development as essential, delegable and non-essential, probably reflecting sharp differences in the economic and social balance from one authority to another. Among those in metropolitan districts only 9 per cent judged this to be an essential part of the chief executive's job.

Table 9.5: OTHER TASKS CONSIDERED DESIRABLE BUT DELEGABLE BY OVER 40 PER CENT

	per cent classing task as: essential	desirable but delegable	not essential	(base)
Conduct and arbitration				
Ensuring probity	47.1	40.5	12.4	(259)
Propriety matters	43.2	44.2	12.4	(258)
Arbitration standing orders etc	26.4	51.0	22.6	(261)
Information				
Information and analysis	45.5	43.8	10.6	(256)
Information to elected members	32.3	47.7	20.0	(260)
Information to the public	22.3	52.5	25.3	(257)
Ensuring implementation of council's decisions	39.1	50.8	10.2	(256)
Other corporate policy matters eg equal opportunities	30.4	44.6	25.0	(260)
Budgetary process	37.2	45.6	17.2	(261)
Services to mayor or council chair	33.6	43.5	22.9	(262)
Economic development	27.5	47.3	25.2	(262)
District Audit matters	19.5	52.6	27.9	(251)
General personnel matters (eg recruitment,promotions)	10.5	55.1	34.8	(247)
Organisational efficiency units eg O&M	14.2	44.6	41.2	(260)
Leading/coordinating inter-departmental work on special problems (eg vandalism)	13.7	52.2	34.1	(255)
Discharge of functions delegated by council	12.0	48.0	40.0	(250)
Dealings with arms-length agencies	10.8	48.6	40.6	(251)

We now come to those functions which tended to be viewed as of central importance to the chief executive's job before the 1960s. Organisational efficiency units, especially o&m, which were given so much importance in the recommendations of the Treasury O&M unit in its report for Coventry in the early 1950s, are now rarely rated as central to the job. The survey results show that hardly any chief executives in the London boroughs and metropolitan districts saw this as an essential task, although a third or more saw it as desirable but delegable. Direct involvement in personnel matters (not including the recruitment of the senior management team referred to earlier) is another such task. It was rated non-essential by most respondents irrespective of authority type or size.

The Tasks Considered Non-Essential

Ironically in view of the way the job of chief executive has developed, the jobs that were historically the basis of the traditional clerk's job - legal and secretarial tasks - were least likely to be considered essential to the role (table 9-6). Fewer than ten per cent of chief executives considered any but establishment functions amongst those listed in Table 9.6 to be essential, and a sizeable majority considered all except establishment functions and legal advice not even to be desirable.

Table 9-6: TASKS CONSIDERED BY LARGE PROPORTION TO BE NON-ESSENTIAL TO THE ROLE

	per cent classing task as:			
	essential	desirable but delegable	not essential	(base)
Establishment functions	20.3	37.5	42.2	(261)
Legal aspects of action & non-action	9.8	41.9	48.4	(246)
Secretarial work	3.8	21.4	74.8	(262)
Other administrative procedures	3.0	36.3	60.8	(237)
Registrar for certain legal purposes	2.7	18.7	78.6	(262)
Legal work	1.5	13.7	84.8	(263)

In general there was little difference between the balance of views by type of authority or party. London borough and metropolitan district chief executives were more likely to believe that the secretarial role was essential or desirable - 40 and 45 per cent respectively as against an all authority average of 25 per cent - because, it has been suggested to me, it gives them the support they need 'to insert themselves into the management process by their relationship with the politicians': it provides re-assurance if this breaks down or if the politicians are ineffective. It also tends to be valued most in Labour controlled authorities. As may be anticipated, lawyers and administrators tend to value the direct control of law and secretarial work more than those from other professions. Nevertheless only four out of the 121 chief executives with legal backgrounds considered legal work essential and only nineteen as desirable but delegable; and none of those with a secretarial or managerial professional background considered secretarial tasks essential although twelve out of the 36 thought them desirable.

Conclusions on the Response to the Questionaire

The response to the survey showed that the role of the chief executive was conceived quite differently from that of the role of the clerk of the council. Its core is now seen to lie in the creation of a management team or chief officer group of high proficiency consisting of members of outstanding managerial talent, together with the promotion of good working relationships between members and officers.

Close to this lie three other sets of tasks. The first is responsibility for the policy-making and implementation cycle, including policy advice, ensuring that political requirements are translated into action within the framework of a strategy, and policy evaluation and appraisal leading into the redefinition of policies and programmes. The second is promoting commitment to key values and objectives. The third is protecting the rights of minority party groups and individual members.

Between these tasks and those that are not regarded by a large majority of chief executives as being essential to the role lie a number of matters that are seen by many to be delegable and which, it may be assumed, they might devolve in order not to dissipate their efforts at the expense of what they see as their core responsibilities.

The Monitoring Tasks: Evidence from Interviews

In view of the debate amongst chief executives at the time of the interviews about the desirability of assuming the monitoring role it seemed appropriate to take the opportunity to sound officers about their individual thoughts on the matter. The oral replies for or against the filling of the role by chief executives were roughly in proportion to what might have been forecast from the response to the questionnaire. Views were divided fairly equally between those who expected to assume the monitoring role and those who were determined that it should be carried out by another officer.

Of those who had decided that they themselves should assume the role, all but one of the eight had long experience as chief executive or director of administration, or in one case as deputy chief executive and clerk in a very large authority prior to his present appointment. All but two were lawyers by profession. Their reasons for undertaking the statutory role were various. Of two in small authorities with large Conservative majorities one said that he did not want 'people going behind others' backs', and that if the chief executive was sufficiently respected the members should have enough confidence in him to appoint him to the statutory role. This was the only case in which it was implied that the members could possibly take a decision on the matter that was not consistent with the chief executive's own, although it seemed unlikely. In the other instance the chief executive said that he would need convincing that the monitoring officer should not be himself, but he would need help if he took it on. One problem of taking any other decision in smaller authorities is that there is often no-one else on the staff with the professional knowledge and understanding of the issues involved in a particular case to fill the role convincingly.

The chief executives of two large boroughs were well established in their roles and felt, like others interviewed, that they had always filled the monitoring role in practice and did not see that it was necessary to place this elsewhere. One believed that the statutory role could be very divisive and that if the secretary were required to undertake it, it could set him and possibly other officers against the members. He believed that the function required a central view but one that took in different criteria from those of a council secretary. He intended 'to get designated as monitoring officer and then forget it'.

Three county chief executives also found the innovation irrelevant to established practice. One said 'If something's wrong, I say so', and 'If councillors do not follow advice, that's their own can of worms'. One without traditional departmental responsibilities was taking on the statutory role because he felt that it needed detachment from the services expected of the chief executive's role, as did advising on ombudsman cases.

The five chief executives who wished the monitoring role to be carried out by another officer all came from authorities with active inter-party politics. They all in different ways argued that the legal view was too narrow a one to be identified with and that they should be in a position to stand back from responsibility for the interpretation of the law in order to help members to find their way round the points raised. One believed that to appoint another officer for monitoring would clear up any ambiguity about the chief executive's functions. He needed to be free to exercise a proactive, initiatory role. Another believed that three different issues could easily be confused: that of legality, which should be with a lawyer; that of probity, which came up mainly in connection with appointments, which should be with the personnel officer except perhaps in the case of the appointment of chief officers when the responsibility should possibly rest with the chief executive; and unfairness, which was essentially the chief executive's issue, he being the only officer in a neutral position. He would have hated to be monitoring officer in a previous authority which he had served because this would have cast him all the time in the role of policeman. In practice there were few problems which he had found he could not defuse while unhindered by a statutory role.

No chief executive considered that the statutory requirement was helpful in his own case. One thought that it was reactionary in returning to a traditional view of the town clerk and chief executive as 'keeping everything proper' - which was 'a blind-eye view'. Another believed that the provisions were almost counter-productive: it could encourage members to test the system. In general those who were taking on the post thought it was unnecessary and those who were not felt that it was divisive and could undermine the nature of the role.

The Personal Objectives of Chief Executives and how they Saw what Members Expected of them

Chief executives were asked in the questionnaire what they rated as their three most important work objectives and what were those they thought members expected of them. These question were pursued partly to identify how far chief executives saw differences with members on their role which might be the cause of strain.

In 26 per cent of the cases chief executives' personal objectives were identical with those expected of the members. There was more perceived agreement in shire and

Scottish districts than elsewhere. The match was lowest in London where only one respondent indicated that his own objectives and those of his members matched. There were no significant differences relating to type of political control.

Matters relating to policy and decision-making came first, being named by over half the respondents (53 per cent). The most prominent aspects of these are policy information, advice and the steering of decisions, followed by policy-making processes and procedures.

Perhaps it is surprising that nearly half the chief executives did not include policy matters among their three main objectives. A clue may be found in what they thought members expected of them. While almost 51 per cent believed that members expected policy matters to be amongst their three main objectives, more (63 per cent) believed that members rated efficiency and effectiveness as a top member concern. The latter came second among chief executives' personal objectives, being given in 45 per cent of their replies.

The effects of government legislation, including compulsory competitive tendering, were not included in this category but in that of 'managing change'. There was hardly any difference between the proportion of chief executives who gave this as among their top priorities (25 per cent) and the proportion who included it among their members' expectations.

Leadership and management style came third in chief executives' priorities, being given by just under 45 per cent, as against fourth (28 per cent) among elected members' expectations. Possibly this is because chief executives are so immediately dependent on leadership as the primary means of securing the behaviour conducive to 'value for money' and other aims, while to members it is a less direct concern. The aims grouped under the leadership head included catalysing new attitudes, improving style and performance and, most often listed, morale and motivation and good internal relationships.

Chief executives tended to expect their members to give a higher priority to securing good relationships than they did themselves (46 per cent as against 40 per cent). In matters of internal relations the chief executives' stress is on the improvement of those between themselves and members and among members, followed closely by those between members and officers generally. The responses reflected the central position of the role not only in achieving a spirit of cooperation but also in mediation over clashes of interest, settling disputes and overcoming blockages in the decision-making process. (The insights on this part of the role given in interviews with members are described in chapter 6).

Slightly more responses related to the chief executive's role in external relationships than to that in internal ones. The emphasis here was on improving those with the public and the media and achieving a better 'image' for the council generally.

Chief executives were slightly more likely to see the improvement of services and meeting local needs as among their own main priorities than among those of their members (27 per cent against 24 per cent). It is surprising that these objectives do not figure higher. This may be because they see members looking to heads of individual services rather than themselves as far as the quality of the services is concerned. More gave staffing and staff performance as among their own main objectives than expected them to be among those of the members (12 per cent against 8 per cent).

Members' objectives tend to be seen as rather more general than their own, as reflected in the fact that 11 per cent of chief executives saw the members as expecting them to 'carry general responsibility', while only two per cent of the chief executives gave answers which were expressed in similarly broad terms.

To summarise, the analysis indicated that in a few matters there seemed to be a significant difference in emphasis, particularly in that chief executives tended to give more priority to policy and strategic planning and leadership and management style while the members placed the achievement of efficiency and effectiveness higher. The extent to which the chief executive should or could intervene effectively in detailed departmental matters in the short term without undermining formally or informally delegated responsibility and morale is at issue. Complaints can be passed on and certainly significant failings in public service pursued, and of course important audit findings discussed. But in a complex authority with responsibility for the major statutory services, performance must surely be influenced through balanced appraisals under arrangements of the kind that have been increasingly set up by authorities in the late 1980s. This may cause frustration for members who expect immediate remedies. The ultimate goal is to have the whole organisation pursuing the ideals of quality and responsibility to the public, and this puts a major emphasis on capacity for leadership through the management team and otherwise.

Because the demands made on chief executives are so extensive and complex it was feared that they might be too great and therefore a cause of serious strain within the system. Respondents were therefore asked whether they considered the expectations of them by their members - and by their fellow chief officers - were reasonable, too high or too low (the last being also sometimes a cause of frustration).

TABLE 9-7 MEMBERS AND OFFICERS. EXPECTATIONS OF WHAT A CHIEF EXECUTIVE CAN ACHIEVE AS UNDERSTOOD BY CHIEF EXECUTIVES

	Members expectations (%):			Chief officers expectations (%):		
Per cent of respondents from:	too high	reas-onable	too low	too high	reas-onable	too low
Shire County	3.7	85.2	7.4	7.1	85.7	7.1
Shire District	14.0	81.9	3.5	4.1	90.1	4.1
Metropolitan District	18.2	77.3	4.5	4.5	81.8	9.1
London Borough	20.0	66.7	6.7	6.7	73.3	13.3
Scottish Region/Island	-	100.0	-	16.7	83.3	-
All authorities	13.2	81.3	4.3	5.0	87.6	5.4

The results (table 9-7) show that in over 80 per cent of cases they are considered reasonable. However in 13 per cent of authorities members' expectations are seen as too high. Chief officers however are thought to expect less: they were considered too high in only five per cent of cases. A few chief executives consider their members' expectations to be too low (four per cent), as also those of their chief officers (five per cent).

There were significant differences in the balance of replies according to type of authority. Members' expectations are seen as too high above all in the London boroughs (20 per cent) and in the metropolitan districts (18 per cent). In these most purpose authorities of course the 'span of control' and often a highly-charged political atmosphere compound the pressures, reflecting the particularly intense problems of the modern city. In the shire counties on the other hand members' expectation are more likely to be considered too low (seven per cent) than too high (four per cent), while the replies on chief officers' expectations are split evenly between too high and too low at seven per cent each way. In view of the fact that at the time of writing all national parties appear likely to include local government reorganisation in their next election manifestos and that there is a wide wave of political opinion in favour of all or most purpose authorities, this result has a certain significance. The executive problems of the most-purpose authority should be given special consideration with a view to establishing whether such innovations in the form of the executive function suggested by the models described in chapter 13 could help to overcome them.

What do Leading Councillors Expect of the Role?

The picture of chief executives' tasks and objectives given above is entirely based on the views and perceptions of chief executives. How far is it consonant with what their political masters feel they require from the job in the 1990s? The following account of members' views is drawn from evidence collected in the interview programme. It covers the qualities required of chief executives as well as the functions of the role.

Communication

The quality most generally required of chief executives by leaders was the ability to relate well both to members and officers, that is to be 'link-man' between members and officers. Several leaders considered this to be a first necessity. The leaders are of course also themselves 'link-men' between the chief executive and their group: they are to some extent in the same boat as the chief executives. On many matters however leaders expected the chief executive to communicate not just through the leader but directly. In terms of skills the ability and motivation to communicate well in both these as well as other directions is clearly a first necessity.

In one city authority a leader defined the chief executive as the main link between the chief officers or directors and the non-executive directors, who were presumed to be the committee chairmen and group officers. In an English county the leader described the chief executive's linkage function more narrowly as through the political leadership. In the first case the relationships between the chief executive and the chairmen were frequent, and in the latter case less than monthly.

In nearly all instances the chief executive addressed the controlling group on matters of importance - normally in an introductory part of their agenda, leaving before discussion within the group.

Several opposition members felt that the chief executives should be doing more to help the opposition to be effective. They were most concerned about increasing the information flow between the chief executive and their group members. They stressed the chief executive's responsibility for making information available to members, and also for giving them advice. One referred to the need for guidance to elected members individually. He gave as a recent case the need for the chief executive to help the opposition group to understand the features of contracts involved in compulsory competitive tendering procedures.

The evidence in previous chapters shows that the frequency of member-chief executive relationship differs widely between authorities. The subject of how far chief executives can strengthen the democratic aspect of local government by raising members' understanding of issues beyond what is normally possible in committee and council is one that may be thought to need close consideration and perhaps innovative approaches.

Good and sympathetic listening is a very important part of communication which several leaders singled out as highly appreciated in a chief executive. One for example said appreciatively of a chief executive, 'he will listen - and always wanted to listen'.

For communication to be two-way and to develop into discussion was said to require 'someone members can trust with their views'. A chief executive needs to understand what leaders consider to be confidential and what they regard as open to onward communication - by no means always an easy task but fundamental to a relationships of trust. One Scottish opposition leader believed that the chief executive 'should reveal matters as far as he can without revealing them' (sic). The role needed, according to a leader in the North-East of England, 'a very well developed political sense'. The chief executive should certainly, he said, not be a party politician but someone who understands 'the politics of inter-group relationships'.

During the recent years of change many leaders needed all the help they could be given in understanding the content and its implications. Failure to give such help, especially regarding its impact and opportunities for elected members, in terms members could understand and without condescension, could lead to feelings of alienation and impotence. (One Welsh politician commented that communication 'was a most difficult role for a professional in that professional men are sometimes academically arrogant and therefore apt to spark off conflict between profession and political machine'.)

The ideal chief executive was said to be one who encouraged communication by being 'human and not too aloof' and 'who could make people feel that their opinions were respected'. He should be straightforward and command respect and totally loyal to decisions of main committees.

It should be borne in mind that the leaders' responses reflect a period in which expectations about roles have been severely disturbed by legislative requirements and in some cases by the impact of hung council situations: a period in which role change was inevitable. While chief executives were fully cognisant of the demands involved, many members, including political leaders, had difficulties in accepting them and in envisaging the implications for the elected member.

Advice, guidance, policy-making and innovation

The giving of information shades into the giving of advice and guidance. According to the conservative leader in a large London borough the chief executive should be the 'mouthpiece for advice to senior members'. One leading member in a shire district said that he 'would like to think that you could lean on your chief executive; that he was there to advise. The chief executive should put up alternatives without councillors suggesting them.'

Leaders demanded political awareness and understanding from their chief executives, including an understanding of the difficulties of the leader's job. They should be 'very close to the political machine and have an understanding of aims and aspirations'. There was a need to be able to recognise disguised consensus between parties, obviously in a hung authority but also to some extent elsewhere.

In one Labour authority, not typical of those visited, the leader held to a conventional political model of the group as policy originator and the chief executive's job as being a largely administrative one of achieving corporate implementation - 'someone who can push things through'. Other Labour leaders held a very different view. In the words of one council leader, 'negative advice is bad'. Another said that they expected to have an executive who could work on policies.

A minority leader referred appreciatively to a chief executive who had bright ideas about what members should be doing and pushed them along. A senior Labour politician in a county said that in the light of current resource problems they needed 'at least a man who will be able to bring departmental heads together and from their ability achieve one type of decision and action that will benefit the people' of the authority 'as well as possible'. He should 'point the way in which money available can be spent best, help us to see common sense and guide our expenditure'.

Another approach was by politicians who saw the chief executive's job as one of opening up areas of debate and promoting free discussion on policy to evaluate whether they were right or wrong. He should 'be able to analyse problems across the board'. According to one leader, 'He governed in council by his presentation of issues'.

A Labour leader in a hung authority saw it as very important for the chief executive to ensure that 'the (political) administration was problem-solving'. The chief executive 'should be able to define priorities'. A council leader said that the chief executive should be strong enough to go to political masters with changes and prepared to negotiate them.

In a hung authority a leader saw it as necessary for the chief executive not only to coordinate and direct the team of officers but also to sort out disagreements between them and the parties and chairmen in pre-committee meetings, resolving differences and act as arbitrator, referee and policy broker. 'He had to construct a kind of consensus', aiming for 'the middle way'.

In most circumstances very much rests on officer reports. One leader stressed that the chief executive must ensure that fair reports are presented and have 'the ability to assess a subject, evaluate and give his support to a project'.

Some leaders looked to their chief executives as a source of original thinking and innovative ideas. It was thought that they should have the ability to propose action in new areas that the majority group could put before the council - and act as a catalyst for new initiatives - 'green initiatives' were given special mention. Leaders in two authorities stressed in particular that chief executives should let matters flow upwards, feeding ideas to members that came from lower down in the organisation.

A lead on policy review was required, where the chief executive should lead a team in the analysis of most key issues while being 'guardian of the corporate approach' and responsible for presentation.

Coordination and control

Another function repeatedly emphasised was interdepartmental coordination and general control. The chief executive, it was said, should be 'pulling all the strings together, able to over-ride any department and supervise and report on the working of the officer organisation as a whole'. He should achieve 'more centralisation, more tie-ups between departments and a strong commercial approach'. He should have a 'coordinating corporate approach'. More mildly, in a district operating more on traditional lines, he was seen as responsible for 'mediation between officers - possibly in conjunction with the council'.

One leading county politician believed that the chief executive should be 'co-ordinating other officers - and members - by persuasion on the way we should be going'. This was seen to require 'a total understanding of the needs of our authority. He needs to ensure that the authority is working in an efficient manner under the management team and that no individual department was behaving inefficiently'. The monitoring function was referred to specifically by only one member, a Labour council leader.

Management qualities

Some leaders placed heaviest stress on management skills. A Liberal Democrat leader in a hung authority said that the chief executive should be primarily a manager - essentially an executive and not have to defend the current state all the time. A Conservative opposition leader in a fairly large city wanted a chief executive who would 'run the council like a tight ship'; another saw the job as 'to keep the numbers of employees down'.

Amongst the qualities sought by a Labour council leader was skill in modern management techniques, budgetary control, budget-making and allocation of resources.

A leader, it was said, should have the confidence to delegate to the chief executive, expecting him to delegate on down the line. Decisiveness was sought: he should be responsible, not hesitant. It was said that he needed to be 'a very brave man'.

Personnel management

Only one leader specifically referred to personnel work, but he regarded this as very important. In a crisis with the trades unions it was said that the chief executive should be regularly involved and should be looking to the long-term as well as the short-term effects of decisions in this area.

The chief executive 'should have managerial experience and capacity combined with trustworthiness'. He was expected by one leader 'to assess the value of each of the officers and find out what they're good at'. He should be able to pick up the way in which they react to different situations, drive the reticent and hold back those that are over-enthusiastic. He 'should ensure that staff grievances were not allowed to fester'.

Public relations and outside representation

A Conservative party opposition leader in a shire district authority said that he would like chief executives well known as public figures, adding that certainly town clerks were much better known in the community than chief executives. A Labour council leader in a similar authority also saw the external relations role as essential. He should 'be a PR man - a projectionist and good communicator, maintaining very positive relationships with press'.

He should 'develop a wider perspective for his own authority: linking with other tiers, regional, tourism and sports bodies'. He would encourage him to be leader in regional and national issues: liaise with national government and take part in national debates'. It was vital he thought that he should be available for comment and promote the philosophy of the local council - its identity and image. His personal presence at functions was important and an awareness of what people expect of him.

The need for power

There were views that the chief executive should have 'very strong powers', that the council needed 'a good strong chief executive', that he should 'exercise a strong corporate role - a general leadership role', that members would look in the future 'for a strong person', and in another case 'a very strong man, able to put the brakes on'.

As statutory head of paid services it was expected that he would have far more authority and power. The powers assumed to be acquired by chief executives under the new legislation were regarded with displeasure in authorities where there had until recently been a heavy member involvement in the allocation of houses and appointments - 'a real hot potato' as a group secretary called it. In the same authority a Liberal leader felt that the chief executive now exercised too much power. This he believed resulted from 'the calibre of members'.

Other requirements

According to other leaders a chief executive should have 'flair and enthusiasm to implement within the law the policies laid down by the council', 'faith in his ability as a manager', 'keenness', 'efficiency', 'general competence'. He or she should be expected to change the way the council worked, and desirably to have 'personality, charisma', 'imagination and generosity of spirit' and be 'a very high flyer, very strong'.

According to others he must be respected by fellow officers and generally for professional skills. He should set an example of diligence in his work. According to an opposition leader the ethics and morality of the council were ultimately in his hands.

A summary of leading politicians' requirements of a chief executive

Senior councillors' strongest and most general emphases were on the ability of a chief executive to relate well to both members and other officers and to act as link between them and as mediator where desirable. They should contribute to the democratic process by enhancing the effectiveness of both majority and minority groups. They should be good and sympathetic listeners with political awareness and clear exposition of the implications of new developments outside the authority. They should be fountains of policy advice including innovative ideas and alternatives for action, feeding up ideas from other levels within the organisation, promoting policy review and leading the officer team in analysis of issues while being 'guardian of the corporate approach'. They should promote inter-departmental working, exercise management skills and accept delegated power from the council and delegate to others.

The Nature of the Role

Senior politicians tended to use the concept of the private sector managing director as a description or point of comparison for a local government chief executive. A chief executive of a large local authority in which political relationships did not bring the difficulties found in some highly politicised urban boroughs accepted the limitations of the term. He would not expect it to include the reallocation of funds from one use to another for example. He saw the chief officers as the executive directors of the organisation. 'Achieving quality', he said, 'needs someone to deal with them in an executive role: the members cannot do this'. One reason why the analogy breaks down is that the roles of committee chairmen and chief officers of large statutory services are not matched in industry. When a leader in hung authority said that the chief executive had acted as chairman of a board he illustrated the fact that the nature of the board is remote from what can be found in the private sector.

Another leader described the role as one of responsibility for the overall running of the authority, using it in a sense in which it lacked the policy and public service dimensions. Elsewhere chief executives had reservations about the description. One said that it was not a useful concept in terms of pursuing a broad mandate. Another thought that the private sector manager was 'so specialised' and would seek 'to be a dictator'.

There is bound to be an ambivalence in that a critical chief executive, committed to public service and his or her concept of the public good is unlikely to find that the council's services, as seen by the members, altogether coincide with his own ideas. As reported above, it is commonly very open to him to use powers of persuasion but he lacks the criterion of commercial success as the yardstick of achievement which is usually the clinching argument in the private sector. The exception has been in competitive tendering by the authority's own workforce which, as seen above, has been espoused with enthusiasm by many chief executives and members to show how competitive direct services can be.

Policy-making involves many different pay-offs, few of which are of a purely commercial nature - certainly not those of setting the community charge or charges for services in quasi-monopoly areas. The social implications of choice spill over everywhere. It is perhaps insufficient to define the job as making the management decisions of the council unless an area can be defined in which the legitimate concern of the members about the impact on the public does not impinge. That is not to say that extensive delegation of responsibility to officers is not desirable: only that it must be done subject to a very complex range of accountabilities. The term 'general manager' which three of the politicians interviewed preferred has similar limitations as a useful analogy.

One county chief executive felt that his present title was more apt than that of managing director, and another thought that 'the executive bit was really meaningless. All is by management and influence. I can't decide things'. (A district chief executive put first, perhaps cynically, 'the need to manage members').

One council leader saw the job as that of city manager or a chief administrative officer who can work closely with the leader 'to bring down to basic sense what might be thought "highbrow" or professional, so that the members can go forward with the advice of the professional officers: but with a 'logical sense', keeping the management team firmly on the ground'. This implies a 'chairman of the board' role different from that which I understand to be general in the private sector. Certainly business 'chief executives' whose tribulations have been much publicised in the early 1990s provide no useful analogy.

Leaders against the business analogies argued that the conception of managing director in commercial life was based on the 'very narrow remit' of maximum profit' and that it should not be money-orientated. One said that the chief executive's was an efficiency role plus a community-serving role.

How far do Job Descriptions Relate to Realities?

As noted above, 21 per cent of the chief executives in England and Wales and all but three in Scotland informed us that their job descriptions were substantially the same as those in the Bains and Paterson reports (see chapter 1). Sixty-five per cent of those in England and Wales reported that theirs were substantially the same and sixteen 'not very'. The figures do not take into consideration the inclusion of departmental responsibilities described in chapter 7.

There are however some areas of responsibility which large majorities of chief executives regarded as essential to their role and which are not specifically part of the Bains and Paterson models and appear in only a small number of job descriptions - in particular chief officer appointments and performance appraisal; strategy formulation and planning; the positive promotion of collaboration; quality of service and other council objectives; building organisational culture; protecting minority groups' and members' rights; and, to mention only matters which at least three quarters of the respondents believed to be tasks that were essential to the role, dealing with complaints not met at departmental level and promotion of innovation in services, organisation and procedures. There are also some matters the Reports include which a little under three quarters of the respondents considered to be desirable but not essential direct responsibilities: organisation development, manpower management and external relations.

The responses showed that at least five English authorities adopted the Paterson clause which excluded from the chief executive's authority over chief officers matters which involved professional discretion or judgment in preference to the Bains version. Conversely it was found that in at least two Scottish cases the chief executives worked under the Bains version. It would be interesting to investigate whether this resulted in any differences in practice.

In nine cases chief executives reported that they had no job descriptions, including four of them from metropolitan districts. It can be said from personal knowledge that in some cases at least this did not appear to have hampered the effectiveness of the chief executives concerned. In one such instance the office-holder was exceptionally powerful and in others the role had been given a strong interpretation. One chief executive wrote that he could not say anything about his job description since he had never read it since he applied for the job. He added that 'the job was self-explanatory: I head the organisation'. It seems probable that in most cases where the Bains and Paterson texts were used they tell us little about local practice or the concepts of the members about the job. We concentrate in the following paragraphs on responses that are different from those in the national reports since at least they may be assumed to have been carefully considered in the light of real local circumstances.

There are two or three instances where responsibilities are limited to the implementation of services and no reference is made to the policy element. These are however strongly counterbalanced by those in which the authority of the chief executive is far more sweeping. Most of these job definitions are fairly recent, but one that came from an area which was formerly a New Town dates from 1974. Here the head of the services was given the power at any time 'to give instructions to any Head of Department who shall comply with them'. It is his duty to represent the corporate view of the Team to elected members but 'he/she shall not allow advice or information to be given with which he/she is not in agreement'. No provisions of this nature were found in any other job specification. (I have decided with regret that I should not name the authorities involved as two or three of the job descriptions were marked confidential and others came under confidential cover, although I believe that there is no good reason for such confidentiality: rather the opposite if there is to be sufficient appreciation of where responsibility and accountability lie).

The responses from the non-metropolitan and Scottish districts included the most cases where a more sweeping general responsibility had been defined. Thus one respondent was 'to exercise personal responsibility for all officers and activities undertaken and also, amongst other things, 'to maintain morale'; and according to an attached 'key areas' report, 'to take initiatives in respect of the Council's role in the Community' and 'to develop, advise and take initiatives in respect of the Council's corporate plan'. No reference was made in this instance to a management team or even to chief officers. In more than half the cases however chief executives had a duty to work with or through the team or through a team.

In one case the chief executive was 'to direct, co-ordinate and control services within the Borough', and in another to accept overall responsibility for the management of the Council's services and set objectives and targets with each Chief Officer and Divisional Director'. In one job description recommended by a firm of consultants the chief executive 'As leader of the Corporate Management Team' had, amongst other things, 'to develop and implement service business plans for each Director and monitor effectiveness of services in meeting stated objectives'. A Scottish district specified that its chief executive was, 'as sole officer in the authority to create a priority to ensure that any such priority is examined, acted upon and any follow-up action is investigated immediately'.

Performance appraisal of chief officers is part of the job description in several authorities. One chief executive had the responsibility to 'develop Members' involvement in policy making'. In some other cases the job description explicitly demanded that the chief executive should put forward policy, or that the management team should do so under his or her leadership - in one case taking collective responsibility for initiating major policies and strategies and having 'to bring forward 'policy proposals as and when requested by the Council and its Committees and establish monitoring procedures'. In another it was the chief executive's responsibility 'to take initiatives in the Community and in respect of the Council's corporate plan'. Strategic planning is becoming part of the chief executive's specific job responsibilities, as in one case where there was a duty to 'propose and implement a 5 or 10 year strategic plan' for the authority'.

One district had attempted to work for four years without a chief executive and, apparently in reaction to the problems encountered, appointed one who was 'to be responsible for ensuring that the Council makes policy decisions that are both timely and effective'. He was required 'to identify issues pro-actively' and 'advise the Council on how decision-making processes should deal with them'.

In nearly all cases the line of relationship with the council was undefined. Only one reference to party leaders was found in all these documents. Here the chief executive was required, as principal adviser, to give 'assistance and guidance to the leader, the leader of the Labour group, the leader's Co-ordinating Panel and, from time to time the party Groups'.

In summary it can be said that in a few cases the job descriptions go beyond the Bains recommendations in defining a responsibility for the chief executive to take a strong lead in policy-making, give a stronger definition of his authority and require him to set and agree officer objectives and carry out performance appraisal.

All except three of the London borough and three of the metropolitan district job descriptions were the same or substantially the same as that in the Bains Report. They tended to differ from those of smaller authorities in being sensitive to the circumstances of an authority with a wide range of large departments. In only one case was the chief executive given unqualified authority over all directors and their departments, although he was required to take full account of directors' professional expertise and their views. In a description of his job by a chief executive himself he included 'establishing short, medium and long-term corporate policies embracing all local authority services with an implementation programme prioritised, costed and communicated within the organisation'. His role interpretation emphasises direct involvement in the budget process service by service; strategic policy planning across all services and ensuring that their corporate impact on the community is defined, understood and reflects the council's policy commitment. He was also to be concerned with 'the establishment and maintenance of best practice in managerial, financial and personnel terms in all aspects of the Authority's work'.

In one very large city the chief executive was given the opportunity to define the scope of his job after appointment. He obtained the support of the council for a role based on the following functions:

- promoting good effective resource management, involving the development of a framework of control which freed the 'Council's managers' while setting a basis for performance and ensuring the best use of resources
- monitoring and reviewing performance
- co-ordinating council policy and activity
- developing and motivating people
- thinking ahead in the light of expectations of developments over the next five to twenty years ('At all costs no one wants or needs a detailed 'corporate plan' but

rather a concentrated examination of key strategies and future proposals.')
- good communications ('the Chief Executive needs to be in control of this process.')
- regulating the formalities of Democracy ('It is inconceivable that the Chief Executive should not be concerned with the constitutional and legal basis of the whole operation.')
- relating politics to administration - providing 'a bridge between policies formulated by Members and the achievement of those policies by officers. It implies an authority in relation to other chief officers and a need to ensure that the organisation understands and acts upon the policies and values of the Council.'

The London borough job descriptions are in general close to the Bains model, but in two cases the responses raised the question of political relationships. One chief executive wrote that the Bains specification was 'silent on political sensitivity. That is a vital ingredient of the job here'. Another's job description makes it a duty 'to maintain and develop close liaison with the Leader of the Council and committee chairs'. In this case the chief executive was amongst many other things 'to identify and develop, as appropriate, corporate policies, priorities and overall objectives for member consideration, giving a positive direction in line with manifesto commitments to the work of the authority, and to present appropriate solutions for developing a corporate strategy for this authority'.

Finally one London borough chief executive had carried the ideal of transparency between himself and the rest of the organisation a long way by circulating every six months a statement of his aims and revised objectives. The objectives in the latest issue were 76 in number. There is obviously no space to do justice to these here, but at least a few of the nine aims which go beyond Bains may be quoted:

- To lead the Corporate Management Team, setting the tone of the officer management style and creating a work environment which encourages team work and a sense of worth
- To ensure a consistent approach to corporate strategy, the development of objectives and performance measures and the implementation of plans
- To promote a customer-centred approach to the planning of Council services
- To keep under review the organisation and management of the Authority and as head of the paid service to have authority over all other officers whilst respecting the duty of Directors to manage their services and to advise Committees on matters within their professional responsibilities.

One English county had adopted the Paterson rather than the Bains definition of the chief executive's authority. Four of the seven other county job definitions submitted with the questionnaires were within the scope of the Bains prescription. One chief executive has a duty 'to ensure the efficiency and effectiveness of his chief officers' and to promote the implementation of the structure plan for the county. Another in a minute to an appraisal sub-committee set out a role closely related to the Bains model and had in his opinion most of the roles within it defined in the Audit Commission paper.

In the remaining county case a statement of the chief executive's 'principal accountabilities' was sent bearing the imprint of a major consultancy firm. Exceptionally the list leads with accountability for strategy, that is to 'ensure that the Council has the decision-making machinery, the advice and assistance, to identify the County's longer term economic and social needs and to determine a policy and resource strategy which enables the identified needs and statutory obligations to be addressed realistically within available resources'. It follows with the preparation, monitoring and review of all the Council's plans so that they provide a consistent and intelligible framework within which the Council's and other agencies' services may be developed in an integrated way and publicly promoted. Accountability for presenting major policy options, performance indicators and cost consequences and for the preparation and submission of the revenue budget and other responsibilities follow. Of all the documents received this is the closest to prescriptive management theory. In another case the chief executive has a duty 'to ensure the effectiveness of Chief Officers' and also 'to promote the implementation of the structure plan' for the county.

In general it is clear that the Bains and Paterson Reports set a framework which comprehends the main elements in nearly all the job descriptions. They created norms which are perhaps more appreciated at the end of the 1980s than they were when new. In a few cases the authority of the chief executive over other officers was no longer limited by the somewhat vaguely expressed purpose of the efficient management and execution of the Council's functions. Some chief executives wrote in comments to the effect that there was now a positive leadership and management role beyond what was envisaged in Bains. In some cases compulsory competitive tendering and budgeting crises have taken chief executives with the support of the members into internal restructuring within large service departments. Strategy formulation, the promotion of collaboration and quality of service and other council objectives, building organisational culture and performance appraisal have been included.

Respondents' comments showed that their job descriptions simply did not reflect the reality of their position. In some cases important new areas of activity had been developed and retained by chief executives, especially in non-metropolitan district leisure services and, above all economic development (an unrecognised addition reported by eight districts, mostly in Wales and Scotland). Policy initiatives and finding innovative solutions to problems have greatly extended the practical range of the job. Performance review, energy planning and training were amongst various new developments mentioned in the districts. In the counties and regions considerable changes in the job are reported: matters around compulsory tendering and decentralised resource management are prominent. One county chief executive said that his role was very broad, relating to all areas of the council's activities. Another complained that the Bains description did not fully recognise the many day to day issues in which he has to be involved.

The metropolitan districts and London boroughs undoubtedly showed signs of the greatest strain, with chief executives conscious of the irrelevance of the model to current contingencies: political matters and trouble-shooting, the role on policy advice going wider and deeper than what was envisaged in Bains, involvement in major local authority functions, the need to anticipate problems in time for them to be manageable, the race relations area becoming one that needed continual involvement and other issues that cut across all department. Most of all perhaps the Bains and Paterson Reports fail to reflect the implications of the political will - or often the divided will - in many authorities, especially obvious in those that are serving large and socially divided city areas, but also many other, and not least the relatively small rural district with interventionist members of varied style and character.

The Job as Advertised

The unprecedented number of retirements of chief executives in 1989-90 is reflected in the many advertisements and re-advertisements of vacancies in the post. These and the particulars of the post circulated to candidates reflect a new pattern of demand that in some cases goes beyond the standard job descriptions. In certain instances they go beyond the implications of the conclusions on the analysis of tasks and objectives given above. One for example at the end of 1989 looked for a chief executive capable of 'Leading Lambeth Council into the 1990s, overcoming current problems and building on past achievements'. Wigan in the previous September addressed itself to the prospective occupant of the post with the words, 'You will have total responsibility for leading the Council through a challenging period of fundamental change, in the provision and delivery of services. Your priority will be to formulate and implement realistic and cost effective policies, designed to enhance the prosperity of the Borough whilst maintaining our quality of life philosophy.' Suffolk County Council announced that they were looking for 'a Chief Executive to lead the Council through the challenges of the 1990s'. It is remarkable that in these advertisements by authorities so different in character and all with substantial majority groups the chief executive is expected to become the leader of the council, if only leader with a small 'l'. Other councils in which the political leadership wanted a chief executive who would lead them have been described in earlier chapters. It was however commoner in advertisements to look for a chief executive who would 'guide' the council.

In some cases there is an emphasis on working closely with members, as for example in Hyndburn 'in identifying needs and then achieving and managing major change'. In this case the title Chief Executive/Managing Director had been introduced 'to emphasise the qualities required' in such working, although it seems that these have generally been accepted as an essential part of the chief executive role in 1989. Other advertisements refer to the chief executive as manager of the services. Here and there political sensitivity is mentioned. Some counties and Welsh authorities in particular mention the need to relate to local culture: as Cheshire put it, 'the ability to capture the culture and ethos of this distinctive county'.

Councils look repeatedly to the successful candidate for vision, imagination, innovation, commitment, self-confidence, innovation, initiative and drive. They look for candidates to lead responses to the challenges presented by new legislation, the changing role of local authorities, the economic development of the area and the needs of the community. Responsibility for leading or directing, co-ordinating and monitoring their council's activities and use of its resources and for turning policy into action is explicit or implied.

In some cases key tasks are defined such as 'ensuring the integration of competing demands from committees/departments against a framework of corporate objectives and priorities, and the management of chief officers' performance through formal objective-setting and performance appraisal' (North Yorkshire). The following relatively humble demands made in an advertisement by the London Borough of Havering in May

1989 were unusual by then: 'vision and skills to help them to review and improve if appropriate, the working of the committee and departmental structure. As Head of the Chief Officers Team the Chief Executive need not have any particular professional qualification, but financial literacy, legal knowledge and a strong record of service to the public would all be useful'.

In view of the demands made, candidates of quite exceptional quality are sought who can 'demonstrate exceptional leadership and management ability' (Somerset), and who have a 'record of achievement at senior corporate level in changing policy into management action' (Powys). The latter case limited the field by specifying the need to have the qualifications to combine the job with that of treasurer. Limitation to someone who could also be solicitor or head of finance still occurred but was comparatively rare. The requirement of success in senior management in a complex organisation, usually in the public or private sector, was a frequent specification. In many cases the need for local government experience is emphasised, sometimes specifically with regard to working with elected members. Little is said of the personal impact of the job beyond frequently calling it 'demanding'. Cheshire is an exception, stating that the candidate must have the 'physical and emotional resilience and stamina to cope with life at the top'.

Conclusions on Tasks and Objectives

Bringing together the conclusions of research on the chief executives' own views on essential and desirable tasks of chief executives with the leading objectives they perceive to be demanded of them by their members and the functions and qualities sought by senior politicians interviewed, a fairly consistent pattern of the role emerges.

Four areas of achievement predominate:

- leadership, most generally of and through the team of chief officers but also in a number of cases leadership of the elected members themselves in an intimate relationship with the council leader
- securing sound internal and constructive relationships and an effective decision-making process among and between members and officers
- policy advice, policy-making, strategy and the planning of policy implementation, including appraisal of extant policies and their impacts
- coordination, effectiveness, efficiency and restructuring, including organisational development.

These functions inter-relate, each demanding the others. Certain others stand high and are closely related:

- innovative thinking and bringing into the arena of debate ideas from outside the authority and from lower levels among the staff
- promoting agreed values and objectives.

Public relations, other than representation, also stand high amongst elected members' expectations in many authorities. The 'enabling' functions described in the preceding chapter came low in the listing, but the 'management of change' area of activities much higher among both chief executives' objectives and those they credit to their members.

Improving services figures lower, as does meeting needs within the community although this is a primary justification of local government. The tasks and objectives defined above are all arguably means to these goals. A refocusing of ideas on the nature of individual needs and how they can be met seems to be required in the early 1990s.

The Aptitudes for the Job as seen by Chief Executives Themselves

As shown above, the tasks of the chief executive's job are extremely varied and the demands beyond exhaustive definition. The chief executive role is one that in theory needs general competence since it may be called to deal with any unforeseen contingencies that arise - in fact especially with such unforeseen contingencies since job definitions of other officers are likely to cover most of the others. It is also highly dependent on the situation and attitudes of the councils served. These would appear to fall mainly into three classes:

- those with unrealistic or frustrated commitments
- those that are supportive and able to set clear and agreed objectives and give their backing to their chief executives to pursue them, and
- those that need much help in adjusting to a new situation and constraints on action and who may lean heavily on the chief executive's ability to define objectives for them.

Stress was seen to arise especially where managerial needs conflicted with members' demands. There were clashes between short-term demands and achieving long-term results. Reluctance to delegate in some cases frustrated managerial objectives. Nevertheless there was a great deal in common in the demands of the job in different types of authority, although the intensity of those demands varied greatly. The following paragraphs bring together quotations from individual chief executives on what is required to do the job at least adequately.

One requirement was said to be experience in senior management - in particular experience of local government of at least a few years duration (although the case in one authority visited appeared to contradict this). For an outsider to local government it would appear that a very close understanding with a strong political leadership can be a great help in overcoming the complexities and culture shock, although the need to achieve a new set of working relationships and the capacity to master the practical demands of knowledge assimilation are extremely challenging, even when given strong political support. Moreover a movement from one type of political or organisational culture to another can present many unforeseen difficulties. A general requirement is the ability to cope with high levels of uncertainty, both about changes in the political situation and in what the chief executive may be called upon to do.

Secondly there are the skills of leadership which have risen in importance as team management has become central to the job. It is necessary not only to maintain the trust and confidence of leaders and officers but also to draw the best from them. The art of listening to what people have to say was regarded as essential to their success by several chief executives as well as politicians. The chief executive should 'look for a solution out of what others say', 'draw out of members what they want in practice', 'balance things' and quickly 'see the common ground between members and officers'.

On the other hand it is necessary to have 'clear purpose and commitment', 'positive attitudes', 'a vision of where the council is going', 'belief in having a large contribution to make', 'to be able to drive through a new concept' and 'to be assertive'. Thus it is necessary not only 'to get on with people - both members and officers' and 'to work with them', but also 'to persuade' and 'to demonstrate ideas', and sometimes 'to crack heads together' and even, as a new county chief executive said, 'to be a street-fighter'.

The job 'does not need a dominant personality' - in fact there was sharp criticism of the dominance of the council and organisation exercised by predecessor chief executives who were mentioned in the interviews both by chief executives and group leaders. For example, 'Problems arose from professional zeal', 'There was a need *not* "to run a tight house", and 'to stand just criticism - and unjust criticism'. The needs for objectivity and the pursuit of fairness were emphasised as well as acceptance of accountability and 'commitment to public service and local democracy'.

The job at the top is unique in its kind and was said to be 'terribly lonely'. When things get out of control 'there is no-one to whom the chief executive can turn'. Such a situation appeared to be rather unusual as far as can be judged from the research evidence, but it may nevertheless happen where there are political conflicts that cannot be resolved.

There was a need for 'excellent health', 'great mental energy' and, it was very clear from a number of cases, considerable resilience. Two chief executives had in the past experienced serious political harassment in their job. A capacity for detachment was important. One chief executive referred to the desirability of writing reports in a monastic cell.

Chapter 10

THE CHIEF EXECUTIVES: BACKGROUNDS, DEVELOPMENT, CONDITIONS AND SATISFACTION

In mid-1989 504 of the 514 principal local authorities in England, Scotland and Wales employed officers carried the title chief executive or one with equivalent or stronger implications such as town manager (Basildon), general manager (Harlow) and borough director (Rossendale). The number includes all 47 county and Scottish regions and island authorities, all but one of the 31 London boroughs, all but one of the 36 metropolitan districts, 327 of the 333 English and Welsh non-metropolitan districts and 50 of the 53 Scottish Districts. Five hundred of these posts were held by men; four by women. Those held by women were undoubtedly among the most demanding, two of them being in London boroughs and two in metropolitan districts.

The twelve months up to the autumn of 1989 saw a unique turnover in the occupants of the post: 110 new chief executives had been appointed as against an average of 32 in the previous 14 years. A large proportion of the changes in 1988-89 appear to be attributable to early retirements. Some chief executives reported that one of their chief objectives had been to reorganise to ease the task of their successors. However it is clear that the average retirement age had dropped substantially and the custom of retirement at 65 had now commonly gone into abeyance. The rate of turnover appears to have sunk markedly in 1990.

Most of the following figures are drawn from the 263 replies to the research questionnaire. As remarked above, comparisons of the response with data for all British authorities on population size, area, political control and the professional characteristics and length of service in office of chief executives suggest strongly that they are typical in main respects of all British chief executives at the time.

Conservative-controlled authorities are slightly over-represented. Authorities with large populations are represented strongly while those controlled by independents, geographically very large and with small populations are somewhat under-represented. The highest response rates (excluding from the total cases where was no chief executive or comparable post) are from the shire counties (64 per cent) and metropolitan districts (63 per cent); the lowest from the Scottish districts (34 per cent) and the London boroughs (48 per cent).

The youngest respondent was 36 years of age and the oldest 64. Six and a half per cent were under forty, 53 per cent in their forties, 35 per cent in their fifties and five per cent over sixty. The average age was 48.5. The younger chief executives responding to the survey tended to be in the shire and Scottish districts.

Table 10-1: OCCUPANCY OF POSTS BY PROFESSION OR MAIN PREVIOUS OCCUPATION

Background	Eng CCs	Wlsh CCs	LBs	MDs	Eng s NMDs	Wlsh Ds	Scot Rgns	Scot Ds	Scot Is	GB	%
Law	22	5	8	14	123	16	6	22	-	216	42.9
& sec/admin	-	-	1	2	5	5	-	2	-	15	3.0
& mngmnt	1	-	-	-	1	-	-	1	-	3	0.6
Accy/finance	9	1	9	7	48	9	1	4	1	89	17.7
& sec/admin	-	-	1	-	7	1	-	-	-	9	1.8
FRVA only	-	-	-	-	1	-	-	-	-	1	0.2
Sec/admin	-	1	1	-	39	1	1	1	-	44	8.7
Sec/ad&mngmt	-	-	-	-	1	-	-	1	-	2	0.4
Sec/ad&persnnel	-	-	-	-	1	-	-	1	-	2	0.4
Planning	2	-	1	2	20	1	-	1	-	27	5.4
Architecture	-	-	-	-	1	-	-	-	-	1	0.2
Engineering	-	1	2	3	9	1	-	-	1	17	3.4
Eng&plan	-	-	2	-	2	-	-	1	-	5	1.0
Eng&sec/ad	-	-	-	1	-	-	-	-	-	1	0.2
Eng&mangmnt	-	-	-	1	-	-	-	1	-	2	0.4
Economic dvt	-	-	-	-	2	-	-	-	-	2	0.4
Housing	-	-	1	-	1	-	-	1	-	3	0.6
Education	1	-	1	1	-	1	-	1	-	5	1.0
Env health	-	-	-	-	3	-	-	2	-	5	1.0
Eh&sec/ad	-	-	-	-	1	-	-	2	-	3	0.6
Eh&trdgsrvcs	-	-	-	-	1	-	-	-	-	1	0.2
Leisure srvcs	-	-	-	-	-	-	-	1	-	1	0.2
Personnel srvcs	-	-	-	-	2	-	-	-	-	2	0.4
Pers srvs&mnt	-	-	1	-	-	1	-	-	-	2	0.4
Civil service	1	-	-	1	1	-	-	-	-	3	0.6
HM forces	-	-	-	-	1	-	-	-	-	1	0.2
Management	1	-	-	1	3	-	-	2	-	7	1.4
None & non-prof	-	-	3	-	1	-	-	1	1	6	1.2
Unknown	-	-	-	1	12	1	-	6	-	20	4.0
Vacancy	1	-	1	1	7	-	-	-	-	10	2.0
Totals	39	8	32	35	292	37	8	50	3	504	

Sources: *Municipal Yearbook 1990* supplemented from othersources including SOLACE records

When they become chief executives, with or without a service department, officers tend to emphasise that their professions are irrelevant to the role, but they cannot avoid taking with them something of their profession - at least in the eyes of their departmental colleagues. The invasion of what was until fairly recently almost a monopoly of the first officer's post by lawyers and a few accountants and administrators has also heightened interest in the subject. Its extent shows how far the opportunity of aiming at the chief executive's job by other than the 'dominant professions' has been opened up since 1973.

Table 10-1 shows that legal qualifications still predominated, being held by 234 (46.5) of all chief executives compared with 48 per cent of respondents to the questionnaire); followed by 98 accountants (19.5 per cent against 18 per cent among respondents). There were 47 with secretarial, administrative and managerial qualification not combined with any other major professional one (10 per cent as against 15 per cent among respondents). However some other chief executives, especially lawyers and accountants, have one or other of the main secretarial/managerial qualifications by examination, and including these the total rises to 79. There are 32 planners including five who are also engineers, 25 who are engineers (including the five planners), nine environmental health officers, seven with backgrounds in general management, five educationists, four from personnel services, three former housing officers, three former civil servants, two economic development officers and one each with architectural, leisure services and HM forces backgrounds. Six respondents to the questionnaire claimed to have no professional backgrounds.

Lawyers formed the largest group in all types of authority regardless of political control. Labour controlled councils have a greater than average proportion of chief executives with accountancy or financial backgrounds, while chief executives located in authorities controlled by independents are more likely to have administrative or management backgrounds.

Sixty-three per cent of respondents had at least a first degree, most commonly law, followed by history and economics, although the range of subjects studied was in fact very broad, including for example philosophy, social sciences, engineering and the physical sciences. Twenty-one per cent had a higher degree, mostly a master's, when again law was the most frequently reported subject of study. In addition over 30 per cent reported a diploma or other further qualification. Of the 18 per cent without degrees or diplomas most mentioned GCE 'O' or 'A' levels as their most senior educational qualifications. Eighty-three per cent had professional qualifications or memberships of professional bodies.

The percentage of chief executives with at least a first degree is lowest in shire districts (58 per cent) and highest in the Scottish regions and islands (83 per cent). The latter group are by far the most learned: all but one of the six had a higher degree. The chief executives who replied from the shire districts were most likely to name three or more professional qualifications excepting those in London boroughs where one third did so.

Previous Careers

Over half the chief executives had spent their complete careers in local government.

Over three quarters of those in counties had done so. Ten per cent (and as many as one third of those in London) had worked elsewhere in the public sector. About a quarter had private sector experience. Fewer of those in Conservative authorities have worked in the private sector than those in Labour ones (18.6 per cent as against 31.2 per cent) or in those without overall control (33.3 per cent). Chief executives in Scotland were much more likely to have worked in the private sector than those in England and Wales: 69 per cent in Scottish districts and 83 per cent in the regions and islands compared with 14 per cent in the English and Welsh counties. Over three quarters of the county respondents had spent their whole careers in local government. The average age at which respondents had become chief executives was 41.7. The earliest age of appointment to the post was 28 and the latest 59. Nearly three quarters of the respondents had become chief executives before the age of 45. In the shire districts 81 per cent had been appointed as early as this. Nearly 86 per cent had worked for more than two earlier employers; 70 per cent between three and six, and over 15 per cent for more than six. Forty-five (17 per cent) had served as chief executives elsewhere, three of them in two previous authorities.

The respondents had spent an average of seven years and four months as chief executives and about six and three months in their present authorities. About a quarter had been in a chief executive post for over ten years, including one appointed 21 years and nine months before.

County chief executives had served longest in their present posts, averaging over eight years in their present authorities and nine years altogether. The shire district chief executives are the second longest serving, averaging six years and five months in their current posts and seven years and four months in all. The lowest average service was found in the metropolitan districts: an average of four years and eight months. Some metropolitan chief executives however had served elsewhere before they came to their present authorities, bringing the average for total service as chief executive to six years and eight months. Those with legal backgrounds had served longest on average (over nine years), 40 per cent having been in post for more than ten years. They are followed by those with secretarial and administrative qualification (a little over seven years). By contrast those with planning, engineering and technical backgrounds averaged only five and three years respectively, due largely to an acceleration in recruitment from these professions.

The number and diversity of background of chief executives appointed from non-traditional public service backgrounds in the late 1980s would seem to prove that the job is now 'open to all the talents', but it by no means follows that every job is necessarily accessible to them. Some posts are bracketed with departmental responsibilities, councils in such cases being biased towards a new chief executive who can take over the department of a predecessor or one of another retiring chief officer. This may appeal to their sense of economy but may also be linked with the fact that they believe a lawyer or in some cases an accountant will have the best qualifications to fulfil their objectives.

Profession can still be important and the advantages of appointing lawyers and in some cases accountants were stressed by political leaders in the interview programme, but it is quite clear that openness to all professions has greatly increased. Any local government recruit who can develop high managerial ability and the capacity to appreciate and relate well to the local government environment is a possible chief executive. A degree is helpful: a professional qualification very much so, but to the very managerially able and well experienced a degree or postgraduate qualification is not essential.

Certainly long and widely based experience in local government in a senior capacity is likely to be expected. It will help to have experience in working in a large organisation outside local government as well (this is something that seems most likely to be valued in Scotland for some reason), but the primary demand is for ability to relate to the nature of the political situation. This will normally have proved by rising to and filling with distinction a chief officer or deputy role, although now that the post of assistant or in a few instances deputy chief executive has become established, usually linked with good postgraduate qualifications, a new and often shorter ladder has been opened up.

Normally long enough service in a senior officer post is required to prove outstanding ability in management. Obviously a majority group will want someone sympathetic to its objectives, but no case was found where identification with a political party was said to have influenced an appointment.

Who Can Hope to become a Chief Executive?

What factors then increase the probability that an authority will appoint a man or woman to the post of chief executive and what kind of previous experiences help them to cope with the post?

It seems that being aged somewhere between the late thirties and the mid-forties is helpful. Changes in the job and good retirement conditions have resulted in careers ending earlier: very commonly now by sixty years of age. This has tended to bring an upper limit appointment age of at least 55 except where internal candidates with exceptional reputations are concerned. Similarly the expectation of professional qualifications and excellent performance in a senior post have led to appointments of candidates in their thirties being rare, although they appear to be increasing. But there is no good reason to suppose that younger or older candidates cannot in some instances perform at least as well as the middle-aged. This can be said with some confidence after meeting chief executives near and above 60 who have responded with great effectiveness to the demands of the late 1980s. (It is worth remembering that Churchill became prime minister at the age of 65 (and Pitt the Younger at 24)).

Chief executives without local government experience have in some instances adapted well to the singular demands of the job, although there are cases where they certainly have not. On the whole entrants from the civil service appear to have been most successful from outside local government despite great difference in the work involved. A strong sense of public service, ability to relate well to politicians and community cultures and to grasp the complexity of a political, multi-service and multi-professional organisation, with a sure touch in human relations, would seem to be virtually essential.

Should the post be combined with that of head of department?[1]. There can be no doubt that many have filled a departmental role not only to their authority's satisfaction but with distinction. No evidence of significant differences relating to their performance have been found between those with and those without traditional departments. However in known situations departmental responsibilities can be delegated to a deputy or section-heads with confidence in their ability to carry out the work without any but exceptional need for help from above. This is easier for someone who stays with his own department when appointed than someone appointed from elsewhere.

Unfortunately it seems not uncommon in smaller authorities for a chief executive to be appointed from a particular profession as much to meet a head of department vacancy as to fill the post of chief executive. Reforming a weak department is certainly not to be regarded as an 'add-on' job to that of chief executive, although very able officers may overcome the difficulties.

Certainly the leadership of a team of professionals and able managers needs no particular professional qualifications. A new chief executive should know in advance where weaknesses may lie in such a team and that he will have the members' support if necessary if he decides that one or more must be replaced because of poor performance.

The potential requirements of the job may give the impression that it needs a 'universal man - or woman'. Clearly this is not so, and in any case it is impossible. It needs someone who can meet the essentials of the job effectively and - as some recent advertisements have specified - is strong in the ability to delegate while at the same time drawing on talents wherever they exist or can be cultivated within the organisation. Experience belies any belief that good academic qualifications are essential: excellent chief executives have been recruited without degrees, although it seems that in nearly all these cases they have performed very well in professional examinations. The ability to expand interests and understanding well beyond the confines of a professional job is also necessary - and there is convincing evidence that this happens in some cases.

A postgraduate degree usually identifies a hard worker with analytical ability and in some cases with a wide measure of social understanding. Management qualifications may help and give confidence if a candidate is sufficiently cognisant of the implications of serving in a local democracy and is backed by broad qualifications and experience, since, as the above analysis of the role shows, organisational management is only one aspect of the job although a very important one. Most important of all a chief executive must meet the various requirements of elected members in the job as set out in the previous chapter.

The Development of a Chief Executive: 1. Experience on the Job

It seemed important to examine what experiences helped chief executives to acquire mastery of the job, not least as a guide to how other prospective and serving chief executives what might be of help to them. The research questionnaire asked, 'What experiences do you feel have contributed most to your ability to carry out your work as a chief executive?' Most of the 256 chief executives who answered this question referred to work situations of different kinds. Above all they referred to working closely with a particular chief executive - sometimes on specific kinds of problem such as 'complex and sensitive issues', 'in the role of a personal assistant', 'working for and with a respected chief executive', 'working in close support to four chief executives during the later stages of my career for' an authority and 'helping the chief executive of my previous authority to develop the organisation and achieve cultural change'. One said his motivation in applying for the post arose from having seen how effective it could be in practice. On the other hand two chief executives wrote that they had learnt from experience of certain chief executives how not behave in the role.

Another valuable form of experience well represented in the replies was work as members and leaders of teams; for example 'a series of project team tasks'; and 'working as Docklands co-ordinator shaped my career and gave me confidence to proceed... and developed my vision. From then I had the range of skills and the confidence to succeed'. Experiences as a co-ordinator and managerial adviser were also mentioned.

Political experience was repeatedly cited - for example 'learning how to operate in a political environment', ' committee work - understanding the committee process' and 'how to 'handle members', 'working for councils of all political complexions' and 'experience of "difficult" authorities'.

There were relatively few references to working with or acquiring knowledge of people outside the local authority. Those there were included acquiring experience of areas with acute social and economic problems and 'a thorough knowledge of the people of the area and the problems of mid-Wales'. Their fewness may well be explained by the self-contained nature of the management culture and terms of reference which seem to have been typical of the world of many senior officers of local government in the late 1980s as far as can be judged from the information collected about outside relationships, although there are of course not a few exceptions.

Over 70 per cent of respondents gave work experiences of the types described above. The second main group of responses was of types of work, instanced by 49 per cent of the respondents. They included practical management experience, policy-making tasks, strategic planning, 'practical planning and resource allocation', 'planning an Inner-City Programme' and 'early involvement in a public/private sector partnership'.

Ex-treasurers were by far the most likely of all the professionals to give working as a chief officer as their main formative job experience. There were references to specific types of professional work such as advocacy and property development by 23 per cent of the respondents. Another seven per cent referred to professional practice generally.

About 23 per cent referred to experience in particular sectors outside local government, including government agencies, the armed forces, the private sector and a mixture of these. Seven per cent gave activities at national level - most frequently in local authority association and LGTB activities.

Three chief executives said that little or none of their previous background was relevant to the job, and two others referred somewhat irrelevantly to 'native cunning'! But, to summarise, it is clear from the answers to this question that most chief executives feel they have benefited most from working with stimulating chief executives and colleagues, being given challenging tasks, working in multi-disciplinary and sometimes multi-sectoral teams and working with elected members. There seems every reason for developing a 'fast track' for those who want to develop themselves for the job and appear to have the abilities, and so ensuring that they have opportunities of this kind that they might otherwise miss in departmental work. Rapid learning experience could be provided by short periods of planned work experience for chief executives and prospective chief executives in other authorities, or possibly simply by attachments as 'shadows' for at least two or three weeks at a time if this could be arranged, both to similar authorities (which in practice are rarely very similar) and to different types of authority.

The Development of a Chief Executive: 2. Training and other Planned Development

A parallel question asked about training and development experiences. The reference to 'development experiences' opened the door to the inclusion of practical experiences that overlapped with the work experiences described above. Forty per cent of the respondents gave 'on-the job' learning in their replies. In most cases it appeared to be probably incidental work experience entered in the absence of any planned training or development situations. As in the case above, respondents were able to cite more than one experience and the total of all coded responses was 406.

Forty per cent of the responses referred to general training, educational or academic experience, 17 per cent to specific professional qualifications and 55 per cent to particular courses or institutions which provided such courses. Eight per cent reported that they had had no such training or development experiences. Seven (three per cent of the total) gave experiences abroad - mainly as voluntary service officers in developing countries or on study visits arranged to the United States.

The response from shire districts showed a particular lack in training and development activities. Simply taking at random thirteen responses from districts in eight different shire counties representing all the civil service standard regions, seven gave incidental 'on the job' experience, some reflected different attitudes such as 'totally inadequate formal training and development', and some dismissed the value of training and planned development despite having never experienced it.

There is a miscellany of other types of experience - for example as a planner, as a lawyer, DOE inspector training, army and overseas experience, a mixture of Industrial Society, SOLACE and Law Society courses and 'occasional specialist seminars', an in-house management development activity organised through private consultants and an INLOGOV training activity with other chief executives. One wrote 'none' and another 'survival'.

Among the responses from county chief executives, seven gave 'on the job' experience; two training in the forces - the Army and national service in the RAF ('This suggested to me that I was not as thick as I thought I was and might be able to pass the additional GCE '0' level'); six, meetings with other chief executives; three INLOGOV courses, four Henley, one Ashridge and one at the University of Kent; one SOLACE and ACCE conferences; one an in-house course; two professional training; two a variety of courses; and one an RIPA study tour in North America. One wrote 'sadly none' and another 'pass'.

Taking all most-purpose authorities together the largest number is of chief executives who have been on courses at INLOGOV longer than short seminars (nine in all). Only one noted a course at Henley. Two gave the Diploma in Management Studies and one an MSocSc qualification by correspondence. Six refer generally to a variety of courses and seminars and one to a Greater London Council course at Oxford. Also significant are three references to management team building activities and, in London, three GLES activity learning sets and one at Ashridge. There were three references to professional backgrounds alone. Of four who wrote 'none' or gave 'on the job experience', three came from London boroughs. In all, the replies from most-purpose authorities showed a higher rate of qualifications, but one that is perhaps less 'elitist' and more multi-sector than that from the counties.

Responses from Scottish regions and districts show an exceptionally wide diversity. Those from districts showed more appreciation of the value of courses internal to the local authority and other management development courses, with more diversity and proportionately fewer cases of 'on the job' and 'none' responses than those from districts south of the border. One exceptional response came from a singular source - one of the all-purpose Scottish island authorities. Here a graduate in philosophy, politics and economics with an associateship of the Institute of Linguists, 25 years of experience in industry and 19 years working for community health councils gave eleven years working as a councillor in South-East England as invaluable, together with a range of short courses. It is Scottish appointments that seem to be breaking down pre-conceptions more than any others.

What can be concluded? Perhaps nothing without a careful study in depth of the relationship of particular planned training experiences to the job, with careful control of any tentative conclusions against matched chief executives who have little more than 'on-the -job' learning to claim. The INLOGOV, SAUS, Henley and Ashridge courses have clearly been highly valued and found as relevant by those who reported them. So have 'action learning sets' and, much more widely, in-house training courses, usually organised by academic or commercial bodies. We can add to courses mentioned above those on transactional analysis, group behaviour, counselling skills, human development, performance management and review, marketing, people management, the management of change and others, and to the courses in the Cabinet Office Top Management Programme, the British Transport Staff College, Dale Carnegie College, the London Business School and Bristol Polytechnic, and others.

What seems likely is that if local government experiences a new general reorganisation in the 1990s with drastic changes such as would be involved for instance in the institution of all-purpose authorities, or if there is a radical change in executive and management arrangements such as the introduction of accountable political executives, it should be of great help to chief executives to re-orientate to the new challenges through a thorough and well-planned educational and training programme that enables them to seize all the opportunities armed with realistic ideas of how they can be put to best use. At the same time the management of the amalgamation and all the logistical problems involved in a nation-wide reorganisation will need to be studied, as happened quite widely in the run-up to the 1973-75 reorganisations. It would be inexcusable if government and local government bodies failed to do all in their power to provide the means for such programmes to ensure that councillors and officers go into the new era with a thorough understanding of what is involved and how the new opportunities can be wisely exploited.

Departmental Responsibilities and Support for the Role

The response to the questionnaires showed that a large proportion of chief executives still had departments similar in their scope to clerks' departments before 1974. They fulfilled directly many of chief executives' needs. They contained staff who helped them in the central functions of the role. Deputies would undertake large areas of their responsibilities; assistant lawyers and committee clerks would be 'their eyes and ears' in the authority and assist with reports on central issues; and there would normally be other highly experienced staff who could be confidently expected to cover the various tasks which fell to their office. There would be an establishment officer, now replaced by a personnel officer with a much more extensive role, and possibly an estates officer - all concerned with central resources as well as others responsible for members' services and the miscellany of tasks beyond these that did not fall naturally to lawyers and legal assistants. This was still the case for many chief executives at the end of the 1980s, both those with secretarial departments and those who worked in an intimate relationship with the head of such a department.

The Bains Report advocated that the chief executive should be above departmental level and thereby above departmentalism, and that the other chief officers should be his or her deputies. Preferably he or she should stand alone with no more than one or two personal aides. The report added that in some cases this pattern had begun to emerge. How have matters developed subsequently?

Although the words clerk, secretary or director of administration were included in only 50 of the chief executives' titles, chief executives in fact headed over three times as many departments with names which made clear that they covered the traditional clerk's functions. There were 24 clerk's departments, 93 chief executive and secretary's, six secretary's, six administration and 21 others that fell into this group. In comparatively few cases (eleven) did an accountant chief executive head a treasurer's or finance department. These might include also management and corporate or strategic planning services. A few other professionals had carried their departments with them when they became chief executives: two kept environmental health departments, two housing departments, one an engineer's and one a planning department. We found that in only 30 per cent of authorities did chief executives have no departmental staff; in 37 per cent they had from one to 20 non-clerical officers and in 57 per cent over twenty.

Only about 20 per cent of chief executives were free of departments in the Midland, East Anglian and Yorkshire and Humberside regions, but a larger proportion elsewhere. In the southern regions about 32 per cent were 'free'; about 28 per cent in Wales and in the North West around 72 per cent. Further north the proportion increased - to 43 per cent in the Northern Region and 48 per cent in Scotland. Amongst respondents from the Scottish regions and islands only one had a department. The lowest proportions by type of authority were a mongst respondents from the shire districts (25 per cent) and the London boroughs (27 per cent), although in the latter case some of the functions in these departments were not of the traditional kind.

The departments varied greatly in size. Chief executives in independent-controlled authorities were twice as likely as others to have small departments of under 20 non-clerical staff. In a quarter of the cases the departments had over 50 non-clerical members - not necessarily more time-consuming than smaller departments since they are more specialised and likely to have staff equipped to take fuller responsibility.

Much the commonest grouping of functions under the chief executive, whether within departments or through specialist units, was one very familiar in the 1960s as including personnel, management services and occasionally estates or property management, together sometimes with public relations. A hundred and ten chief executives had a direct responsibility for personnel services which was often grouped with a secretarial or a financially based department, or in individual cases with leisure services, management services and public relations. In 59 instances personnel services were provided by a specialist unit. Management services were similar, 49 respondents being responsible through departments and 35 through units; the position was similar for those with estate management responsibilities (23 through departments and ten by way of units). Chief executives relied on these means for maintaining control over human and property resources. Responsibility for public relations was classed as departmental by 22 respondents and administered through the head of a special unit in 25 cases.

Even more central to the priorities indicated by chief executives in their replies to the questionnaire are the policy advice and policy implementation roles. Thirty-six of the respondents had special units reporting to them concerned with policy development and review, including four with corporate planning in their titles and four research and development. This is a small number considering the prominence given to policy advice and planning. They are mainly in the large authorities: in nine of the 34 counties and regions in the response, in two of the 15 London boroughs and in four of the 22 metropolitan districts.

Some had found other means to help them in their policy and planning role. One chief executive who also headed the finance department of a large authority looked to his departmental staff to do most of the corporate planning work including an assistant treasurer who helped him with his corporate responsibilities. Another relied on the planning department where the main resources for the analysis of the problems of the area were concentrated. Another approach much closer to the Bains ideal was to share the responsibility fully with the whole management team and to have, as in new arrangements in one county, a corporate planning and budget work group working to and under the management team. More than one chief executive had faith in the extent to which a talented assistant chief executive could aid him in keeping the complex machinery of inter-departmental working groups and other sources of policy advice effective.

Relatively new areas of personal responsibility included economic development with 23 departmental and 29 special units reporting direct to the chief executive, as well 'arms-length' and mixed sector economic development bodies in which chief executives were involved in some instances); marketing and publicity (13 departmental and two units leaving out those where this is combined with tourism services); employment training (six and three with units); and equal opportunities and race relations (five and ten with units, mostly in the London boroughs and the metropolitan districts). Some chief executives justified giving special attention to particular functions of this kind because of the importance they and their leaders gave it, its political sensitivity, or a personal interest in the matter.

Compulsory competitive tendering introduced a complication in that the duties of 'in-house' contracting bodies should not in principle be under the control of the client department in the traditional sense and their separateness may be emphasised by requiring them to relate directly to the chief executive. These were however named in only 13 cases.

The majority of chief executives had only one or two unit heads reporting to them but in an extreme case eight. A very few of these appeared to form a novel kind of 'strong centre'. An examples is a county chief executive who had reporting to him a unit for executive support, one for corporate support and one for public relations. Another had one for policy planning and one for systems and efficiency. What is comparatively rare is the chief executive detached from any common services and dependent on working through the management team to the extent that Bains envisaged.

Of the 76 chief executives without departments 13 had deputies, including two who had more than one, and 50 had personal assistants (in three cases two or more). Out of the 180 with departments 66 had deputies (nine two or more); and 94 personal assistants (six two or more). Thirty-seven had no personal secretaries, including fifteen who had no department, but 17 had at least two. Eighty-nine had other non-clerical staff: 47 one only and 42 more.

There were significant changes in progress in a number of the authorities visited in the research which suggest a level of innovation which the questionnaire was too early to catch. Two county chief executives had strong and efficient policy units. One district chief executive felt the need to integrate financial and policy planning and was proposing to bring together personnel services and management services with political coordination in a small department. Another was setting up small specialist units headed by an officer of chief officer status responsible for examining and reviewing policies which were was to act as 'service client' in representing the interests of the council. Another was about to ask his council to appoint a high level corporate assistant to help with control and policy. Elsewhere, as indicated above and perhaps most significantly, the management group had been greatly strengthened so that, led by the chief executive, it was able to use its combined resources to set up ad hoc machinery to meet each purpose. A highly able executive officer working to the group, or if justified more than one, could be expected to undertake monitoring of services and report back to the team on the functioning of the machinery and ways in which it might be improved.

Some respondents understood 'specialist units' to include those providing services of the type usually contained in separate departments. We had no way of distinguishing where a department ends and a 'specialist unit' begins. Clearly, as in the case of a London borough where it was reported that there were 300 staff in 'units', the matter needs further investigation. The average of the reported non-clerical staff in chief executives' departments worked out at 46, ranging from 17 in Scottish districts to 165 in London boroughs. The average number in units worked out at 19.5, the largest average being 42 in counties and the lowest in metropolitan districts at 13. London borough and shire district averages were the same at 17 units.

The need felt to strengthen the chief executive's resources was reflected in many advertisements for assistant staff in the early '90s. Thus, to take a somewhat random sample, from 1989 to 1991 Carrick in Cornwall advertised for a 'Central Co-ordination Officer' in the Chief Executive's Office, 'preferably with media experience', 'a self-starter with an enquiring mind' to assist the management team in formulating and achieving the Council's Capital Programme' as well as cost-centre management, improvement of internal and external communications, customer orientation and market research'. Brighton advertised for a 'Head of Corporate Analysis and Development' as part of the intention 'to change the very culture of the organisation'. They needed a 'forward thinker and initiator of change', working closely with the chief executive and the elected members and assisted by a small team. Part of the job was 'the formulation of both short and long-term policy strategies'. Newham advertised for a 'Capital Programme Officer' subordinate to the head of the Central Policy Unit within the chief executive's department. Wolverhampton advertised for an 'Assistant Chief Executive - Development and Employment', to replace an existing officer in the post reporting to the chief executive on the work of 'four substantial teams covering strategic planning, business development, training and employment, inner areas and the voluntary sector. The officer was to have responsibility for a 'Unitary Development Plan' and the 'European dimension' amongst other things. Berkshire advertised for a 'Management Adviser' to assist the chief executive in shaping 'the policy planning and management style of our multi-million pound business'. These examples suggest a tendency towards the rapid widening of chief executive's staff and a quickly widening avenue for promotion to the chief executive's job that by-passes the traditional professional structure.

The growth of personal staff was illustrated by developments in progress in four of the representative sample of 17 authorities visited in the research. Four of the chief executives of these authorities at the time of the visit were about to put forward innovative proposals to their councils that would strength their capacity to lead in matters of policy-making, strategic planning and service evaluation. Five others already had strong although differing arrangements to ensure that these aspects of their role were effective. In those visited to study new approaches on the specific recommendation of members of the advisory panel for the project, two of the chief executives were at the time presenting new proposals and four already possessed special although differing arrangements for the implementation of innovative concepts of their roles. These findings suggest that the surprisingly high degree of conformity to earlier practice was changing rapidly under the influence of the contingencies of the late 1980s, with changes in the role to an extent that were not fully reflected in the evidence from the responses to the questionnaire sent several months earlier.

The Personal Demands of the Job

The estimated working weeks of the 263 chief executives in the survey averaged 52 hours (see table 8-1 p110). More than a quarter said that in a typical week they worked more than 55 hours. Fourteen estimated that they worked a forty hour week or less; 69 worked 60 hours or more. There is considerable variation by type of authority. The shortest average was found in the Scottish districts (48 hours). The average rose to 51 hours in the shire districts, 52 in the counties, 54.5 in the regions and islands, 56 in the metropolitan districts and 57 in the London boroughs. Over a third of metropolitan district chief executives and over half of those in London boroughs worked a week of more than 55 hours, and in both cases over a quarter worked more than 60 hours.

The average working week is about the same for chief executives with departments as for those without. According to an analysis of 106 cases however the average number of hours worked increases with the number of staff reporting directly to the chief executive. Chief executives with more than ten years' experience work two hours below average as against those in their first year who work about an hour more. The longest working chief executives on average are those in the Labour controlled outer London boroughs; the shortest in the small Scottish districts.

Interviews in authorities indicated to an extent that the questionnaire survey did not that heading a department can detract seriously from the time that a chief executive can give to the chief executive job, especially in a large authority or, as shown in a previous chapter, where in a small authority a new chief executive had a difficult task in reforming a department where senior staff were reluctant to adapt to new approaches.

The answers on evening meetings suggest that on average chief executives attend five evening council and committee meetings a month in London boroughs as against hardly any in the counties and 0.5 in the regions. Those serving Conservative-controlled authorities had on average more evening council meetings than those in Labour ones. However, regarding other types of evening meetings connected with their work the position is reversed: 36 per cent serving Labour controlled councils attend more than five such meetings a month as against 27 per cent in Conservative-led authorities. Taking these together with council and committee meetings the average for London borough chief executives is over twelve evening meetings a month, for metropolitan and shire district eight and for counties and Scottish regions and islands six.

A district chief executive who was interviewed contrasted the situation in a previous highly political authority he had served not far from his present one where he worked about 48 hours a week. In the previous case most committees went on till midnight. Now he had no evening meetings and 'it was a great relief'. He was able to let his deputy attend service committees other than one in which he had a special interest. Another chief executive in a fairly large Scottish district authority that had evening meetings enjoyed a great reduction in the drain on his energies when members accepted that a competent solicitor or committee clerk could handle a meeting competently in his place. He commented that he was 'very fortunate in having an understanding wife'.

Fifty-three per cent of all chief executives who replied to the survey said that they often worked at home in the evenings and 45 per cent said that they did so occasionally. Numbers working at weekends were slightly lower than this. The groups most likely to work at home were those in the counties and still more so in the regions and islands. All in both groups worked at home in the evenings and 67 and 83 per cent respectively did so often. Seventy-seven per cent of county chief executives often worked at weekends and 83 per cent in the regions and islands. London borough and metropolitan district chief executives were also more prone to work at home regularly than not: 60 and 62 per cent regularly in the evenings and 67 and 52 per cent at weekends.

The time involvement in metropolitan districts in 'unsocial hours' is extraordinary, and even more so that in London boroughs. This was predictable from the political, functional and organisational complexity of their jobs. Size of authority does not emerge as a significant factor in this matter.

A new chief executive full of bounce and with good political support can evidently thrive on a twelve hour day while also working weekends, as in one case visited. Others where the politics of the job are difficult can be under strains that demand exceptional qualities. These may be 'no-win' situations where the need to take a strong role is resented politically and sometimes also by officer colleagues. It was said to be extremely stressful when a leader was told by his colleagues (quite unjustly) that he could not control his chief executive and when there is no way of making what are seen as 'proper decisions' about priorities; or in some situations when there is no alternative but for the officers to take a strong line which is frustrating to the politicians. Three cases of this kind were found in the seventeen authorities visited in the representative sample.

One chief executive who was fortunate in having a good corporate team of colleagues emphasised the need to be able 'to switch off' from it all. Another, less fortunate in officer support, said 'so often there's nowhere I can turn'. Another, new to the job and self-confident about it, commented that the job was vulnerable. It could be 'terribly lonely'. These are exceptional cases. Two chief executives in the structured sample had moved from authorities which were politically difficult in the ways described to ones where they enjoyed strong leader support and the trend was towards consensual decision-making, and in both cases they had found it a great release. The job was still very intense and one in which they could hardly ever afford to relax. Yet it could have great satisfactions.

Conditions of Employment

Most salaries advertised in the press during the period of the research were based on the Joint Negotiating Committee (JNC) agreed scales, but some authorities had broken away from the system in order to offer stronger incentives - especially in the south where costs of living and general levels of salary were particularly high. The basic salary rates for posts advertised in the press during the period of the study ranged from around £20,000 to £40,000 in smaller and average size districts, but they rose sharply with size of population to, for example, £55,000 in Cheltenham and over £60,000 in Bristol - well above the maximum on the JNC scale. The scale set for county, London borough and metropolitan district chief executives was only marginally higher. The smallest county offered around £45,000 and medium-sized counties from about £50,000 to £70,000. Most London Borough appointments advertised ranged from about £40,000 basic at the bottom of a short annual scale to £50,000 basic. Hammersmith and Fulham however in late 1990 offered a figure of around £78,000 (negotiable) plus a car and benefits package. Metropolitan districts paid from around £40,000 to £65,000 according to the evidence in 1990 but in 1991 Liverpool was reported to be paying well over £80.000 in practice. The City of London and one other authority were understood to be paying over £100,000.

Thirty per cent (78) of the respondents to the questionnaire had conditions differing from those set by the JNC, and 58 were said to relate to salary arrangements. The most frequent differences were local pay scales (17). These included salary plussages of ten per cent (3) and 20 per cent (in the latter case 'to compensate for fixed time contracts or 'special responsibilities') (2), 'market salary linked to private sector chief executives' remuneration' (the INBUCON scale was mentioned) (3), special MBBC (LACSAB/MSU) scale) (1), performance related increments (6), 'annual renegotiation understood to be currently available only in the South-East of England' (2), higher salary population rating (4) and overtime conditions (1). Two referred to 'local conditions with sacrifice of appeal rights', presumably implying higher salaries.

Just over a quarter of the 263 chief executives who returned the questionnaire reported that they were subject to performance appraisal, and a further 20 per cent said that they had discussed the possibility. Sixteen per cent said that their pay was performance related and an additional 16 per cent had discussed the possibility. Another development in the 1980s was a sudden increase in the use of short term contracts.

Thirty respondents (about 11 per cent) were on such contracts and five per cent reported that they had been considered. Nearly a third (32 per cent) of those appointed in 1988-89 had such conditions as against six per cent in 1986-88. The proportion in 1986-88 had actually dropped below the level before 1984.

Some authorities were offering successful applicants a choice between a regular contract and a special one for several years, the salary in the latter case being negotiable. It seems clear that moves towards a short-term contract are not unusually led by officers rather than members. Some of the more experienced chief executives had chosen to move onto a new short-term set of conditions, probably associated with higher salary awards and in some cases preliminary to retirement. A London chief executive on indefinite tenure said in an interview that short-term contracts seemed to him a reasonable way forward. A county clerk believed that a four year contract was too short for maximum achievement. A district chief executive who was not on a limited contract but very concerned about achieving results for the authority through his personal performance said that he could not see the difference in practice: he would go if he was not seeing eye-to-eye with the members. He could not see that contracts were relevant to the relationship. 'There are occasions when you need to stand up, and then you need to feel free to do so'.

The point was not made in interviews but, just as in the case of the run-up period to elections, there can be adverse effects on the ability of elected members to deal firmly with matters that may cause short-term criticism, so that the approach of the end of a term of office may cause real difficulties in some cases. Some chief executives may become weaker than normal in some instances and stronger in others. The subject deserves serious study.

Performance appraisal was not strongly related to length of service, being commonest among those appointed between 1984 and 1986, 34 per cent of whom had accepted it against an average for all cases of 26 per cent. Performance related pay also showed an indefinite pattern, those appointed recently being slightly less likely to possess it than the overall average of 16 per cent. It was commonest among those appointed between 1986 and 1988, 22 per cent of whom enjoyed it.

The attractions of moving to an agreement that brings better remuneration has clearly paid a significant part in encouraging these arrangements, but there does not appear to be a close relationship between short term contracts and performance-related pay. Chief executives with accountancy backgrounds were over twice as likely to be on short term contracts as lawyers or administrators, but they were less likely to be on performance-related pay than the latter and only slightly more so than the lawyers. The incidence of performance appraisal shows hardly any differences between these groups although it is much more likely in the case of those with professional planning and technical backgrounds.

Behind these changes, which are particularly characteristic of the south east of England, lie the influence of a more competitive labour market and a tendency to break nationally negotiated norms, both characteristic of the 'Thatcher decade'.

'Plussages' of different kinds raised incomes above the salaries quoted. Fees as electoral registration officer and returning officer for local elections and for clerkships to police authorities and outside posts undertaken with the agreement of the employing authority could also raise some chief executives' levels of income considerably.

Other non-salary benefits detailed were a free car (15), higher car allowance (1), car-lease and loan schemes (12), lump-sum travel allowance and subsistence (3), periodical medical check-ups (14), free private health insurance schemes (5), hospitality allowances (3) and professional subscriptions (4).

In addition there were single references to an 'effective no-strike clause requiring maintenance of service at all time' and 'renewal of contract subject to a two-thirds majority' on the council, a private sector directorship, and special provisions in case of redundancy, unfair dismissal and early retirement.

The Satisfactions of the Job

The material rewards of the job may be important to some but seemed much less so with others. Some found great satisfaction in serving local communities, public purposes and, as some put it, democracy. The post leads to service with lieutenancies, police authorities, metropolitan joint agencies and regional and national bodies and in many other ways outside itself which can be of great interest and satisfaction. One chief executive of a county authority however found his job gave him much less satisfaction than one in a basic level authority where he knew every service well and everything he did seemed relevant. A similar feeling may lie behind the fact that many chief executives for county and regional councils declared themselves in favour of all-purpose authorities.

Being able to run an organisation from the top instead of a subordinate part of a bureaucracy can be in itself be a great source of satisfaction, be it simply the sense of 'being at the top' (frankly expressed by some in the questionnaires), or the opportunity to fulfil social and other objectives in a way that was not possible from a subordinate position. In not a few cases political leaders are happy to see an officer take up the ball and run with new policies which they feel can only bring credit to the authority. Successful innovation can carry great rewards in itself. One county clerk commented that he found the job 'wholly-satisfying. One lives with conflicts and ambiguities, but that is all right as long as you understand them.'

Note

1. Over 40 per cent of the respondents said that they retained direct responsibility for legal services, 91 per cent for administrative or secretarial services, 61 per cent for committee or legal services, 17 per cent for central or common services and 29 per cent for parliamentary matters, elections and registration. These terms overlap in meaning and indicate that in nearly all these cases the arrangements are similar to those of a clerk's department before the Bains Report.

Chapter 11

THE CHIEF EXECUTIVE IN NORTHERN IRELAND

Note

I am deeply indebted to SOLACE (Northern Ireland branch) for the information they gave me in preparing this chapter. But the responsibility for the text falls on me alone and that they must not be blamed for its content or imperfections.

Background

Northern Ireland has a population of roughly the same size as Hampshire. Its area is roughly equivalent to that of Cornwall, Devon and Somerset combined. Its history has been traumatic in the last few decades, and not least in the 170s and 1980s. The role of its clerks and chief executives has been conditioned by the fragmentation of its politics and the violent opposition of extreme 'loyalist' and 'republican' groups who have rejected the politics of reconciliation. Since 1972 the country has been under 'direct rule' from London through the Secretary of State for Northern Ireland and the Northern Ireland Office (Stormont).

A reorganisation of local government in 1973 followed on the heels of the failure of attempts at representative democracy. A British style system of six county, two county borough and 67 borough and district councils was replaced by a division of the responsibility for services between Stormont, five area boards for health and personal social services, four for education and libraries and 26 district councils. Each board includes a minority of local authority representatives, the majority being made up of nominees appointed by government.

Most infrastructural services, including planning, roads, street lighting, water and sewerage, are the direct responsibility of the Department of the Environment, but the law provides that draft programmes for the services must be presented to the district councils for consultation. Housing is the responsibility of the Northern Ireland Housing Executive, an appointed board which is also required to consult districts on its proposals. This leaves the district councils with direct responsibilities for environmental health, waste disposal, cleansing and sanitation, arts and museums, safety, pollution control, cemeteries and crematoria, parks and countryside, markets, abattoirs, building control, community services, leisure services, tourism and recreation, and otherwise what local authorities have found space to develop on their own initiative within their legal competences. Two authorities are responsible for local airports. One important area of growth has been economic development, a cross-party matter supported by members generally and usually exercised through special agencies.

Authorities' effectiveness has to a great extent been dependent on their ability to develop an 'enabling' role in the community, drawing the necessary support for development from other agencies.

The districts, apart from the City of Belfast with a population a little larger than that of Leicester, range from about 17,400 to 95,700 inhabitants. Two-thirds of their authorities serve populations of below 60,000.

The appointment of district chief executives is monitored by a government appointed staff commission. A local authority is required to prepare a short-list of selected candidates for the post with the Commission, which has the power to remove names from consideration. The Commission can raise objections and take action if the proper procedures are not followed. Under the Fair Employment Act penalties of up to £30,000 may be imposed if there is discrimination on grounds of religious or political discrimination. Short-lists are prepared by a trawl for suitable candidates in accordance with conditions laid down by the Commission. Appointments tend to be internal to local government but lately more posts are being advertised.

A Northern Ireland Act of 1972 protects chief executives from suspension, dismissal, changes in conditions of service and salary etc by giving force to decisions of a council on these matters only after approval by the Department of the Environment: a provision that is said to be both a help and a hindrance but, in present circumstances, more of a help.

Ten of the principal chief officers of the councils carried the title of clerk and fifteen that of clerk and chief executive. Here they will all be called chief executives since the difference in their titles bears little relevance to the role in practice, even less so than in Great Britain because of the circumstances in which they work. Out of the 26 chief executives the Municipal Yearbook shows five to be chartered secretaries and five chartered accountants. There were also in 1988 one qualified in environmental health and an engineer with a diploma in public administration. At the beginning of 1990 roughly 40 per cent of the 26 chief executives were among those originally appointed to the new authorities in 1973, showing a remarkable lack of turnover in seventeen years in demanding circumstances. But by 1991 the figure was down to 15 per cent.

The committee structure is similar to the English. In one case there was a committee for general purposes and finance supplemented by a policy abd resources task group, and planning, amenities, development, technical services committes with a number of sub-committees dealing with specific matters such as arts and culture. For corporate working at officer level there was a management team made up of the chief executive and chief officers, including the personnel officer. It is generally the rule to have a chief administrative officer, leaving the chief executive free for his leadership role.

The Politicians and the Chief Executive

The appearance on councils of the political wing of Sinn Fein, a party supporting the IRA, challenged traditional relationships and was accompanied by abuse of standing orders and the calling of the police in some cases. In addition Unionists used local government to oppose the Anglo-Irish Agreement and in some cases boycotted council. A substantive case for statutory protection of chief executives became obvious - not least to preserve a base for the continuation of the public services.

Especially since 1985 chief executives have been exposed to great pressures by those seeking to move them away from an apolitical and public service role towards a political one. It is reported that many councillors have lacked an understanding of the members' role in recent years and shown an increased insistence on being involved in management, accompanied by a lack of respect for standards that had previously been expected of public representatives. A distrust of officers had developed in some cases that showed itself in an inquisitorial style of display at meetings, motivated probably by the seeking of personal publicity. Nevertheless members would give healthy consideration to experienced and well prepared advice. Outside meetings relationships were reasonably good. Those with party leaders were reasonable, although their standing had quite changed since the early 1970s.

One party majorities existed on no more than one or two councils. The single tranferable vote system very accurately reflects the public choice but that choice is split in nearly all cases between four or five parties, a range which reflects factionalism and fundamentalism that is resistant to coalition or consensus except on the broad basis of 'nationalist' or 'unionist'. The role of council leader has therefore failed to emerge, which has deprived chief executives of the opportunity to work with a political administration or leadership which can make a strong policy contribution and deliver political support.

The elected members are largely dependent on what officers put before them. Matters that would normally in Britain go to a leader or chairman have to be resolved by officers. The ensuing officer leadership has proved itself able to make things happen. Members see officers as making the main decisions and have generally accepted officers' advice. In respect of the infrastructural services they accept that their role is to be consulted and to influence officer decisions. The best the chief executive can do in many cases to gain the benefits of an enabling authority is to present benefits and possibilities which the council can accept or reject. Those presented are in general based on the best interpetation of what the authority and government should be providing, and in the circumstances it is appropriate that the possibilities are fully examined by public representatives.

Due partly to a lack of understanding of policy matters members have shown much greater concern about being involved in management detail than in the past, and some seek to lay down the rule on staff and other administrative matters. They have in general been reluctant to delegate to officers.

External Relationships

Chief executives' relationships in the local community were said to be generally very good. In most instances the chief executive was looked upon as a key figure in any initiatives or undertakings that were about to be launched. Given the relative smallness of Northern Ireland districts the chief executive is well placed to develop outside relationships throughout the community.

Relationships between chief executives and central government are close and reported to be very good. It was said that 'there was a mutual respect amongst those in the public service which had probably arisen because of the strong common bond that had arisen out of the trauma of the past years'.

The Demands, Skills and Satisfactions of the Job

The most important objectives members expected of chief executives were reported to be reliability on procedural matters, sound advice in all matters and the initiation and development of policy. A chief executive interviewed was more outwardly orientated than was often the case in Britain: not only did he see one of his most important objectives as the management of the organisation but also included amongst them addressing the problem of economic development and raising the quality of life in the area.

The skills seen as necessary for a chief executive in Northern Ireland were similar to those often quoted in Britain, but there were more of them than any British chief executive cited and some at least seemed necessary to a greater degree: diplomacy, sensitivity, lateral thinking, 'what management experience can be mustered', vision and readiness to take up a leadership role in various circumstances and, to underwrite these, courage and integrity. Other needs for the job were said to be inexhaustible patience, some maturity, ability to see ahead, flexibility along with a comprehensive understanding of modern management methods, commitment and being good at human relationships, especially with staff, and ability to cultivate loyalty to and from them.

A chief executive said, 'You live with the job all the time. I have no private life outside the job and am continually trying to rethink the situation. There are some seductive merits in it, but also, at the end of the day, responsibility will be laid at the door of the chief executive'. The real satisfaction in the job, he said, was 'making good things happen'.

PART C

THE FUTURE OF THE ROLE OF CHIEF EXECUTIVE

Chapter 12

THE CRYSTAL BALL

As the Audit Commission has put it in its Management Paper No 2 of 1989, chief executives are agents of change. At the heart of their job lies advising on the response to unpredicted contingencies of the present and the uncertainties in the future. This is true of all chief officers, but others have defined fields whereas the chief executive's field of concern, as we have argued above, is limitless.

At the time of writing the changes arising from demands outside local authorities have accelerated rapidly and that acceleration appears likely to continue. In the first two years of the 1990s there has been a sudden shift in the values professed by the new government leadership of 1990 from Thatcherism towards collegialism and increased sensitivity to social values. The concept of the social market has entered into Conservative thinking, although at the time of writing its implications seem little understood or acted upon. A major review of local government finance, functions and structure has been launched by the Secretary of State for the Environment with the intention of including a commitment to a comprehensive reform of local government in the pending election manifesto. A new fiscal system is being introduced which allows local authorities to levy only 14 per cent of their revenue locally and deprives them of control over vital parts of the secondary and further education systems. The state of the national economy is such that continuing pressure on local government expenditure seems set to continue, including local tax capping. The future may well lie in a new 'social conservatism' or the takeover of power by the Labour Party with or without dependence on other parties now in opposition.

Whatever may happen a new social concern seems likely to bring a new emphasis on action to overcome social squalor and unacceptable levels of disadvantagement, with or without significant central government support. On the other hand severe problems with the national economy may result in harsher control of local authority finance than is consistent with social objectives, whatever party or parties are in power. Such developments will place a great responsibility on chief executives in guiding their authorities to cope with a new set of contingencies.

The most confident prediction that can be made about the prospect for local government in the 1990s, but also the most trite, is that it will be full of uncertainty; and that demands for change may be of a different and unexpected nature. More specific forecasts are given below, both from chief executives point of view and from that of the author. Events may well disprove these forecasts before this book is published, as they may or may not disprove the views of chief executives on the future of their role expressed at the time of the survey in 1989. The title of chief executive may vanish as a result of a new approach to local authority management. Whatever happens, the role of local authorities' head officers, whatever they may be called, will be central to the adaptation to change and therefore to the future of local government.

This last part of the book considers possibilities of structural change in the light of comparisons with other local government systems and business analogies. Foreign models are reviewed, and the effects that the introduction of similar arrangements in the United Kingdom might have on the definition of the role of their first ranking officers. Business analogies are taken into consideration and the general implications of the discussion, including the means which may be needed to develop and attract executives able to fulfil as well as possible the demands of a role which may be expected to be at least as demanding as in the past.

But first the perceptions of the role's future by chief executives themselves are considered, as expressed in their responses to the research questionnaire and what those interviewed in local authorities - leading local politicians as well as chief executives - wanted or expected to happen to local government structure.

Chief Executives' Concepts of the Future of the Role

The research showed that British chief executives' concepts of their role had in many cases been reconceived and strengthened in the late 1980s. A new sense of mission was abroad in response to the policies of the third Thatcher administration. The pressures of the period had undermined traditional ideas on local government's role: the emphasis had moved from the maintenance and delivery of services to response to legislative challenges.

Repeated intervention by central government had stimulated a wave of innovation, bringing a need for organisational restructuring and the remotivation of officers and elected members. Financial crises arising from the impact of central government's administration of local government finance accentuated the case for reshaping priorities and finding new means to deliver them within the new legal framework. Elected members, although often antagonistic to central policies which they saw as downgrading local government's role, were ready and in some cases eager to support new approaches which would give their councils a reconceived mission. In many cases they looked to the chief executive to define such a mission.

Concepts of the new role included an increased and more direct responsiveness to local public demand, analogous to that of a private firm to the market. The language used by chief executives in their responses to the research questionnaire included phrases such as customer or consumer consciousness and service quality, conveying a new emphasis on fitting provision to the choice of individual members of the public. It reflected the idea of an adaptive, competitive market-orientated local authority, as put forward in the publications of the Audit Commission, the Local Government Training Board, INLOGOV and others. The new message provided a means for inspiring and remotivating staff; for moving from bureaucratic behaviour to behaviour based on an ideal of service to individuals of a quality better than the private sector could provide within the financial resources available.

The new demands on local authorities reinforced the case for a strong role at the centre of the authority to achieve such a response and for chief executives to take the lead in redesigning structures, instituting new procedures and promoting commitment to service delivery with increased efficiency and effectiveness throughout the organisation. The restructuring provided the opportunity to break through traditional practice and to introduce innovative approaches designed to achieve the new ends.

The response of individual local authorities varied greatly according to their situation and their political and administrative cultures and practices; but the evidence collected in the questionnaires and in the interviews confirms this general picture. In some cases there was a breaking of the ice. In others the changes brought no more than a mild thaw. Much depended on the values and concepts of chief executives; how they shaped their objectives; and the level of support they found in the political leadership of their authorities.

The chief executives' replies tell more about the past than the future. Most of those answering however expected to be involved in the making of the future: their views and attitudes will play a major part in creating it. The replies show also the opinions of those who were soon to retire, based on long experience of the job's fortunes against a changing reality.

Chief executives are of course by no means the only players on the stage and their views are inevitably moulded to a large extent by their expectations of what might happen in the central and local political arenas. They reflect back an image of their present beliefs and states of mind as people whose work is or should be constantly orientated towards the future. They help to widen the debate and set the picture for discussion of the role's future. Readers during the 1990s may find it instructive to learn how far the often conflicting assumptions made by them about the future are being borne out by later experience.

The responses reflected especially the experience of the previous few years and of a present in which local government was undergoing the early effects of the 1989 Local Government and Housing Bill as a climax to successive measures designed to effect drastic and lasting change. In most cases the chief executives identify closely with the councils they serve in this matter. It is often difficult to distinguish whether they are writing of the future of their role or that of their employing authorities, or indeed of the future of local government in Britain as a whole. What follows is a synopsis of over 200 views and their variety. Where the number of responses is quoted it does not of course imply that other chief executives who replied would have agreed or disagreed with the predictions. Respondents may be assumed to have usually recorded those matters foremost in their minds rather than attempted to be comprehensive. One or two commented that a real answer would need a book.

The impact of new legislation and government constraints. Fifty chief executives saw a primary influence on the future of the role to lie in the impact of central government policy, legislation or control, including the results of the next general election. One county chief executive saw a change of government as the route to public sector growth and therefore to higher expectations of local government; others seemed happy in the expectation that there would not be such a change. Since the head of paid staff has been given statutory recognition it was thought that his role might be extended.

The continuation of current legislative trends is likely for some to lead to the building up of the 'centre' in the local authority, to identification with central government purposes, to becoming 'more removed from working as part of a local team to that of manager with increasing responsibility to a centralist system of government', if not to becoming the direct agent of central government and being 'bogged down in rules and regulations from central government while coping with the frustration of councillors'.

Disquiet is expressed about the statutory monitoring role as it was understood in the summer of 1989. At the extreme it was thought it could alienate the chief executive from his members and diminish his influence. Other reactions connected with central government policy include expectations of radical structural change within authorities and without, a shrinking of authorities, the increased riskiness of the role, a period of 'stop-start policies' and a more positive role in some areas, depending on 'the reality with the politicians'.

The members of the council and the chief executive. The commonest topic after developments in competition and 'enabling' was relationships with elected members. These fell into two main groups. The largest was characteristic of the situation in the more politicised authorities, and also in authorities where control by party institutions was expected to increase - perhaps crossing a threshold where, in the words of a Scottish region chief executive, 'the role will be virtually totally changed'. The second group was of those where inter-group politics was at a low level or virtually non-existent.

Most responses on member-chief executive relations were concerned with the development of the party political local authority. The usual expectation was of highly politicised local authorities, the relationship with the leaders being the critical factor. Several chief executives expected that there would be increasingly strong identification of the chief executive with the controlling group's policy. Their replies included such statements as 'politicisation will not go away', 'the aims and objectives of elected members will drive them ever closer to the management of local government' and 'the reality of the Political Executive has to be recognised'. One half of the 66 assumed a situation in which political power would be strong; twelve on the other hand expected a party organisation that was weak or non-existent. Where party political control was strong the future of the chief executive's role was commonly expected to lie in working closely with the political leadership, and even in one case accepting identification with its policies and interests.

Some responses envisaged political control by a small board, with or without a larger assembly of elected members. According to one district chief executive, 'The only local authorities that will survive are those that are effectively led. Effective member leadership can only come from a small group which is either regularly mandated via the party group system or given considerable freedom - the chief executive needs to become the managing director of an executive group of directors'. Distinct from these is the view that there will in the future be fewer elected members but these will be 'paid and virtually full-time', 'acting as though they were ministers' (seemingly without an elected council), with the chief executive serving as adviser'.

The responses in general however go no further than to foresee a strong and recognised relationship between the political leadership and a chief executive with a status similar to that at present. It is generally assumed that the post of chief executive will remain whether or not there is strong party leadership or structural change. As certain respondents from districts in England and Wales put it, 'success in promoting partnership with leading members on a personal level will determine the role in individual authorities'; and 'real scope will depend on the reality with politicians: anything more fundamental is only likely to come via legislation on local government reform'.

Party politicisation is seen as a positive and challenging development for the role as 'originator and developer of policies, plans and programmes', growing 'in tandem with the role of elected members, with increased delegation' (from a Scottish islands authority). Such views appear to be based on recent experiences. In some cases however sharp changes are expected in the future. A Scottish region chief executive sees no basic change in the role until his council becomes organised on a political basis 'when it will be virtually totally changed'. It could be, as one respondent puts it, that 'there will be less direct member control in day to day functions' although the chief executive is closely aligned with the controlling party group'. Some respondents however expect more, not less, involvement in day to day decisions than the business analogy might suggest. Vulnerability to political identification is forecast with consequent insecurity.

The future, it was suggested, lies 'in working with paid political appointees' and, in another response, 'under a Labour council increasingly with political appointees'. There is concern about the difficulties of the role where there are full-time politically motivated leaders and chairpersons. One view is that 'more positive political involvement/ commitment will develop' and that the job will mean 'working with parties to achieve political objectives'. An opinion from a 'hung' county was that, 'Chief Executives, willingly or unwillingly', will become 'closely involved with the political process of [politicians'] demands'.

Where strong party control is not expected, responses suggested that the chief executive would take responsibility for contracting arrangements, which would become the central activity of the council. If Conservative control continues this would, in the opinion of some, lead to the chief executive operating in a commercial environment - and even to responsibility and accountability centring on him or her 'to the exclusion of the local democratic process'.

One chief executive believed that the increased responsibilities of the role arising from new legislation would require 'more sensitivity to elected members' and management of 'a potential conflict of interest between commercial operations and democracy'. A major part of the chief executive's role would be 'easing the transition to the changed role of councillors'. Others believed the members 'will be satisfied to simply judge performance on output' and that there will be more executive management and less member involvement in management or, as two county chief executives put it more specifically, members 'will need help in accepting a new role', 'with more discussion with them and more preparation and support'; and, from a district, that the chief executive will need to work with elected members in better defining the relationship between them and paid officials 'in the inexorable move towards local government rather than local administration'.

New commercial procedures are seen as reducing the role of the elected member to judging performance or, at the extreme, playing the role of shareholders with little to do in practice. Analogies are made with the role of the county and city manager in the Republic of Ireland or in the United States described below.

A county chief executive saw the need for careful monitoring of officer/councillor relations in the light of the new legislation. A respondent from a district saw himself preparing members for their changing role as delegation increases and members become less involved. Another from a county with a 'hung' Council, using another business analogy, judged that 'on balance' there will be 'a shift towards members playing a reduced role closer to that of shareholders - but shareholders with some real influence'. But will members be content to be at arms-length from operations where they directly affect their constituents?. One district chief executive questions whether 'local government will not lose abler members and become too complex & insufficiently rewarding for real strategic control by members, with the need for the chief executive 'to more openly fill this vacuum than in the past'.

There are much more positive responses, such as that from a London borough council which wants 'a more public relations conscious "political" figure to give the administration a credibility it has not had in recent years'. The respondent sees the 1989 legislation as 'hopefully' re-establishing 'the "proper" relationship between the policy makers and the executive'. Another London chief executive comments that 'for those who view their task as supporting political process and their colleagues and who view the future with hope it will be the best years they ever had!'. (Both these boroughs were Conservative controlled.) A county view was that new positive challenges may transform the relationship, as in the case of those springing from the acceptance of recommendations relating to a new role for local authorities in the Griffiths Report (Giffiths,1988), a view sadly irrelevant to the community care situation in 1991.

Behind these quotations appear to lie varying concepts of the role that chief executives see themselves helping members to fulfil. There is a fundamental question of the nature of the elected members' role which they can surely never ignore if it falls to them to explain it. The job needs well-developed concepts of the nature of local democracy as well as the ability to convince members if the chief executive's own views conflict with theirs, but to accept the members' views (providing that no legal impropriety is concerned) if they do not.

In most respects the chief executive is in the same boat as the council although not necessarily at the tiller: he is seen as continuing to meet situations where reduced resources, primarily the result of central government policy, conflict with public expectations for better services. As one chief executive put it, 'The job is 'increasingly becoming more difficult because of the erosion of local democracy. But the challenge must be met.'

Compulsory competitive tendering (CCT), competition and contracting. Seventy-one chief executives made references to contracting and competition: five from counties, three from London boroughs, six from metropolitan districts, two from regions, nine from Scottish districts and 49 from English and Welsh non-metropolitan districts. The chief executive of a large Conservative controlled non-metropolitan district wrote: 'The role of the contractor, whether in-house or not, is now firmly established. A company ethos is beginning to prevail. Looked at dispassionately, there is not much that local government can do that cannot be treated similarly. Where does this leave staff and councillors? - running, I would suggest, commercial operations.' There were a number of similar comments. A district chief executive writes of a 'powerful officer-led thrust to achieve new commercial approaches - particularly housing provision... with countervailing pressure from action groups, interest groups, possibly town councils'.

Local authorities react to the gospel of competition for local government services in various ways. The commonest, to judge from the responses, is one that fits well the interests of their employees - that is, doing what they can that is proper to enable employees on the contractor side to compete successfully with the private sector to win the contracts offered for tender by the client side of the authority, and obtaining what benefits they can for the authority in terms of enhanced efficiency. In some other cases the expectation is that private provision will virtually replace 'in-house' provision. To quote a response from an English district, 'most of my professional support will come from the private sector, as most of my services will be private'. The role of chief executives will be 'to manage the transition as painlessly as possible. Another chief executive from a 'hung' authority refers to 'a hard-nosed management style. Workforce resistance to change won't be possible'.

Some chief executives showed unease about developments relating to competitive contracting. One respondent wrote that fair competition would be 'a tremendous boost for local government services' but feared that 'it will get less fair as the years go by'. Another expressed unease that a business approach to most services might lead to a lowering of standards and values. One expected that competition would lead to 'disputes between warring factions within the authority'; another employed by a borough with dominant Labour control saw CCT as 'the most divisive of recent local government measures, placing a strain on inter-departmental arrangements and potentially between members and officers, especially where there is a strong tendency to retain work in house'. Another feared that sector/departmental committees would tend to pull apart'. The general feeling however was that competitive tendering was well established and likely to survive a change of government.

The weakening of members' power was referred arising from the 'managerial' approach. A chief executive in a south coast Conservative controlled town wrote: if the chief executive is 'continually letting and monitoring contracts, what are the implications for members engaged in it?'. Specific management demands on chief executives were identified in this context, including 'the art of decentralised management', negotiating delivery and 'ensuring efficient contacts and activities on behalf of client departments'. and greater intervention of the centre to ensure that standards were being met.

Many chief executives looked with some enthusiasm to the opportunities competitive tendering offers for the role of central management. In most cases there was little expectation that it would lead to the general loss of 'in-house' services, although a mix of public and private sector services was expected to become common.

Ensuring quality of service. The need to define service provision and conditions with 'unprecedented precision' in contract specifications' was seen to demand a more critical attitude to service provision in future years. This was believed to require an expanded role for chief executives both in the setting of standards (a corporate issue involving both members and departmental officers) and monitoring the quality of services provided by external and internal contractors. A considerable change was forecast in the type of service provided as well as the method of provision. Some respondents from districts emphasised the search for, promotion and comparison of innovations in this context. Evaluating and judging alternative means of provision was seen to be part of the job. Setting standards of performance, performance monitoring and measurement were more specific tasks identified by some as leading parts of the role. One district chief executive saw himself as 'much more orientated towards comparison of "best performance" issues'.

The chief executive as 'enabler' and 'catalyst'. Sixty chief executives gave the 'enabling authority' as a principal development in the coming years. One chief executive of a large non-metropolitan city for example saw the way opening out to 'greater enabling commercial partnership' and, 'in the broader view, encouraging innovation and flexibility'. There were qualifications. A chief executive in a Conservative controlled London Borough gave the view that 'enabling will not automatically take over'. Another in a Labour controlled district expected that there would be a return to direct provision. One with a hung council expected 'enabling' to lead to the chief executive 'becoming more of a politician in a non-party sense'; while another, also with a hung council, suggested that the 'enabling trend' might lead to directly elected chief executives.

'Enabling' was associated with closely related activities, including influencing and persuading, facilitating, 'fixing', guiding, brokering, seeking of external finance, entrepreneurship and 'getting things done'. Few of the responses indicated the context in which enabling would take place or its scope, although one respondent saw it as extending to the coordination of 'all sectors of the community (public and private)'. It could expand to 'the central coordinating role in any authority' which 'must come from the town hall, and which the private sector was 'never likely to undertake no matter how many services it provides'. While one saw enabling as an 'aggressive and entrepreneurial role', another saw it becoming, 'if this government remains in office', the post of 'a monitor - not a doer, risk-taking post'.

The use of the word 'enabling' was questioned by one respondent who chose to use terms he thought likely to have more permanent currency. Another related term, 'catalyst', came under similar criticism. Certainly both words are neologisms which may mean different things to others than what their users intend unless defined at length (see Rodney Brooke, Managing the Enabling Authority', 1989).

Eight of the nine references to the role of catalyst use it in the sense of effecting a change of relationship with or between external bodies. One chief executive defines it as 'bringing together various agencies to effect change'; another as promoting (increasingly by indirect means) 'varieties of service provision to meet public needs'. A development of the role of coordinator of multi-agency projects was also foreseen - presumably implying a clear leadership as well as servicing function.

Other aspects of service provision. References to specific services were rare, but individual district chief executives referred to economic and tourism development, 'meeting the demand for leisure facilities', and from Scotland "quango" housing for the unemployed and social cases'. There were only two references to physical planning: one from Scotland to the reduction of planning and building control with an emphasis on the certification method; the other to placement of planning and development proposals 'in a substantially longer time frame'.

The need for more emphasis on market research and marketing and the development of resulting strategies was given as an important area of development by a Scottish chief executive, as was the significantly different stress on 'the need for assessment of problems and alternative means of service delivery to respond to them' from an English district.

The chief executive and the community. Relations with the community may refer to contracting, 'enabling' or 'catalysing' relationships with other public or private service providing bodies or to the inhabitants of the area generally or, more narrowly, 'customers'. A growth of 'customer-consciousness' or its propagation was expected of chief executives in some of the responses: for example, from a northern Labour controlled borough: the 'need to ensure that the council treats people like customers'.

There were only eight references to community relationships as distinct from customer-consciousness, and four to market research or customer consultation, although some were concerned with the quality of local government's relation with its public. (Use of the word 'public' other than in the phrase 'public relations' was virtually non-existent, while the word 'citizen' did not occur at all). However a few responses indicated a range of attitudes, with chief executives expected 'to become more proactive vis-a-vis the community', 'to ensure that the local authority is perceived not merely as a provider of services to the community but is of the community', to place a stronger accent on contact direct with the community, speaking on behalf of the Council and relaying expressed views to members'. A view from a Scottish Labour controlled region was that there would be greater emphasis on finding out what the customer wants, devising programmes to implement this and persuading others that this is necessary'.

Managing the organisation. The responses referred little to the traditional departmental work of the chief executive and clerk of the council. One prophesied 'an increased move away from departmental responsibility' and others had the same implication. The task of 'adapting the organisation to new modes of service delivery' was the central challenge to a large proportion of the respondents, both in counties and districts. In several cases a smaller corporate core organisation was forecast. A county chief executive wrote that 'The Chief Executive must be leader, innovator, and must lead a small team of directors accountable for the whole thrust of the achievement of the Authority's objectives', and another that 'Departmentalism and professional hierarchies will give way to flexible, adaptable multi-disciplinary team-working'.

Only five responses referred to strategic management as a developing part of the role (which does not of course imply that many chief executives who responded did not view it as important). One wrote that the need for strategic planning of policies would increase, and another that chief executives would move towards corporate planning and involve themselves less in detail.

A district chief executive forecast 'greater devolution of control to departmental heads and lower, with responsibility for their budgets'. A London respondent expects 'more accountability of chief officers to the Chief Executive'. A county chief executive expected to have not only 'greater responsibility for departmental operation through a directorate' but also 'responsibility for efficiency and implementing savings'.

A district chief executive gave as a major part of the role 'the management and development of smaller numbers of better paid staff on fixed terms and performance related salaries/contracts'. Others looked to 'leaner and fitter authorities' and 'a smaller team of officers; reduced staff overall'. Three forecast greater emphasis on value for money and review of performance to justify expenditure levels' and 'identifying the performance of individuals'. Another serving a district council in the south-east of England with a very dominant Conservative majority painted a vivid picture of the effect of a clash of political objectives : 'In the political tension which will exist for the foreseeable future between the demand for the provision of public services, and measuring everything in terms of value for money, the Chief Executive will be like a rabbit paralyzed between the headlights of two advancing vehicles'.

There was concern about relations with other chief officers. A metropolitan district chief executive wrote, 'the centre in organisational terms becomes ever more important...' and there is 'danger that ... senior chief officers will become disillusioned and suspicious of a chief executive working ever more closely with the leaders and senior chairmen and effectively reducing their traditional autonomy and discretionary spending'. A shire district chief executive foresaw a major problem in 'handling chief officer disillusionment'.

The maintenance of morale figured as a prominent task in a number of replies, for example 'positive leadership is paramount as staff face uncertainty as government legislation continues', 'maintaining morale in an endangered species will become increasingly difficult' and, from London, 'the need to rebuild and re-establish the image of local government and the morale of those in it'. In one view, 'the role 'will need more direct support if it is to be carried out properly as motivation, performance appraisal and strategic management become more important'.

Replies from the North, Midlands and South Wales as well as (most often of all) the South envisaged that various influences and the increasing mobility of staff would make recruitment and retention of staff a critical problem, despite reductions in staff numbers. Problems of motivation and calibre were mentioned. 'The Chief Executive will have to assist in the recruitment of high calibre officers in the face of demographic change'; and 'Staffing control and skills shortage... will require greater skills and initiatives from the Chief Executive'.

A number of chief executives believed that they would be 'more involved in management succession and development planning' and there would be 'much more personal counselling of senior staff and exhortation and encouragement', with 'greater time spent on manpower matters eg organisational development to retain good employees, and recruitment drives'.

The power, authority and influence of chief executives in their authorities. There were 38 references to the power, authority or influence of chief executives: five from metropolitan districts, three from London boroughs, two from counties and one from a Scottish region - the remainder coming from non-metropolitan districts. Twenty-seven out of the total envisaged an increase in the power, influence or authority of the chief executive. In five cases - two of them from counties - his or her authority or power was seen as increasing generally or accepted more widely. One saw it increasing particularly in relation to politicians, and in two other cases in comparison with other chief officers. A London chief executive wrote that he expected to have 'greater delegated power for the management of the community'.

Twenty-one other officers saw the role as becoming more that of a managing director or general manager, and if these are included, at least 59 expected that chief executives would become more powerful. This question is inseparable from the problem of relationships with the political leadership, already considered above. Several responses point to a sharp constriction of the members' role following from the development of the managing director role. Another states that the chief executive would become the 'manager of a business organisation'. One saw an inverse relationship between the chief executive's management role and the member role. The chief executive of a Labour controlled London borough believed that the managing director role 'may be accepted with the consequent vulnerability to political identification, shorter appointments and more turnover, and consequent insecurity'.

On the style of future management, one county chief executive saw the role being more managerial and less professional; another from a district that chief executives must be 'professional managers, not professionals who manage'; and two that the role would become more business orientated. A strong view from a metropolitan district was that 'the last vestiges of professionalism would give way to pure managerialism'. One from a shire district on the other hand challenged the commonly expressed view with the statement that 'under present trends' the role is more likely to become a coordinating role and less that of a manager'. A Scottish region chief executive believed that the 'monitoring role' under the 1989 legislation would prevent him from adopting the managerial and entrepreneurial approach needed.

The general impression is that the extension of the authority and influence of the chief executive was seen to be related to a clearer definition of the managerial role, and that the main qualification must be the extent to which elected members would accept such a development. The managerial role in its turn was related closely to the development of competitive tendering and its demands, and occasionally to the activities of the chief executive in the multi-sectoral forum of local enterprise.

Conditions of employment. Short-term contract appointments were identified as increasingly a feature of the 1990s by thirteen chief executives coming from all types of authority excepting the Scottish regions and islands. References were made to 'high paid specific contracts', five year contracts and contracts that are performance related and assessed against agreed targets and priorities. Other chief executives mentioned higher turnover and 'shorter periods in the role springing from political identification'.

The difficulties of the role and response to challenge. A few chief executives expected the role to become 'even more difficult'. Concern was expressed about the prospect of being at the centre of conflicting pressures and having to serve two masters. The chief executive is seen as continuing to have to cope with the challenges of reduced resource resulting mainly from central policy, conflict with the public and party expectations for better services.

Typically difficulties are seen as challenges. As one English chief executive wrote, 'he must be ready for the challenge and make the most of it for the benefit of the service' and a London chief executive, 'only continuing adaptability will bring success'. Response to new challenges was believed to require innovations of a kind far beyond those forced on authorities by new legislation, but ones that genuinely serve local democracy and the quality of local life. It is a period that will demand 'greater willingness to adopt non-conventional action'. One respondent said, the role is a 'more exposed, risky occupation, but more rewarding'. On the other hand, returning to the question of recruitment, 'if central government continues to undermine local government, candidates of the right calibre, training and experience will not be drawn to the job'.

The skills required. The skills seen as required in the coming years reflect the perceived demands of the new tasks, for example 'innovative ability', 'sustained leadership' and 'the management of large-scale organisations', together with skills in inter-personal relations and motivation. To quote some of the responses by district chief executives on the subject: 'there will be a need for an 'increase in importance of managerial and innovative ability'; and the 'emphasis on non-risk management skills will perhaps shift to a requirement for sustained leadership skills. One remarks that 'professions must recognise that managers can be made'.

Skills and qualities seen as required in special measure are 'much finer interpersonal techniques than those at present exhibited and less theory and more practical understanding of the difficulties faced by the human resources', 'motivating and dealing with people' as 'the most significant part of the job', performance monitoring, 'client, strategic and financial management', 'vision and lateral thinking', 'persuasiveness and salesmanship', and, from a Scottish islands authority, 'entrepreneurial skills... both to seize the best from what the legislation permits, and to capture opportunities for financial and other joint undertakings with other public bodies, with private interests and individuals within the community'.

The role in general. Some chief executives saw themselves in the future as 'still managing major organisations with the predominant role of service provision', and otherwise doing the same job. But these responses are untypical. The weight given to the competitive approach and 'enabling' indicates a substantial shift and the beginning of a new definition.

Why did the main traditional planks of management action receive so few mentions? It may be that they are too familiar and not seen as areas requiring exceptional attention. Yet with the disintegration of many assumptions it may be that they will need radical rethinking. It may be that outside and 'arms length' suppliers of services are expected to take over the burden of service management, leaving chief executives more remote than before from the problems of service delivery. They may have simply been crowded out of respondents' minds (or due to the limited space provided on the form) by the current salience of the themes of competition and enablement, especially at a time when a major task was seen as guiding elected members and officers to respond constructively to the current legislative agenda. Speculatively, the cultivation of an effective response from the members, the paid staff and key elements in the world outside the authority will be of the greatest significance, although only possible in an intimate relationship with the political executive.

The Chief Executive Between Four Worlds

The problems of the 1980s have led some to believe that structural change is not only necessary within local authorities but needs to be enforced by legislation in order to overcome fundamental problems in the relationships between the worlds of local government politicians, local government officers, local communities and central government. In a great majority of cases the major difficulties reported by chief executives revolved around the relationships with local politicians and officers and their management. Failures in these areas may give cause to question the present nature of the powers, status and relationships of local government's twin heads: the council leader and the chief executive. The need for much deeper structural changes than those brought by the legislation of the 1980s may be indicated if the existing system is failing to serve the community as effectively and efficiently as may reasonably be expected and change can promise genuine improvement.

Politics are of their nature competitive, and in a plural society must and should represent a variety of values and motivations - both within as well as between parties. Officer values and interests are also divided and involve competition between groups for limited resources. It demeans the interests on both sides to describe them as political or professional selfishness, since pursuit of higher values - what is believed to be right and good - cannot often be disentangled from self-interest. The energy and effectiveness of an organisation at senior levels derives in part from championship of conflicting points of view on means and ends and in competition for resources. But there are also values and interests with which a chief executive must be concerned that more or less transcend the variety and enable the authority to achieve temporary resolutions of the conflicts in the general good. This is the dialectic of a democratic society, and one that allows and respects criticism of points of view but is sufficiently civilised to accept positions reached through dialectic in the common good.

The task of leadership in this sense is to represent the interest of the whole against the parts, resolving these interests through the pursuit of integrative values that are acceptable and that conserve the energies that would otherwise be frittered away in conflict. This is likely to be difficult even when the rules of the game and the authority of leadership are accepted without question. But in recent years changing values, structural change and straitened resources have made the difficulties of leadership more demanding in both the political and the officer worlds.

Politicians and chief officers not infrequently place a high value on solidarity among themselves and leaders and chief executives find support in using their authority to achieve that solidarity in pursuit of shared goals. The authority they need to exercise is likely to derive from a number of sources: respect for their accepted prerogatives as leaders exercised for the good of all, their ability to put forward values and arguments that transcend divisions, and other human qualities that are mixed and difficult to analyse - not least among them perhaps decisiveness when they are the only members in the group in a position to resolve conflicts.

The heads of the political and officer worlds need to give each other mutual support in this situation: the politician to know what the officers believe to be feasible, and the chief executive to know that the leader can deliver political support. In a hung situation when political leadership is divided the mutual dependency is likely to be stronger, often involving mediation between leaders by a third party who is usually expected to be the chief executive. There are also cases known where the leader has mediated between chief officers.

The normal situation is one where the nature of change is determined from within the authority, but changes may be imposed from without, or demanded by powerful political forces from within against strong opposition. On the officer side chief officers may dig their heels in and fail to deliver, whether or not delivery is feasible. Both leader and chief executive need to find the influence or power between them to formulate a viable strategy with colleagues and to execute it. Such challenges can provide the stimulus to drop preconceptions and to think boldly. The evidence presented above shows that in such circumstances leading politicians are likely to look primarily to a chief executive to lead the way. As shown above, they may actually advertise for a person of vision to fill the post of chief executive, not only to direct the implementation of agreed policy but also to provide new ideas and inspiration for the fulfilment of a shared vision.

But there are abnormal cases. The chief executive's authority may depend on a fragile consensus. He or she may be seen as at one with the political leaders and too far from the traditional apolitical role. Support may break up amongst politicians or amongst chief officers who will be responsible for execution of policy, or both. There may be logrolling between committee chairmen and chief officers protecting their services or their personal interests. Chairmen and/or officers may be incapable of delivery because of lack of feasibility, entrenched values or simply incompetence. The chief executive may find that the required level of support to carry out the changes that he or she believes to be desirable is simply not there, however strong the persuasion or thorough the search for agreement.

The potential points of strain in relationships are many: between chief executive and leader, between leader and other leading politicians, between chief executives and entrenched chief officers. Removals from office may be necessary to achieve an outcome satisfactory to the chief executive and/or the leader. It may be impossible for the leader to deliver the support for this. The executive function may go by default, morale deteriorate and no outcome be possible that carries a satisfactory level of support or that does not bring other acute problems in its train.

These are black scenarios but close to what can happen, as illustrated in Part B above. When the situation is critical key politicians or officer actors may be replaced. But if the problem is deep-rooted and may justifiably be blamed on the nature of the local authority structure, radical structural solutions may be sought within or outside the scope of a local authority's powers.

The frequency of these problems must not be exaggerated. In few cases do they appear to be critical. A heartening aspect of the research is that relationships appeared to be working well and to the satisfaction of leaders and chief executive in a high proportion of cases. As shown in part B, over two-thirds of the chief executives who answered the questionnaire met the leader of the council twice a week or more often and one in five at least daily; and seventy one per cent described the relationship as a very good one. Only five per cent described it as less than good. It is also a sign that chief executives are achieving results that are not frustrating on either side, and that the relationships between the governing political and chief officer teams are in general reasonably satisfactory.

Developing the Role to Fit a New National and World Context

The evidence points in general to the political element in local government continuing to be strong and central to the chief executive's role. A reduction in the political character of British local government would require structural changes of a kind that seem unlikely and are not generally expected by chief executives beyond the extent effected by and under the Housing and Local Government Act 1989. The principle of proportionality in committees has been introduced, and although it may bring clearer recognition of the interests of minority parties within the legislation, there seems no likelihood that it will depoliticise local politics: rather, together with the provisions for political advisers, it would seem to give them a new degree of legitimacy. The argument that a system of inter-sectoral contracting for services responsive only to market forces will make politics at local level largely redundant (Mather, 1989) denies the central political role of local government in the community as accepted throughout the other nations of the European Community.

A reaction from the policies of the 1980s seems likely to call for more social intervention, particularly in areas where reliance on the non-public sectors has been shown to be insufficient without public backing. Initiatives will have to be undertaken against a background of continuing economic stringency - a situation likely to confront a new government of whatever political composition. The sharpening of priorities seems likely to continue, with redoubled efforts to increase internal efficiency and to mobilise human, property and financial resources within the local community wherever they are available and relevant to public aims. The 'enabling role', as redefined above, may be seen to demand joint working at all levels in the local community: with those in patent need of support, voluntary groups, business interests, government agencies and wherever resources of all kinds can be generated. This implies a stronger outward orientation to generate self-help of a different kind from that of Samuel Smiles, involving subsidy to enable people to help themselves and others.

There is no reason to expect that the beneficial effects of competitive tendering will not continue to be accepted, but with an increased realism about where they produce 'value for money', result in desired standards and do not lead to the loss of essential flexibility in delivering policies. The same may be said of the decentralisation of schools, the voluntary provision of housing for people with low-incomes and other areas of public policy affected by Thatcherist initiatives. Centrally established instruments of urban renewal, such as Urban Development Corporations and City Action Teams, have been in existence long enough for critical review, and an attempt is due to relate the learning derived from their experience to the fundamental democratic principle that the local community should carry responsibility for its own future, taking into account the interest of all groups within it. The time is one for reassessment. Chief executives in the 1990s are in a leading position to promote a new approach of a wider nature than the word 'managerial' suggests to most people. But at the very least they are there to show how new approaches can be 'managed'.

John Stewart has elsewhere analysed the role as based on two key themes which broadly coincide with the analysis in this book (Stewart, 1988). One is building the relationship between the political and the management processes. He writes that 'The chief executive relates to the political leadership and can assist the leadership in giving political direction to the organisation'. He 'increasingly needs wider relationships to build political understanding': 'organisational understanding and responsiveness to political purpose' on the one hand and 'political understanding of organisational constraints and opportunities' on the other.

A shared understanding is desirable in the first place between the leaders of the local political world and leaders of the officers' world if either or both are to be successful. Both are dependent on their ability to develop approaches with their senior colleagues in ways that are widely acceptable. The process can be difficult and may in some cases involve a reconstitution of the leadership group on either side as has been achieved in some cases described in chapters 5 and 6. How far party leaders can and do reconstitute their own top teams within party groups has not been investigated, but this certainly happens. On both sides the process is likely to be strainful to the participants but it is most problematic on the political side because whereas the chief executive can usually obtain the support of the council leader, the leader owes his authority to his ability to satisfy the party group.

Things have moved fast in the short time between John Stewart's interpretations of the role quoted above and that in the research on which this book is based. Achieving a new re-orientation to change of both members and officers in the face of new challenges depends on a strong relationship with both the political leadership and the officer team. Achieving the restructuring of the officer organisation into client and contractor interests and developing the potential for control and efficient working that this theoretically contains, along with the institution of performance appraisal, give a much enhanced status to the role.

Changes in local authority structure are not in themselves important: their justification, like any other aspect of a local authority, lie in service to the local community. Action in the world outside the organisation is the third world of local government. It gives it its basic resources, its purpose and its justification and legitimacy. The development of its relationship with this world will, it may be hoped, mature during the 1990s to inform and guide more surely the objective setting, strategic planning and operational approach.

There is no ground in the results of the research for predicting that the requirements of the 1989 legislation for a monitoring officer to be appointed to serve as 'whistle blower' on the propriety of members' decisions will make any significant difference to the role. Chief executives in authorities where they believed it would were determined not to undertake it. The chief executive's first responsibility, as the servant and guide to the council, is to ensure understanding of issues and to participate with its members in the design of a new future, contributing ideas and innovations to benefit the full spectrum of interests within the community, and not least those of its members who may in some cases lack an effective voice within the council. The role can be used to promote legitimate shared values and goals. The argument of social solidarity which has such general recognition in continental western democracies may be one such value and goal.

The temptation is to state an ideal role in general terms, yet it is a fundamental requirement of the current chief executive role to adapt continually to the particular situation. As shown above local situations vary extremely, and with them the role of chief executive that is acceptable to the political world may vary commensurately. Certainly one primary need is to assist the political process as strongly as possible and to see that both the political leadership and the opposition are as well equipped to fulfil their roles as possible without breaking confidences. The need is central both within the classical British adversarial system of politics and in a system with a strong orientation towards consensus such has been found in some of the authorities described above.

These matters and many others - not least that of being the 'last resource' on some relatively trivial matters that no-one else is in a position to deal with - are extremely demanding because of the many points at which disagreement and strain can arise. A key question is how far the functions and ambiguities of the role can be stretched, and whether the adoption of other forms of local authority executive in which responsibilities are clearly defined might deliver greater social benefits.

Chapter 13

LOCAL AUTHORITY EXECUTIVES ABROAD

THE CASE FOR A NEW EXECUTIVE STRUCTURE

In 1991 on the threshold of a general election all parties were committed to radical changes in the local government system. The tide of opinion over previous years had been towards the general institution of all- or most purpose authorities which, on assumptions such as had led to widespread amalgamations in the 1970s this would lead to a general enlargement of the non-metropolitan district authorities in order to support the expert staff assumed, rightly or wrongly, to be necessary for the highly professionalised services such as education, social services, engineering and possibly physical planning as well as for economies of scale and other reasons. Some have contested the need for bigness against closeness to the community while others have looked to a system that varies according to the needs and preferences of different areas. Whatever reforms come about they are likely to have great implications for the work of chief executives and the number of posts available.

In visits to local authorities during the research on the role of chief executives a common view was found among leading politicians and chief executives in 'two-tier' areas in favour of such a change. If there are to be single-tier authorities then we should look for guidance to the London boroughs and metropolitan districts, and if smallness is favoured in the end over bigness then to the all purpose Scottish island authorities for what can be learnt about the functioning of the chief executives' role within them.

Larger authorities are likely to imply stronger centrifugal influences within the administration at chairman, committee and departmental level. Fears that contracting out services externally might undermine a corporate approach seemed stronger in the most-purpose authorities visited than elsewhere. Certainly the extent to which the chief executive could exercise a controlling influence and a monitoring role on developments was lower than in fewer purpose authorities on account not only of the nature of the services but also of their number, sophistication and relationship with the community. Increased politicisation may also result in some cases.

Elected mayors have been advocated in the past by Michael Heseltine, the Secretary of State for the Environment in 1991, and by others as a mean of providing a focus of accountability for the management of local authorities. The possibility was raised in consultative paper from the Department of the Environment which inquired amongst many other things whether 'a more "executive" model of decision-making' should be adopted, 'eg management boards; an executive formed from the majority party; directly elected mayors or leaders'.

British local government management structures differ from those in most of Western Europe in not providing for a distinction between the 'deliberative assembly that discusses proposals and makes substantive decisions and an executive that organises its business, develops and where necessary negotiates proposals and carries out the assembly's decisions. This is not to say that members of the council other than those who may play a role within the executive are not involved in the development of proposals: it is normal for authorities of any size to participate in the preparation of decisions through a committee structure where the views of different party groups can be put forward and considered corporately. In multi-party administrations such as are more the norm than otherwise in most countries the process usually results in a high level of agreement being reached between their members on the measures adopted. The executive is of course bound by the decisions made by the deliberative assembly: normally however he, she or they will have already have agreed if not proposed or negotiated them. (It should be borne in mind that party systems are generally more highly developed than in Britain, both locally and nationally).

It can be argued that it is a nonsense that the council as a whole is theoretically the executive as well as the decision-making body of the authority. The council role is representative and deliberative in the sense of delivering decisions after debate, not for taking executive responsibility. For preparing and implementing its business it depends on those who exercise power in its name. Earlier chapters in this book have shown how much it depends on officers to review community needs, formulate objectives and plans, review and assess achievements, supervise the organisation of the authority and its coordination, integrate and restructure the organisation to achieve efficiency and effectiveness, take management decisions necessary for the implementation of the council's decisions, present business and run the management process as a whole.

These functions are largely those that the Maud Committee on Management 1967 had in mind when they proposed the institution of management boards to act as executives for councils *(Management of Local Government vol.1*,1967, para 162). The Committee however largely ignored the vital question of political leadership and accountability.

The introduction of the chief executive concept in Britain before and after the Bains Report has been a move towards meeting some aspects of the executive role as developed abroad: pinpointing corporate responsibility in the administration; providing for leadership and control of business; centralising and simplifying a decision-making process that can be torn apart by departmental interests; internal reorganisation, from a position above departmental interests; representation of the authority as a whole at official level; strategic management and planning for the future in some cases; working with the community; and many other matters.

But the profiles in Part B have shown how problematic the development of the power of chief executives to fill a vacuum in effective political leadership can be in some instances. Even without keen political support the officers' real power is formidable in that they control most of the information politicians depend on to fulfil an effective role and are the sole means of policy execution. Local politicians interviewed in some authorities said in so many words that democracy had gone awry because of their dependence on the officers: they were required to justify the decisions of officers to their electors in which they had no part and with which they did not necessarily agree. The democratic principle requires that decisions made by a council are thoroughly understood by elected members and 'owned' by its majority, or at least have the majority's political support. That they are 'owned' by the responsible politicians is more important in principle than that they are 'owned' by the employees of the council who execute them.

It has been argued above that the chief executive depends on political support, usually through a strong leader, to achieve a high level of effectiveness in these matters. In some respects his or her responsibilities are hard to distinguish from those of a strong leader. Their achievements are joint achievements. As the response to the survey question on where the chief executive owes principal responsibility has shown, the line of responsibility is confused. Neither leader nor chief executive gets proper recognition for their contributions. There is a lack of transparency about the location of power: both leader and chief executive may be mystery persons outside their immediate circle, receiving neither clear blame nor credit, or in the cases where they become household names receive unjust blame or credit for matters that they are not in a position to control. Why should their positions be so indefinite? Does this not reflect badly on recruitment possibilities? Is there not a need for a clearer definition of the role to open up a new vision of local government to the public, appropriate to an authority that seeks to lead the communities it serves in overcoming present problems and achieving a better life.

It has been shown in the earlier parts of this book how a quasi-executive consisting of leader and chief executive has developed and functioned to fill a role analogous to that of the continental executive. This is a typically British institution, existing by convention without legal definition or accountability. There is no defined focus of responsibility for executive responsibilities among the elected representatives nor for the critical functions of the chief executive. It is obscure where the line of accountability lies between the council or its majority and those who execute tasks on its behalf.

In most cases, as we have seen, the present arrangements work, but in some they have worked badly, giving satisfaction to no-one. Proposals for instituting an executive mayor would locate legal and political responsibility. A formal cabinet system is also a possibility. The brief survey that follows of forms which the executive takes in Western European and North American local government should give some appreciation of the possibilities, although it is important to appreciate that the extent to which any form would satisfy given criteria cannot be determined simply by its functioning in Europe or America. That it works well and is accepted as satisfactory in one political, social and legal context does not necessarily imply that it will work well in another. However, forms that work abroad are valuable starting points for considering alternatives for Britain.

Any formal definition of a distinct executive, whatever its form, would have an immediate implications for the job of chief executive. It would not however remove the need for a head of service. I have been assured by a number of experts from countries with different systems that the description of the tasks of the British chief executive is close to that of the head of paid service in their own countries, whatever the formal definition of their jobs may be there will always be a head of service with duties closely analogous to those of the British local government chief executive. Whether the title is secretary-general, *Stadtdirektor* or whatever, a head officer with a general responsibility is needed to carry a general responsibility for fulfilling the needs of the politicians in policy definition, liaison between interests, ensuring that the services function corporately and overall control of staff and the management of services. It is a 'law of the situation' that seems to apply very generally in well-developed systems of local government.

From consultancy work abroad I have found that the lack of such an officer may be a reason for disintegration of purpose and extreme levels of inefficiency in a 'strong mayor' organisation of considerable size: partly because the interests of its constituent services are likely to tear it apart and frustrate corporate decision. Exceptions may be cases of countries where there are collegiate executives with a relatively strong tendency towards consensus formation, as in Sweden and Denmark for example, or where a high level of officer experience combined with a strong corporate tradition is included in a plural executive, as in the German Länder of Hesse and Schleswig-Holstein (I am informed however that Sweden is considering the institution of a chief executive of the British type).

The formal definition of a political executive does not remove the need for a chief executive officer to fill what would in any case be a most demanding, stimulating and highly responsible role in any local government system possessing a formal political executive.

Eecutive Models from Overseas

The functions and powers of elected councils outside the British system are similar in principle but vary according to the amount of power and discretion belonging to the executive. Decisions made by councils tend to be formulated in a quasi-legal form, leaving the executive free to act with discretion in their implementation. Generally the executive prepares the business of the assembly, including the budget, and implements its decisions.

The state constitutions in the United States provide 'off-the-peg' forms which individual local authorities can adopt. North American forms include two models where the decision-making power and the executive are fused as in Britain. Both have been subject to heavy criticism. One is the small elected commission or board, usually of three to seven members, often supplemented by elected officials including a popularly elected clerk. In some cities a chief administrative officer is appointed with responsibility for operations in parallel with the political board's responsibility for strategic policy. It has been not uncommon for there to be rivalry between the 'operations manager' and the chairman of the commission or board. The other model, the 'weak mayor system', is nearer to the British system, although in practice the mayor tends to act as chief executive for the council and so possesses much more real authority than the British mayor.

The American system is un-European in several ways. The representative element tends to be small, councils having commonly only five or six members. A council of 15 is regarded as large, and one of 30 generally the largest permissible. (In Europe they are generally not very different from those in Britain for comparable populations.) Electoral turn-out is commonly lower than in Britain, 20 per cent not being unusual. There is no real party control in most American authorities. The parties hardly exist between elections in most cases, so that there is generally no-one comparable with the British party leader. Functions are in general comparatively narrow, being constrained by the ultra vires principle and the fact that some services are provided by other levels of government or by special purpose bodies.

The only system to be found with some resemblance in outline to that in Britain in the larger countries of Western Europe was set up under the influence of the British authorities in occupation of North-West Germany after the second world war with the intention of blocking the way to the emergence of 'local Hitlers'. The aim was to separate the political from the administrative power: a strange objective to most continentals, especially perhaps in Germany and Italy where lack of political identification among those with power is liable to raise suspicions of non-accountability. The system set up in North-Rhine Westphalia, Lower Saxony and Schleswig Holstein was one of an elected council which held both decision-making and executive power, as in Britain. The council chairman, the *Oberbürgermeister* (*Bürgermeister* in smaller towns) was intended as the equivalent of the British mayor as chairman and formal representative of the authority. The 'business director' and head of service is the *Oberstadtdirektor* or *Stadtdirektor*, (literally 'town director'), a chief executive or administrative officer who has been compared misleadingly with the British town clerk. The *Stadtdirektor* is an appointed official who was intended to be apolitical and neutral. He was however selected from the start with regard to his party membership as well as his proven abilities.

The attempt to split administration from politics was a failure from the start: the German wish was for openness, fairness and negotiation of positions with all cards face upwards on the table. But this could not solve the problem of where the effective leadership would lie and be seen to lie. In practice it could be with the *Oberbürgermeister* although theoretically he lacked executive power; or the leader of the leading political party, although his authority lacked formal recognition; or the Stadtdirektor. The outcome varied from authority to authority. The system received strong criticism from the start for its failure to allocate power and responsibility - a matter that can cause serious problems when the will of the party leader conflicts with that of the Stadtdirektor.

Schleswig-Holstein abandoned the system. Hedley Marshall quotes an official as saying, regarding the position of the Stadtdirektor, that 'men of intellect will not stand it' ('it' being its subservience) (Marshall 1967). The problems have been exacerbated since Dr Marshall's report by the financial stringencies confronting high spending authorities in the 1980s and clashes with political majorities on what constitutes a proper and reasonable budget (Banner, 1985).

Executive boards. The German Länder of Hesse and Schleswig-Holstein require local authorities to appoint an executive board (*Magistrat*) - an institution with a long tradition in Germany. The council appoints a chairman of the board (the *Oberbürgermeister*) and five to eleven members for a six year term, who are re-eligible for a second term of office. The members are a mixture of senior officials and politicians appointed for their administrative abilities. Each member is in charge of a range of services but major matters have to be determined corporately. They are required to consult all relevant departments of the council before bringing any matter before the board. Criticisms include slowness in decision-making. Its good characteristics are said to be collective wisdom, a less dictatorial character than single executive systems and wider contacts with council and community.

In Swedish municipalities the general executive responsibility rests on an executive committee of at least five members appointed by the council. Led by a politician, commonly the most powerful person in the authority, it fulfils an executive role similar to that set out above although with a role less distinct from the council. Some members may be chairmen of other council committees and work full-time on the authority's work. The executive committee is responsible for departmental coordination, often but not always through an official equivalent to the British town clerk. The larger cities in Denmark have a similar executive system.

There appears to be less scope for personal initiatives by the head of the paid service in these systems than in those of the single executive type, although in case of the *Magistrat* it is normal to appoint highly experienced officials to the board itself.

Single political executives: directly elected. The American strong mayor system concentrates executive responsibility on the mayor, who is the only elected administrative officer. He appoints and can dismiss heads of departments, proposes budgetary and policy matters and implements decisions. The system was introduced in the 1880s in order to concentrate responsibility on a strong politician accountable at the ballot box.

In a number of large cities the executive mayor has been supplemented by the appointment of a chief administrative officer (CAO) or chief executive officer, sometimes called the controller or deputy mayor of operations. The CAO may be appointed to serve at the pleasure of either the mayor or the council. He may be specifically responsible for supervision over heads of department and appoint and dismiss employees subject to the mayor's agreement, prepare the budget, direct and make investigations into departments. He may be part of a mayor-led 'cabinet' of officers.

The South German mayoral (*Oberbürgermeister*) system is similar to that of the American strong mayor. The South German mayor has a responsibility to veto illegal decisions by the council and in practice maintains a strong grip on business. Members of his party look to the mayor for their political success, since their own re-election may depend on the *Oberbürgermeister's* performance.

Single political executives elected by their councils. The roles of mayors in the French, Italian, Spanish and Italian systems are similar to each other in principle although the different arrangements at deputy or assistant mayor level limit the direct power mayors can exercise to a varying extent. They are appointed by their councils (except in some cases of direct election in Spain). In practice the name at the top of the successful party list, or the key party list in a coalition, indicates who is expected to be mayor or president. Thus in voting for the party the voter is indirectly voting for the executive. Once the mayor is elected he or she has tenure until the next election.

The president of the council for the department or province is elected in the same way. Deputy or assistant mayors are elected or chosen by the mayor or in Italy and partly in France by the council to be responsible under him for areas of the services. Together the mayor and his assistants form a corporate board. The offices of assistant mayors are normally allocated by agreement proportionally to the parties in the coalition. The deputyships and corporate executive boards limit the direct power of the mayor, although he or she carries general responsibility for the executive.

The Latin mayor retains a vestigial role as servant of central government for certain non-political purposes which prejudices his political independence no more than does the British chief executive acting as an agent for electoral purposes.

In each case there is an official who takes general responsibility for the administration. He is the authority's secretary or secretary-general. His functions are in practice very close to those of the British chief executive.

Heads of staff in most countries in Western Europe are involved deeply in the policy-making process due to organisational arrangements which make them an integral part of the decision-making system. A primary distinction is between those countries which have constitutional and statutory provisions for the local government service and those including Britain that have none, where councils appoint without restriction. Of the latter Denmark is an example where the clerk or chief executive normally heads the finance department and political secretariat of the burgomaster with whom he or she works in a close relationship. In Sweden the clerk or chief executive is responsible to the executive committee as adviser on general policy matters and co-ordinator of the administration.

In the South Mediterranean countries the secretary or secretary-general and the directors of services are generally part of national corps with rights, salaries and conditions of service related to those of the national civil service. They have a status in the law and constitution. The officers who fill these posts have security of tenure and are generally appointed politically from central lists of highest grade public servants, proportionately to party strengths on councils. Though the party to which they belong is a consideration in making appointments they are bound in law and practice to be impartial. The secretary works primarily to the mayor, although in Italy he or she has responsibility to the *giunta* and to the council. He or she is generally required and may have a right, as in Italy, to submit an opinion on proposals submitted to the executive as to their legitimacy which must be included in the council papers. A French law of 1987 provides for a service more in the nature of a 'cadre' than of a corps or integrated body. Germany also, to which most of this general description applies, has an élite cadre rather than a corps. Heads of service in all these cases qualify through demanding education and training courses and have to fulfil high level examination requirements. The point to be emphasised is how much they are integrated partners in executive political-administrative teams responsible for the executive policy and strategic functions at the centre of their authorities.

The functions of British leaders of the council overlap broadly with those of continental mayors and presidents, but the status and power of the latter are very different since they are legally responsible executives for the authority and chairmen of their councils. They generally spend a great deal of their time representing the authority both formally and in discussions and negotiations with community leaders and other levels of government. They have an autonomy once appointed that gives them the power virtually to control the business of the council. Most of the political uncertainties associated with the British leader-chief executive relationship are absent: the secretary-general has a clear point of reference and accountability. The attachment of a 'cabinet' or 'bureau' of experts to the mayor or president provides a source of ideas, advice and policy analysis.

The provisions in the German *Land*, the Rhineland Palatinate, are similar in some respects. The *Bürgermeister* post is open to candidates who are appointed with their regard to their ability. Bürgermeister normally serve for a ten year period, but the councils are re-elected every five years. The *Bürgermeister* cannot vote for the budget or the appointment of deputies, and the administration under him is subject to supervision by the council. He or she has often been a government official and his deputies have mixed administrative, technical and political backgrounds as in the Magistrat system. To quote A.H.Marshall, 'open conflict is unlikely because the mayor (*Bürgermeister*) and council must show a united front. The mayor, having no independent mandate, must take his cue from the council, while the latter are conscious that they possess ultimate sovereignty.' (Marshall, 1967)

Councils with county and city managers. Many medium-sized towns in the United States elect councils of up to nine members, the main functions of which are to appoint the mayor, pass by-laws, adopt the budget and appoint a manager. The manager holds his job 'at the pleasure of the council' but may request a public hearing if a motion is tabled to remove him from office. His duties are by delegation from the council and are similar to those of a chief administrative officer described above except that he appoints and dismisses heads of department and controls their work. This plan was associated with efforts to de-politicise local government and has been adopted with a large variety of variations. Hedley Marshall found that the mayor's role tended to be that of 'chief political broker'. 'A manager who has established good relations with his mayor, and can sense which incidents are likely to have political overtones, has made the first step to success.' (Ibid)

The advantages of the plan are that the manager is chosen for his ability as a professional administrator (often having graduated in public administration) and is in a position to maintain a highly integrated organisation with clarity of responsibilities and efficient procedures. But, to quote Dr Marshall again, 'Conceived in the spirit of business enterprise, it underrates the political aspects of local government... there are many communities in which it is difficult for an administrator to play the principal local government role... I heard many times that the manager system tended to leave a political vacuum... If he takes a firm stand, he is accused of usurping the position of the politician, if on the other hand he adopts the position of an English local government official, he is said to be responsible for causing a vacuum... there is a widespread feeling that whilst it works well in small homogeneous communities, it is not suitable for the rough and tumble of large cities with mixed populations and varied ethnic groups.' The post has been adopted in only a few of the larger city authorities. It is conspicuously weak in terms of representation of a large population.

The Irish Republic has a national system of city and county managers who serve as executives not only for counties but also for the urban authorities within their areas. The authorities have no responsibility for schools or colleges, personal health or welfare functions, their functions according to a National Planning Board report being 'effectively confined to the discharge of functions under the aegis of the Ministry of the Environment'. They are 'almost wholly concerned with environmental infrastructure plus limited cultural activities', although their recognition of them as 'partners' by the European Community implies an importance in their economic development role of which this does not take full account (Barrington, 1991). A National Planning Board report in 1984 said 'developments in recent years have effectively confined local authorities to the discharge of certain functions under the aegis of the Ministry of the Environment'.

The internal structure of Irish local authorities originated in the 1920s, largely under the influence of an enthusiast for the American commission and manager form. The model, in the words of the body which was put forward initially as combining 'control by the people and administration by experts', is based on the classical dichotomy between politics and administration. Certain matters were reserved for decision by the council, leaving the county or city manager to decide on all others. (Collins, 1987). The 'reserved functions' were principally major policy matters, finance, by-laws, bringing legislation into effect and nomination of representatives to public bodies. Anything beyond these is by law an 'executive' function falling to the county or city manager. The county managers are also the chief executives of the 118 municipalities and towns, the basic level of local government whose populations ranged in size at the end of the 1970s from about 600 to 54,000. All but seven had populations of below 20,000, some being under non-elected commissioners and administered by the county council (a theoretically possible arrangement for community councils within the area of new British unitary authorities).

In practice the managers usually initiate policy and the members are very dependent on them for advice. But managers are not dictators: 'The councillors are so close to affairs that a manager who acted dictatorially would be likely to find himself left out on a limb'. More important than that a council can suspend a manager by a two-thirds majority vote, but needs the Minister's consent to remove him. The relationship of managers with the national ministry is a very close one, 'but the Department scrupulously avoids doing anything that is destructive of the authority of the councils' (Marshall, 1967). 'Activities of the manager vis-a-vis his elected representatives... centre on his autonomy... His ability to formulate and conduct policy relies upon an unquestioned acceptance of his leadership by his council.' (Collins, 1987).

Appointments to the county and city manager posts are arranged by the Local Appointments Commission, which consists of three very high level members appointed by the Government. It appoints to all designated posts - in practice virtually all the senior posts in the local government service. Generally a board of expert professionals and others chaired by a layman selects the officers. The commissioners then make a recommendation to the local authority, who are virtually obliged to appoint their nominee. Internal appointments are not permitted and salaries are determined by the minister. The managers are expected to be selected for their professional competence for the job. It is common for them to possess secretarial or accountancy qualifications and to have experience as town clerks in the basic level authorities before appointment (ibid).

On paper councillors have the means to control managers, being able among other things to require them to do any lawful act for which money has been provided except for staff and individual health functions; but the provision has been little used and in practice the relations between members and managers have been collaborative. The budget estimates are generally the managers' affair, the councillors being said to complain that they find difficulty in understanding the budget papers. A problem is said to be that the manager's authority, as in the American system, can cut across departmental matters of which he lacks understanding.

The general view in Irish local authorities is reported to be that the system is much preferable to control by elected members because the volume and technicalities of business could not possibly be dealt with effectively under a committee system, and that in any event members were in general glad to devolve most managerial functions onto the managers. Managers are accepted as 'non-political' (although the policy polarisation typical of many British local authorities is not characteristic of Ireland, so that except on symbolic matters policy differences have been comparatively low).

The dependence of a manager on support of the council for policy decisions preserves the accountability of the members for key decisions. It does not necessarily mean that the elected members and others are not involved in extensive consultation on the documents put before them through a committee process or by other means. The executive must seek to maintain support, not only in the council but also in the community, so ensuring the political benefits of well-informed and sensitive decision making. If a budget for example takes the authority on the road to financial crisis against the manager's advice it will be crystal clear where the responsibility lies.

Conclusions

This international survey of executive structures for local authorities cannot be as critical as would be wished due to the shortage of sources of unbiased evaluation. However it suggests the following conclusions. The American and Irish city or county manager models are inappropriate to the political nature of most British local authorities. Local government controlled through a party system requires full and direct accountability of representatives for policies and delivery of services. It is not inconsistent however with a clear division of responsibilities between a deliberative decision-making body (the council) and an executive that prepares business for such a body and carries out its functions in accordance with the council's decisions. Councils and executives are accountable to electors both morally and through electoral mandates, although the choice in the case of the executive is in most cases exercised indirectly by the council.

A political executive does not remove the need for a head of the paid service, and in fact requires one able to work in a close relationship with politicians, analysing problems, suggesting approaches and assessing alternative means of policy implementation. The head of paid service is in the same kind of symbiotic relationship with the executive, whether it be a single person or a corporate body or a combination of both, just as is a British chief executive with a council leader and other party members who exercise real if informal executive responsibility. In the case of a collegial executive the onus is clearly on the board to resolve its own differences with the help of official advice. In the author's experience officials in large cities play a leading part in the contribution of policy ideas although, as in Britain, mainly behind the scenes and in mayoral systems often as his appointed advisers. Their relationship to the officer organisation as a whole is nevertheless of fundamental importance in policy-making matters.

Chapter 14

THE FUTURE OF THE ROLE: CONCLUSIONS

In the future the term 'executive' itself may seem inappropriate in a time of accelerated change and uncertainty. The emphasis has moved from carrying out defined purposes to a re-identification of the purposes of local authorities. The term 'chief' also bears questioning. It conveys to many a concentration of responsibility at the top of the organisation when in fact responsibility has to be carried throughout the organisation if it is to function effectively. The 'missionary' role implies the teaching of values, which seems inappropriate and patronising to elected representatives. Words that have more meaning are perhaps 'agent of change', '*animateur*' and above all the simple description of 'leader': a word that has regained respectability among organisational theorists in the 1980s. These are all functions however of which no-one in an organisation must have a monopoly.

'Changing the culture' seems generally to have been used in the sense of achieving shared goals throughout the organisation. In a large organisation this requires the existence of many cultural agents or leaders. It is arrogant to assume that the top has a monopoly in the definition of goals: it contains the danger of a new authoritarianism which in a democratic society can result in pervasive cynicism.

But the need has never been clearer for understanding leadership at the top to guide the organisation towards optimum functioning and ensure that new external demands and conditions of success are rapidly understood and responded to. Such leadership appeared to have become an accepted aspect of the role of the chief executive in many of the authorities visited, at least as it was understood by the political leaders interviewed, so that it may be best to remain with the title of chief executive rather than seek a new one provided that it is seen by leading politicians as compatible with political leadership: a complement to the leader of the council's role rather than a substitute for it. The rationale depends on the role being formally subordinate to and in close association with the political leadership: highly sensitive to the maintenance of a political process which provides the bridge with the community on which the justification of local government depends.

The chief executive, head of service, general manager or whatever he may be called, together with a management team and assistants, have unique capabilities because of their centrality in the organisation and their personal choice by the council to carry out its purposes. The position carries its own implications peculiar to the nature of British local government whatever it may be called.

Because of the strategic position a chief executive occupies it seems inevitable that he or she will continue in the strategic position to initiate change and balance this with the maintenance of continuity jointly with the chief officers and in association with political leaders. He or she may be expected to continue to be a leader, working with colleagues not only to respond to changing contingencies and opportunities, whatever they may be, but also to develop the organisation and its contribution to the community in accordance with shared values. This implies a motivation to pursue the best interests of the authority and be at the forefront of thinking about local government's role. The chief executive's role cannot therefore be divorced from concepts of the purpose of local government. While it is impracticable in this context to pursue the implications in detail, perceptions of local government's purpose are clearly central to the future of role if the pursuit of changing values in the 1980s is a guide to the future. Steering the implementation of that purpose is also a natural role of the centre. In its modern organisational form it may be termed 'strategic management'.

Strategic management has become a byword on the threshold of the 1990s. Like other borrowings from private sector management literature it is used in various and usually undefined senses. A paper by Stephen Nicklen, a member of a firm of management consultants, drawing on a definition by an eminent American private sector consultant (Michael Porter), provides a starting point for considering its implications for the chief executive's role (Nicklen, 1989). He distinguishes sharply between a council's relationship with trading units and its other core activities, and in doing so illuminates the ambiguity of the vogue expression 'the competitive council'. He points out that in its most obvious sense it is trading units competing for contracts from a core authority that are the competitors, not the council itself (although councils have commonly invited internal units to separate from their client organisation to compete with outside bodies).

The core authority is a commissioner of services, whether from its own staff or from outside organisations. By this means it escapes from the concept of being primarily a service provider but retains a secondary role as supplier of services which it is best fitted to control directly or can provide most effectively or efficiently. One advantage is that it ceases to be constricted in its functions by the boundaries of its area. It can commission services from public, private, voluntary or joint bodies constituted to provide the catchment area and specialist resources that are most effective and efficient for meeting its purposes in particular fields and hold them accountable (cf the 'core authority' concept in Norton, 1986).

The model seems relevant to the projected intentions of all the main national British parties to replace the present arrangements with a system characterised mainly by all or most purpose authorities. The core council's primary function would be to determine where and how the needs of its area's present and future inhabitants should be met.

Nicklen follows the business theorists in seeing the conception of a 'mission' for the organisation as a prime requisite for strategic management. Local government's mission is clearly different from a private firm's. Its 'missionary' connotations seem less inappropriate than in the private sector case since public service values are of a fundamentally moral character, whereas those of the market are basically for material gain. It seems less confusing to talk of defining values and purpose rather than of a mission.

To draw on a further source on the meaning of strategic management in the public sector, inspired partly by writers on the mission of public government and administration in general, 'It extends beyond the limits of market demand' and involves collective action with the motivation to match provision to 'a publicly established concept of need' in response to a changing environment (Stewart and Ranson, 1988). 'Need' is also a word of which understanding is confused by different meanings. It certainly extends beyond 'wants', 'express demands' or professionally defined need. British local government's greatest achievements were arguably to overcome the environmental abuse of human lives arising from the industrial revolution in the nineteenth century and to develop individual capacities by its educational provision in the early twentieth century, fulfilling in each case both needs of the economy and the restoration of a sense of human worth and dignity. Stewart and Ranson number amongst other matters as the basis of the public sector model of strategic management openness for public action, equity in relation to need, justice and citizenship.

Nicklen sees performance requirements as determined by external economic, demographic and political pressures (to which may surely be added 'social need'), with other councils as comparators and feedback from the public on preferences, priorities and expressions or expectations. The influences comprehend political vision incorporating values and customer group priorities on the one hand and officers' vision incorporating managerial and professional values and standards on the other. This is a bridge to the 'subsidiarity principle' that social tasks should be performed at the level at which they can most effectively be provided, with the rider that they should be 'enabled' by subsidy or other means where performance is best undertaken at another level on grounds of moral development or, arguably less important, efficiency.

Beyond performance requirements lie the development of capability within the organisation: managerial ('directional clarity' and 'managerial grip'); structural capability ('organisational shape' and 'operating systems'; 'cultural capability' ('values' and 'acquired habits') and 'resource capability' (finance, people, equipment and accommodation' and 'information'). It is on these last matters that a chief executive is usually expected to concentrate, but the justification of local government ultimately lies in its outputs towards which these are but means.

All these factors demand not only orchestration but also the active commitment of the conductor of an orchestra. If chief executives are to ensure the implementation of strategic management in this sense their task is even more demanding than the tasks defined in Part B.

The 1980s have seen the opening up of a new value agenda for local government which may be expected to move in new directions during the 1990s. New emphases were already implicit in the Audit Commission's paper *The Competitive Council* of 1988. Taking a rather different approach from the Commission in its subsequent paper on the chief executive in local government (Audit Commission, 1989) but adopting to some extent its framework, we may consider the role in relation to the key factors that were there stated to stand out in a well-managed council:

Understanding its customers. A member of the advisory panel for the research project (David Spiers, until recently a chief executive), has pointed out to me that 'customers 'are by definition an exclusive group. Many services are for people who have no effective choice'. 'If "the market" pollutes or makes the environment dangerous the community has a right to have it controlled by a public body acting on its behalf'. Public bodies are there to create effective choice in the market as a matter of right: to support a moral society concerned with promoting human worth. To return to the same source of comment, 'Perhaps chief executives will do more to articulate the needs of their communities and through the politicians they serve, or personally, become advocates or "champions" on behalf of those communities.'

One may hope that chief executives will in future place a stronger emphasis upon assisting local councils to understand the social and economic factors which are associated with disadvantagement of individuals and groups in their communities so that a better understanding can be reached of where strategic intervention is likely to be most effective in countering the imbalances in resources between an authority's communities and between them and those elsewhere in the United Kingdom and Europe. Policy advice in the 1980s has been to a large extent reactive to the welter of central legislation. The immediate concern has often been far more the softening of the impact of central policies on the community than increased understanding of local needs. The local authority possesses by far the best means to gather and assess information on community needs across the functional spectrum and to consider these in relation to the quality of future society. It has at its disposal information from its employees which is commonly of unequalled depth. The area is the often neglected one of the purposeful integration of available information.

In the 'enabling' context chief executives may be concerned with assisting elected members to open the way for bodies within the community to contribute as effectively as they can to an understanding of the needs of people present and future. The commercial survey, looking for evidence of what people will pay for within narrow fields, is at odds with the nature of a social survey concerned with the public goods which the free market fails to deliver, diagnosing underlying conditions which restrict well-being. They may be concerned with achieving joint working with people within the community, as described in chapter 8.

Responding to the electorate. Working with the political leadership to achieve the successful implementation of party manifestos has been central to many chief executives' concepts of their role. Ninety-five per cent of the respondents to the research questionnaire saw translating political requirements into management action as an essential part of their job. On the other hand a substantial majority of the potential electorate - voters and non-voters together - have not in most cases cast votes for the majority party. The public good extends further than the implementation of the manifesto: it includes giving assistance to the opposition parties to provide the democratic virtue of an effective opposition and also regard to the wishes of non-voters and 'protest voters'. There are large areas of service outside the majority manifesto in which a chief executive and other chief officers may reasonably be expected to promote responsiveness to public wishes with the support of the party group in power.

Set and pursue consistent, achievable objectives. A number of responses indicated the importance of guiding elected members in the definition and support of feasible objectives. Without such objectives a rational management process of programming, implementation, appraisal of performance and evaluation of output leading to a redefinition of policy is impossible. The evidence is that chief executives not infrequently play the leading role in defining and developing objectives within the framework of council policy.

Assign clear management responsibilities. This has been an area of important development by chief executives in the later 1980s along with performance appraisal, and may be expected to continue so. It implies responsibility for restructuring to meet contingencies and to set up a pattern of motivation, as in the case of competitive tendering.

Monitor results. The systematic monitoring of results is a management function which the chief executive must be concerned to ensure.

Adapt quickly to change. Adaption requires a continuous awareness of changes in the environment and the seeking of opportunities. The research studies have shown how the ability of elected members to understand some types of new development depends on the leadership of the chief executive.

Distinguishing clearly between the roles of members and officers. The requirements of competitive tendering and the provisions of the 1990 Housing and Local Government Act's definition of the two officer roles of head of paid service and monitoring officer, in conjunction with the earlier requirement of a chief financial officer, attacked traditional concepts of the members' role without contributing to a new one other than by implication. It normally fell to the chief executive to interpret the implications with the help of the advice of the Audit Commission and others. The centre of responsibility seemed to many to have shifted away from leading members towards the officer leadership. Although a strong case can be made for non-involvement of the members in the management of the contracting units within as well as outside the local authority and the legislation has helped to enforce this, their role in the definition and control of contracts has been less clear. Even more important perhaps is the fact that the executive role of the council implicit in the theory of the omnicompetence of the councils has been thrown into doubt.

In its report of January 1989, *More Equal that Others: The Chief Executive in Local Government* (the main title being taken from George Orwell's *Animal Farm* and carrying an ironic ambiguity) the Audit Commission set out questions which brought out strongly the ambivalence of the chief executive's role in relationship to that of the council. The subsequent legislation did little to resolve the ambiguities. The crux of the problem lies in the fact of the whole council being legally the executive power and there being no special definition of that power. Some tentative replies may be given to the Commission's questions.

'Is there a clear definition of the chief executive's role within the authority?'. Recent legislative changes appeared to the Audit Commission to have made it critical for councils to have 'robust mechanisms for corporate decision making'. They concluded that a 'strong chief executive was essential for the process'. They saw it as helping to restore a sense of purpose and direction to local government in coming years.

The Commission stated their belief that chief executives should be 'the centre of continuity and the agents of change within councils. They must manage relationships with politicians, managers, clients and contractors, convert policy into strategy and then into action, develop processes and management skills to ensure the council can deliver its strategies, review performance and think and plan ahead'. This is clearly the executive role, not one that is only ancillary to the political executive. This appeared to many to minimise the management role of members, overriding the sensitive way in which the Bains Committee had dealt with members when it acknowledged that 'it is unlikely that one can rule out the elected representatives of (the) community from any particular part of the management process'.

The achievement of continuity is a task that town and county clerks had long before been expected to provide as elected members came and went. Some German *Länder* were looking for this when they provided for their executives to be in office twice as long or more than their councils. It has been a justification for the appointment of 'permanent' officers in preference to short tenure. Yet the dependence of the council on its chief executive which the Audit Commission described is such that it may work against the sense of partnership. Partnership requires a 'common possession' of the work of the council. For a council to require their head officer to meet set requirements under threat of termination of contract if there is in the majority's opinion a failure, in the Commission's words, to 'translate its policies into reality', constantly to innovate and promote change and hold the organisation together as a corporate body satisfactorily', could militate against partnership.

Chief executives are inevitably dependent on their councils to approve feasible policies, support them in reorganising the structure, reconstitute the management team where this appears to be essential to efficiency and officer leadership, meet conditions of sound resource management and many other matters essential for success by generally accepted criteria. They depend on the political system to back them in such matters. If the relationship fails because of unreasonable expectations the result may be a quick turnover of senior staff and a downward spiral in morale and achievement. Such cases are rare. As we have seen, in chief executives' judgments the relationship with political leaders has generally been a good one. In itself the chief executive concept appears to have played an essential part in the management of corporate innovation in the 1980s and may be expected to develop to meet further and possibly very different challenges in the 1990s. But it is dependent on co-responsibility with or acquiescence from the political leadership for its success. Both leaders and chief executives are assuming a role that is not backed by formal definition.

The case for a new model executive follows essentially from the lack of a clear status and accountability for political leadership. Arguably a clarification of formal responsibility and accountability within the political sphere is needed, as by instituting a formal political executive taking the form either of a 'strong mayor', directly or indirectly elected, or of a board. If this happens the relationship between such an executive and the head of paid service will certainly change, but probably for the better because the ambiguity of the role of the head of the political administration will have been removed, providing a firmer basis for a partnership between political and officer executives.

It may well be that a radical change in the form of the political executive will not take place, if only for reasons of conservatism. Or it may take the form of the development of the council leader position into one of clear formal responsibility. Whatever happens the maintenance of a corporate approach at both member and officer level will be required if principles such as those set out in the prescriptive local government management literature of the 1980s are to be maintained.

It is not within the scope of this book to go in detail into the problems, possibilities and implications of structural innovations. It seems likely that the best way to explore how the institution of a 'strong mayor' or board executive might develop in the British situation would be to give scope for authorities who wished to adopt such an innovation to lead the way and for others to benefit from their experience. Private bill procedures might be appropriate so that pioneering authorities would truly 'own' the system and take responsibility for its success or failure.

Writing at a point in the history of British local government (June 1991) when radical changes of greater significance than those of 1972-75 may be close, it seems unwise to launch generally upon changes that go beyond boundaries and functions on a national scale. But particular 'shadow councils' in the year before they acquire responsibilities may wish to take decisions that could lead to the adoption of a new form of executive.

Whatever happens, chief executives may be expected to carry similar responsibilities to those they undertook in 1972-74 (Long and Norton, 1971; Richards, 1975; Pearce, 1980), designing and setting up new authorities through joint committees of constituent authorities and shadow councils. It is to be hoped that there will be new legislation or advice to facilitate their ability to experiment with new forms of executive, either immediately on reorganisation or early in the lives of the new authorities.

As stated above, the evidence suggests that a head of paid services would remain, possessing responsibilities at least as wide as those of a 1980s chief executive: in fact in a period of such rapid change the post is likely to carry more responsibility than ever before. The area of staffing and morale will be critical, as will the design of new structures and the relationship to the community, and also the 'trouble-shooting' that goes with a reconstruction of relationships. Ultimately the chief executive is the authority's pilot, guiding it towards its democratically determined goals and dealing with matters with which no-one else has been placed in a position to cope.

To summarise, the chief executive as servant of the council is its adviser on the need and form of action in response to community needs and external demands within the exigencies of its resources, participating in the development of its policies in a dialogue with the political leadership to fulfil its ends. He or she is the council's agent as head of its employees, seeking through the authority of the post the implementation of its agreed objectives to the extent possible through the rational use of its resources. The roles of adviser and agent come together in the practice of strategic management. To fulfil these responsibilities adequately requires the exercise of a general competence to pursue the council's interests within the community as well as within the authority's organisation.

Effective implementation of such a role requires high levels of ability to develop and maintain purposive relations with and within the political, officer and community worlds. It needs high qualities of leadership, intellectual grasp of policy issues and their ramifications and the ability to advise councillors on them in language that is understood together with the capacity to lead a large and complex organisation towards the fulfilment of corporate objectives, restructuring the organisation where necessary to meet changing conditions of effectiveness and efficiency.

The council exercises its responsibility through a leadership which is largely dependent on the chief executive. Mutual understanding and joint working are essential between the leader and the chief executive for the implementation of its will and its effectiveness as an expression of local democracy. It may legitimately expect its chief executive to assist in overcoming difficulties in decision-making due a failure in its internal functioning, and to assist opposition parties to play an effective role in the democratic process.

To fulfil most of these tasks a chief executive is highly dependent upon officer colleagues: primarily on the team of officer colleagues who work with him to ensure advice to council that embodies all the relevant knowledge and ability within the organisation and are in a position to ensure as far as resources allow the implementation of the council's policies, accepting with commitment a high level of delegated responsibility. Through the management team and otherwise he or she should promote a sense of purpose within the council, seeking to catalyse a spirit of initiative and commitment wherever this is lacking.

If the evidence gathered in the research from chief executives and political leaders is reliable, these should be realistic and achievable objectives given the necessary abilities and shared understanding with the political leadership. I started this research without conviction that such demands were reasonable. The evidence in the field has shown that they can be so in many if not all situations when assisted by strong political support.

REFERENCES

Audit Commission (1988), *Management Paper No 1, The Competitive Council, London* (1989), *Management Paper No 2, More Equal than Others: the Chief Executive in Local Government*, London

Banner, Gerhardt (1985), "Budgetary Imbalance and the Politics of Cutback Management in German Local Government', *Local Government Studies 11,4*

Barnard, C I (1938), *The Functions of the Chief Executive*, Harvard University Press, Cambridge, Mass

Barrington, T J (1991), "Local Government in Ireland', Macmillan, Basingstoke and London

'The Basildon Experience' (1965), *Public Administration vol 44*

Boynton, John (1986), *Job at the Top*, Longman, Harlow, Essex

Brooke, Rodney (1989), *Managing the Enabling Authority*', Longmans, Harlow, Essex

Burns, J M (1978), *Leadership*, Harper & Row, New York

Clarke, Michael and John Stewart (1991), *The Role of the Chief Executive, Local Government Training Board*, Luton

Clarke, Michael and John Stewart, (1986), *The Role of the Chief Executive: Implications for Training and Development*, SOLACE and Local Government Training Board, Luton

Collins, Neil (1987), *Local Government Managers at Work*, Institute of Public Administration, Dublin

Committee on the Management of Local Government (Maud Report) (1967), see under *Management of Local Government* (Maud Report)

The Conduct of Local Authority Business (Widdicombe Report) (1986), Cmnd.9797, HMSO *Conference Papers on Management and Administration in the Local Government Service: 1969-70* (ed. R.Greenwood) (1970), Institute of Local Government Studies, University of Birmingham

Curnow, Barry (1980), "The Political Context of the Chief Executive's Job', *Party Politics in Local Government*, Royal Institute of Public Administration & Policy Studies Institute, London (1979), "Town Hall Hot Seats', *Management Today May 1979* (also published in *Party Politics in Local Government* (see above)

Elliott, J (1971), "The Harris Experiment in Newcastle-upon-Tyne', *Public Administration, vol 49*

Greenwood, R. (1973), "Where the CEOs Have Come From - A Survey', *Local Government Chronicle*, 19.10.73

Greenwood, R & C R Hinings, Stewart Ranson, Kieron Walsh (undated), *In Pursuit of Corporate Rationality: Organisational Developments in the Post Reorganisation Period*, Institute of Local Government Studies, University of Birmingham

Greenwood R & C R Hinings, Stewart Ranson and Kieron Walsh, (undated), *Patterns of Management in Local Government*, Institute of Local Government Studies, University of Birmingham

Greenwood, R & M A Lomer, C.R.Hinings and S.Ranson (1975), *The Organisation of Local Government in England and Wales*, Institute of Local Government Studies, University of Birmingham

Greenwood, R & A L Norton and J.Stewart (1969), *Recent Reforms in the Management Structure of Local Authorities - the County Councils*, Institute of Local Government

Studies, University of Birmingham

Greenwood, Royston, Kieron Walsh, C R Hinings and Stewart Ranson (1980), *Patterns of Management in Local Government*, Martin Robertson, Oxford

Greenwood, R. and Annette Warner (1985), *Local Authority Structures*, Institute of Local Government Studies, University of Birmingham

Harrison, Margaret and A.L.Norton (1967), see under *Management of Local Government (Maud Report)*

Haynes, R.J. (1978), "The Rejection of Corporate Planning in Theoretical Perspective', *Local Government Studies 4:2*

Headrick, T E (1962), *The Town Clerk in English Local Government*, Allen and Unwin, London

Hinings, Bob and Royston Greenwood (1988), *The Dynamics of Strategic Change*, Basil Blackwell, 1988

Hinings, C R, P R S Ranson and Royston Greenwood (1974), "The Organisation of Metropolitan Government and the Impact of "Bains"", *Local Government Studies 9*

Leach, Steve and John Stewart (1986), *The Workings of Local Government*, Future Role and Organisation of Local Government Study No.3., Institute of Local Government Studies, University of Birmingham

Lee, J M & B Wood, B W Solomon and P Walters (1974), *The Scope of Local Initiative*, Martin Robertson, London

Local Government Trends (1987, 1989), Chartered Institute of Public Finance and Accountancy), CIPFA, London

Lomer, Margaret (1977), "The Chief Executive in Local Government 1974-76', *Local Government Studies 3:4*

Long, Joyce & Alan Norton (1972), *Setting up the New Authorities*, Charles Knight, London

McVicar, Malcolm (1975), "The Gaffney Affair', *Public Administration Bulletin 18*

Management of Local Government (Maud Report) (1967), *Ministry of Local Government, HMSO*: *Vol. 1, Report of the Committee; Vol. 4 Local Government Administration Abroad* by A.H.Marshall; Vol. 5, *Local Government Administration in England and Wales* by Margaret Harrison and Alan Norton

Marshall, A.H. (1967), see under *Management of Local Government (Maud Report)*

Mather, Graham (1989), "Thatcherism and Local Government: an evaluation', *The Future of Local Government*, Macmillan, Basingstoke and London

Midwinter, Arthur F (1978), "The Implementation of the Paterson Report in Scottish Local Government 1975-77', *Local Government Studies 4:1* (1982), *Management Reform in Scottish Local Government*, Department of Administration, University of Strathclyde, Glasgow

The New Local Authorities: Management and Structure (Bains Report) (1972), HMSO

The Municipal Yearbook (1973,1975, 1979,1984,1988,1990, 1991), Municipal Journal Ltd, London

Nicklen, Stephen (1989), *Strategic Management - Comparing the Private and Public Sectors*, Kinsley Lord Ltd, London

Norton, Alan (1977), "Has the Chief Executive a Future?', *Local Government Studies 3:4*

——— (1989), "From County Clerk to County Chief Executive' in *New Directions for County Government*, Association of County

Councils, London & Institute of Local Government Studies, Birmingham
———— (1986), "The Future Functions and Structure of Local Government' in *The Future Role and Organisation of Local Government*, Institute of Local Government Studies, Birmingham
———— (1986), *Local Government in Other Western Democracies* in series *The Future Role and Organisation of Local Government*, Institute of Local Government Studies, Birmingham
Norton, Alan and J D Stewart (1973), "Recommendations to the New Local Authorities, 1973", *Local Government Studies 6*
Paine, Roger (1985), "Is Excellence Relevant in Local Government?, *Local Government Studies 11:2*
Pearce, Clifford (1980), *The Machinery of Change in Local Government 1888-1974*, Allen & Unwin, London
Peters, Thomas J & R H Waterman Jr (1982), *In Search of Excellence*, Harper & Row, New York and London
A Profile of Chief Executives and Their Jobs (1988), Joint Negotiating Committee for Chief Executives of Local Authorities
Qualifications, recruitment, training and promotion of local government officers (1934), Report of the Departmental Committee (Hadow), Ministry of Health
Recruitment and Training of Chief Executives (1977), Society of Local Authority Chief Executives
Richards, Peter (1975), *The Local Government Act 1972: Problems of Implementation*, Allen & Unwin, London
Royal Commission on Local Government. Final Report (1929), Cmd 3436, HMS0, London
Royal Commission on Local Government in England 1966-68 (Redcliffe-Maud), Vol.I Report (1969), Cmnd 4040, HMS0, London
Selznick, Philip (1957), *Leadership in Administration: a Sociological Interpretation*, Harper & Row, New York
Sharp, Evelyn (1960), "Address to the Association of Municipal Corporations', *Municipal Review vol 40*
———— (1962), Lecture, *Public Administration vol 38*
Stewart, J D (1970) in *Conference Papers... 1968-70*, Institute of Local Government Studies, University of Birmingham Birmingham (1988), *Understanding the Management of Local Government*, Longman, Harlow
Stewart, John (1986), *The Many Roles of the Chief Executive*, Future Role and Organisation of Local Government Study Paper 3, Institute of Local Government Studies, University of Birmingham
Stewart, John and Stuart Ranson (1988), *Management in the Public Domain: a Discussion Paper*, Local Government Training Board, Luton

INDEX

Note

This index does not claim to be comprehensive. It picks out many of the main themes that emerged from the research under particularheadings or groups of headings. All the index items are connected in some way with the chief executive's role, but those of a personal nature or role-types are listed under one heading. Those referring to the chief executive's relationships and to Northern Ireland chief executives are also listed separately.

Index

Index

Index